FORM
IN TONAL
MUSIC

FORM IN TONAL MUSIC

An Introduction to Analysis

Second Edition

DOUGLASS M. GREEN
University of Texas, Austin

Holt, Rinehart and Winston

New York / Chicago / San Francisco / Atlanta / Dallas
Montreal / Toronto / London / Sydney

Cover: Portion of the first page (mm. 24–27) of the autograph manuscript of Schubert's *Impromptu, Op. 90, No. 2.*

Library of Congress Cataloging in Publication Data

Green, Douglass M
Form in tonal music

Includes index.
1. Harmony   I. Title.
MT58.G75   1979   781.5   78–27072

ISBN 0–03–020286–8

How all's to one thing wrought!

—*Gerard Manley Hopkins*
ON A PIECE OF MUSIC

Preface

American college students, upon taking up the study of musical analysis, are often placed under an unnecessary hardship. When attempting to master the disciplines of harmony and counterpoint, they have traditionally been given help of a very specific nature. Before being required to construct phrases in the harmonic style of the nineteenth century, they learn step by step how to fashion chords, how to connect them, how to choose them. Before attempting to reproduce the style of a late-sixteenth-century motet, they may labor pains takingly through the various species, acquiring bit by bit the requisite skills. But on being led to the field of musical analysis, although much of the technique of the analyst is no less an acquired skill than that of the contrapuntist, they are virtually abandoned. The standard forms are explained, but as they try to discover for themselves the structure of a given composition, many students suffer from inadequate directions on how to proceed.

From one point of view this book is much like other form books in that it attempts to acquaint students with what is standard. More important, it begins to equip them with the necessary technique for achieving the real aim of the study of form and analysis: the ability to approach a piece of music unencumbered by preconceived notions about what characteristics it should or should not have and to discover, it might be said in *innocence*, the structure of the music.

For the purpose of developing such a technique, many exercises have been devised and placed at frequent intervals throughout each chapter. The music on which these exercises depend is to be found in the third edition of Charles Burkhart's *Anthology for Musical Analysis* (New York: Holt, Rinehart and Winston, 1979). Occasionally an exercise requires access to music not included in Burkhart's *Anthology*. In this case a choice of a number of different compositions is given so that students can work with music already owned or in which they have a special interest.

In this second edition I have made no attempt to change the original book in any basic way. Though passages have been added, deleted, or altered to such an extent that hardly a page has been left untouched, these revisions are all by way of clarification, correction, or greater conciseness. An *Instructor's Manual* containing classroom suggestions and discussions of the exercises has been prepared; it is available on request from: Music Editor, College Department, Holt, Rinehart and Winston, 383 Madison Avenue, New York, N.Y. 10017.

If certain portions of this book seem to urge the student toward labeling, I make no apology. A label is harmful only if students assume that once a label has been applied the piece has been understood. But a label—that is, a name—can be very useful if the student grasps that it is no more than a means, never an end in itself. The search for a meaningful name necessitates asking questions and finding answers about the structure of the music that might otherwise never have been asked or answered.

•   •   •

Among the many books to which I am indebted, specific mention should be made of the works of Percy Goetschius and of Felix Salzer's *Structural Hearing.* From the former I have borrowed a number of terms still in common use today, though some of these have had to be redefined. From the latter I have taken several important concepts. Although applied in a different way and, indeed, to different ends, the view of form as an interaction of *tonal structure* and *design* owes its origin to Dr. Salzer's book.

I should like to give thankful recognition to my own first teacher of analysis, Dr. Paul A. Pisk. My continued thanks are due to Barry S. Brook of the Graduate School of the City University of New York and to Leo Kraft and Saul Novack, both of Queens College of the City University of New York, for welcome criticism and helpful advice in the preparation of the first edition. The revision of the longer historical notes owes much to the perspicacity of my colleague Hanns-Bertold Dietz. MacWilliam Disbrow, Appalachian State University, and Mina Miller, University of Kentucky, read the second edition in manuscript and offered valuable suggestions. The following users of the first edition also made constructive suggestions: Leonard Berkowitz, California State University, Northridge; Harold M. Best, Wheaton College; Frederic Billman, Susquehanna University; Richard C. Domek, University of Kentucky; J. D. Kelly, Arkansas State University; Bohdan J. Kushnir, Wayne State University; Donald M. Pederson, University of Tennessee; John W. Stewart, University of Montevallo; Lawrence Weiner, Texas A. & I. University; Scott Wilkinson, University of New Mexico. I am indebted to Dennis Libby for his excellent preparation of the final copy and to the editorial staff of Holt, Rinehart and Winston. Finally, I should like to express my thanks to my wife, Marquita Dubach, and to my son, Antony D. Green, for their help in many ways, including the preparation of the indexes.

D.M.G.

Contents

Contents

5

PHRASES IN COMBINATION 50

6

THE ANALYTICAL METHOD: SMALL FORMS 73

7

THEME AND VARIATIONS 98

8

THE TERNARY FORMS 129

9

THE RONDO   153

10

THE BINARY FORMS   167

11

THE SONATA FORM   178

12

FURTHER ASPECTS OF SONATA FORM   220

13

THE CONCERTO   234

14

FUGUE AND RELATED GENRES   257

Contents

15

UNIQUE FORMS 290

16

RETROSPECTION 307

1

INTRODUCTION: FORM, SHAPE, AND GENRE

In discussions of music the word "form" appears frequently, often with more than one meaning. We would do well to distinguish these meanings from one another by the terms *genre, shape,* and *form.*

1–A.
MUSICAL GENRE

The collection of *Encyclopedia Britannica* articles by D. F. Tovey describing the aria, cantata, suite, symphonic poem, and so on, is entitled "The Forms of Music."[1] Bukofzer writes, ". . . the forms of the renaissance, such as the madrigal, the motet, the canzona, ricercar, the dance . . ."[2] Such categories of musical composition are more correctly referred to as genres. Beethoven's *Op. 61* and Mendelssohn's *Op. 64* are identical in genre—both are violin concertos—but different in form. Mozart's *Rondo for Piano, K. 511,* and the *Agnus Dei* from his *Mass, K. 317,* are quite different in genre but happen to be similar in form. Example 1–1 illustrates a composition which is in genre an orchestral dance (a minuet) and which constitutes part of an opera, another genre.

Example 1–1

MOZART: *Don Giovanni,* Act I, Minuet

[1] New York: Meridian, 1956.

[2] *Music of the Baroque Era.* New York: Norton, 1947, p. 351.

1

1–B.
MUSICAL SHAPE

Listen to the Minuet from Mozart's *Don Giovanni* (Ex. 1–1). A melody with accompaniment is heard which gathers tension [measure (m.) 5], rises to a climax (m. 7), then comes to a close (m. 8). After a repetition of this passage the melody continues somewhat higher and is accompanied by a new figure in sixteenth notes. In m. 13 begins a rise toward a new melodic climax (m. 15) higher than that of the previous passage (m. 7). In the following bar the second passage comes to a close. It is then repeated.

We have here a composition in which each of two adjacent passages is built on the principle of a curve increasing in tension and rising in pitch to a point of climax, then quickly subsiding. The increased activity in the accompaniment of the second passage and the more highly placed melodic zenith combine to give the second passage a more intense quality than the first. The general impression that is made on the listener can be approximated in diagram by a pair of curving lines.

The Prelude to Wagner's *Lohengrin* begins with high, barely audible sounds in the flutes and strings. Other instruments enter and the music becomes louder, fuller, and more complex until it reaches a great climax. It tapers off to a low point, then grows higher, softer, and simpler until it disappears in silence.

From the beginning of the prelude to its climax, tension is gradually increased in spite of a general descent in pitch from high to low. Crescendo, increased complexity of texture, fuller instrumentation, and greater rhythmic activity are the elements that have been used to bring about the climax in this case. The shape of the prelude might be graphically represented in this way:

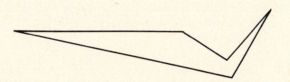

The term "shape," when applied to music, refers to the surface contour of a piece and depends on the action and interaction of the qualities of tension and relaxation. These qualities can be influenced by any of a number of factors:

1. Rise and fall of melodic lines, particularly in outer voices
2. Rhythmic activity
3. Dynamics
4. Texture
5. Instrumentation
6. Relative amount and degree of consonance and dissonance
7. Harmonic rhythm (rate of chord change)

1–C.
MUSICAL FORM

The two aspects of musical form are design and tonal structure.

DESIGN Let us turn our attention once more to Ex. 1–1. The composition is clearly in two parts due to the divisive nature of mm. 7 and 8. The repetition sign at the end of m. 8 is a clue to the location of the division, but does not determine it: The division would be equally strong without it.

Although they contain important differences, the melodies of the two parts run roughly parallel to each other. Rhythmically, they are almost identical and they each rise to a melodic zenith in corresponding places (mm. 7 and 15) and return to their starting points. Caesuras—light breaks in the flow of the music—are found in corresponding places (after every two bars) and each part comes to an emphatic close, or *cadence* (mm. 7–8; 15–16). Yet, the two halves are different. The melodic line of the second half, though almost similar rhythmically, follows a different contour during its first five bars, and the quarter- and eighth-note accompaniment of the first part is replaced in the second by sixteenth notes.

We have observed certain rhythmic similarities and differences, both in the melodic line and in the accompaniment. We have located parallelisms in the placement of the caesuras and cadences and in the location of melodic zeniths. The organization of these melodic and rhythmic factors makes up what is called the design of a composition. The design of other pieces may include such factors as changes of tempo, texture, and even of instrumentation.

Design is the organization of those elements of music called melody, rhythm, cadences, timbre, texture, and tempo.

TONAL STRUCTURE

The harmonic organization of a piece is referred to as its tonal structure.

In the Minuet from *Don Giovanni* (Ex. 1–1) the harmony moves from a tonic chord (I) in m. 1 and cadences in m. 8 on the dominant (V). This V has been approached through a secondary dominant (mm. 5 and 7) and has thus been given prominence as a secondary tonic. Measure 9 begins with V_7 and cadences in the final bar on I.

$$\| : I \rightarrow V : \| \; \| : V_7 \rightarrow I : \|$$

At the first cadence (m. 8), there is a break in the flow of music. In spite of this cadence, however, the listener is not satisfied that the end of the piece has been reached. Surely there is more to come. Repetition of the eight bars does nothing to dispel the incomplete feeling they produce, but with the playing of the remaining eight bars the listener is satisfied. The final cadence (mm. 15–16) is completely conclusive, even though comparison shows that, except for a change in pitch, it is almost identical to the previous one. Why should the same cadence be strongly conclusive at one pitch and only mildly conclusive at another? Clearly because the first cadence, unlike the last, was not on the tonic chord. The harmony moves from I to V but returns in a cadence on I only at the end of the minuet. We have here, then, a single journey—a removal from home to a different point and return. We say that the tonal structure involves a single harmonic movement.

4

1–D.
DESIGNATIONS AND CATEGORIES
OF FORM

Form is an inclusive term which refers both to the design of a composition and to its tonal structure. In arriving at the form of Mozart's minuet, we must consider that the design is, as we have seen, in two parts, while its tonal structure involves a single harmonic movement.

Since the tonal structure has not completed itself when the design has rounded off the first part, the listener expects a continuation. The second part fulfills this expectation, continuing and concluding the piece. The form, then, is one continuous movement divided into two parts. It is called a *continuous binary form.*

The designation "continuous binary" has meaning because it reveals something about both the tonal structure and the design of this minuet. Although it leaves much unsaid, it indicates enough to show that the piece is constructed, in some important respects, like a number of others. It belongs to a general category of musical forms, members of which appear often enough in music literature to warrant recognition as a group. Within the general category of continuous binary forms there are a number of distinct types, of which Mozart's minuet represents one.

Other forms appear often enough to be grouped into other formal categories. Frequently, however, disclosure of the tonal structure and design of a composition results in the discovery that the form is unlike that of other known compositions. Such pieces are said to have free, or more aptly, unique forms.

Our approach will be to consider those forms that occur frequently before directing our attention to the unique ones. We will begin this approach in Chapter 6. In Chapters 2 through 5 we must deal with a prior concern—the way in which music grows and shapes itself from tiny fragments into phrases and combinations of phrases.

2

HARMONIC
STRUCTURE
OF THE PHRASE

2–A.
THE NATURE OF THE PHRASE

Although the phrase is a basic unit of music, it almost eludes precise definition. Writers on music seem to agree only that the phrase (1) exhibits some degree of completeness, and (2) comes to a point of relative repose.

Often there is no problem in defining the phrase structure of folk songs, hymns, and other music of a popular nature, for in many cases each phrase comes but once to a point of repose. But if we listen again to Mozart's Minuet from *Don Giovanni* (Ex. 1–1), we may note a number of pauses in the melodic line (mm. 2 and 4), a slight one in m. 6, and a very distinct one in m. 8. While all of these may be considered points of relative repose, only those in mm. 4 and 8 seem to appear as the completion of a musical thought. We might feel that mm. 1–4 comprise one phrase and mm. 5–8 another.

To pinpoint the exact reasons for this impression is difficult, for it is likely that a variety of factors are at work here. Measures 1–2 may seem to be incomplete because of their shortness. Undoubtedly brevity does play a part, but occasionally one does find two-measure phrases in other music, even when the tempo is faster than that of this minuet (for instance, Ex. 6–9). A more likely reason is to be found in the uneventful harmony of mm. 1–2, expressing only a tonic chord. Measures 3–4, introducing V_7 and a return to I, produce harmonic action, however simple. Measures 5–6 are harmonically active, it is true, but the caesura in the melodic line is too slight to halt its steady upward rise before it reaches its climax in m. 7. Measures 5–8 comprise, then, a single phrase.

With these considerations in mind we can approximate a definition of the phrase in the following terms:

A phrase is the shortest passage of music which, having reached a point of relative repose, has expressed a more or less complete musical thought.

Each of the two essential characteristics of the phrase—its measure of completeness and its arrival at a point of repose—carries with it a further implication that can be of aid in phrase recognition.

HARMONIC ACTION

We have maintained that in all likelihood the chief reason for the incomplete impression given by mm. 1–2 of Ex. 1–1 is their harmonic inactivity. Examination of a large number of phrases reveals that the great majority exhibit a definite harmonic movement. It would seem, then, that harmonic action is a normal characteristic and is certainly responsible in part for the impression that a musical event has taken place in the phrase. Exceptional phrases dwelling on a single harmony are, of course, not lacking in music literature. In Chopin's *Preludes*, for instance, are several remarkable cases (*No. 3*, mm. 1–6; *No. 21*, mm. 17–24 and 25–32; *No. 24*, mm. 1–7 and 19–25). Here the rise and fall in the melodic line and its clear caesuras are enough to express the musical thought.

RELATIONSHIP OF CONSONANCE AND DISSONANCE

A dissonant chord strikes the ear as more active, more restless, than a consonant chord. It might be expected, then, that the final chord of a phrase—the point at which there is a certain feeling of rest—will be consonant. Examination of many phrases reveals that the great majority do end with a consonant triad. Nevertheless, phrases closing with a dissonant chord, especially a primary or secondary V_7, are not rare and occur in certain musical styles, such as the Wagnerian, rather frequently. Yet even here a feeling of relative repose can be present if there is a definite caesura. In addition, the final chord, though dissonant, is often noticeably less so than the chords immediately preceding it. (See Ex. 2–1.)

Example 2–1

WAGNER: *Tristan und Isolde,* Introduction

There is no infallible guide by which every phrase can be recognized with certainty. Much depends on the listener's own insight, and even experienced analysts may hold differing opinions. Occasionally passages occur that might be construed as part of a phrase, as one phrase, or as more than a phrase. Different theorists would almost certainly disagree, and it is doubtful if the composer himself would be able to decide, even if he cared. Such a case is Bach's exquisite *Come, Sweet Death,* in which several possibilities present themselves. The student need not be concerned, however, if he should come across certain passages that defy all attempts at division into a definite succession of phrases. Great poetry and prose are not always written in a syntactically straightforward manner. If by ignoring the "rules" writers and composers can express an idea more clearly or with greater power, they are certain to do so. Students who have learned to recognize and appreciate music which is systematic and precise will be in a better position to recognize and appreciate that which is not.

2–B.
THE CADENCE

The immediate goal of the phrase is its cadence, the chords that bring it to a close. An important characteristic of any cadence is its degree of finality, expressed in terms of relative strength. The greater the conviction of conclusiveness exhibited by a cadence, the stronger that cadence is considered to be. There are a number of factors involved here.

BASIC FIFTH RELATIONSHIP If the roots are a fifth apart, the cadence is stronger when this interval is made apparent to the ear by placing both roots in the bass. In other words, a cadence will be strengthened if the final pair of chords, roots lying a fifth apart, are both used in fundamental position.

POSITION OF ROOT IN FINAL TONIC If the phrase concludes with a tonic chord, it will be stronger if the root, rather than the third or fifth, appears in the uppermost voice of this chord.

CONCLUSION ON A TONIC CHORD A cadence that ends on a tonic chord is stronger than one that does not. This is true even when this final tonic is a secondary tonic, but, as we have seem in Ex. 1–1, the most conclusive chord for a cadence is the primary tonic of the piece.

PRESENCE OF LEADING TONE The chief key-defining tendency note is the leading tone. If a phrase is to conclude on a tonic chord, the cadence in which a leading tone appears in the penultimate chord is stronger than one which lacks it. Therefore, the authentic cadence (V–I) is stronger than the plagal cadence (IV–I). If the leading tone is heard simultaneously with the fourth degree of the scale, the pull of the resulting tritone strengthens the cadence still more. In other words, other elements being equal, V^7–I is stronger than V–I.

STRONG-BEAT
ENDING

When the final chord of a cadence is rhythmically stronger than the penultimate chord, as in the cadences of Ex. 1–1, mm. 7–8 and 15–16, the cadence is more conclusive than it is when the reverse situation obtains. Weak-beat endings are illustrated by Ex. 5–1a, mm. 8 and 13, and Ex. 5–1b, m. 10. Here the V⁷ falls on a stronger beat of the bar than does the final I.

Reference to the cadences in mm. 4 and 12 of Ex. 1–1 reveals a situation midway between the strong-beat and weak-beat endings: the movement of the harmony and the bass line are those of a strong-beat ending, but the melodic line has a weak-beat character. Thus a basically strong-beat cadence can have a considerably less conclusive quality.

BREADTH

A cadence which takes up a greater amount of time will seem stronger than one taking less time, other aspects being equal. Cadences are often broadened by a dominant preparation (the *full cadence*, discussed in Section 2–C) or by expansion of the dominant note in the bass over several beats or more (e.g., V–I$_4^6$–V⁷–I).

SLOWING OF
MOTION

When a cadence is heard simultaneously with a slowing up of the pace, the effect is more conclusive than when the pace continues at the same speed. For instance, in Ex. 1–1 the note values change from eighth notes to quarters at mm. 7–8, adding to the conclusive effect of the cadence. Similarly, at mm. 15–16 the cadence is strengthened by the change from sixteenths to quarters. As every performer knows, a slowing of tempo, too, can have much the same effect.

2–C.
CADENTIAL FORMULAS

CONCLUSIVE
CADENCES

The various cadences, while exerting enough conviction of finality to bring a composition to a satisfactory close, are of very different relative strengths, and, of course, they appear as phrase endings throughout a composition, not only at its close. Any of the penultimate chords may be either a triad or seventh chord. Not infrequently, the composer mixes the major and minor modes within a single passage with the result that various alterations may occur (Ex. 2–2c and e). Example 2–2f is the result of a vestige of the Phrygian mode.

With Leading Tone (Authentic and related)	Without Leading Tone (Plagal and related)
V–I	IV–I
VII–I	(♭)VI–I
III–I	(♭)II–I

Example 2–2

Illustrations of some conclusive cadences

G: V$_7$ I   vii$^o_6$ I   vii$^o_7$ I   IV I $\flat$VI I $\flat$II$_6$ I

Example 2–3a shows a cadence that is often to be found in nineteenth-century music. Although on paper the penultimate chord appears to be iii$_6$, the ear easily recognizes it as a ==variant of V== (see Ex. 2–3b and 4–13, m. 19).

Example 2–3

Authentic cadence with substituted 6th

G: V(not iii$_6$) I   V$^{13}_7$ I

Composers of the twentieth century have regularly avoided the pure authentic or plagal cadence. The chief cadential practices of recent composers of tonal music can be grouped by procedure.

1. Addition or substitution of tones in the cadential chords

Example 2–4

PROKOFIEV: *Peter and the Wolf,* Triumphal March

C: V   I

2.   Omission of tones in the cadential chords

Example 2–5

BARTÓK: *Quartet No. 2*, Finale

3.   Contrivance of new penultimate chord made up of notes that resolve stepwise into the final tonic

Example 2–6

SCHOENBERG: *Variations on a Recitative for Organ*

4.   Approach to final tonic by systematic descent or ascent of seconds, thirds, or fourths

Example 2–7

HINDEMITH: *Das Marienleben* (revised), *No. 15*

PERFECT AND IMPERFECT AUTHENTIC CADENCES

When the V of the authentic cadence is in fundamental position and the root of the final I appears in both outer voices (as in Ex. 2–2a and Ex. 2–4), the cadence is considered perfect. Otherwise it is imperfect. The strongest cadence is an authentic perfect cadence with strong-beat ending.

THE FULL CADENCE

When the authentic cadence is enlarged by a prefix functioning as a preparation to the V, we speak of a full cadence. Most commonly the bass of the prefix is on the fourth scale degree, supporting IV, $ii^6_{(5)}$, $\flat II^6$, or even vii^o_4, thus leading smoothly to the root of V. At other times the bass of the prefix moves by descending fifth or ascending fourth to V, supporting the ii in root position. Not infrequently the prefix moves down from the sixth scale degree to V, in which case it supports a vi or IV^6.

CADENTIAL ELABORATION

The cadences in m. 7 and m. 15 of Ex. 1–1 are full cadences using the formula ii_6–V–I. The student may note that no mention has been made of the I^6_4 which both times precedes the V. The reasoning behind the method of harmonic analysis employed here is that, since the I^6_4 is heard not as a I in its own right but as an ornamentation (two accented passing tones) of the V, only one real harmony, the dominant, has actually sounded. Indeed, the nomenclature I^6_4 is misleading, since it indicates a tonic chord, whereas the entire harmony is in fact dominant. The I^6_4 merely delays for a moment the unqualified appearance of V. This delaying action is a method of elaborating the cadence.

I^C_4 *

Another commonly used elaboration of the full cadence involving a delay in the appearance of V is the connection of V with its preceding chord by means of chromatic passing notes (Ex. 2–8a).

Example 2–8

Illustrations of cadential elaboration

A delay may occur not in the appearance of V, but in the appearance of I. Example 2–8b shows how a delay by means of nonharmonic tones might take place. On paper the aggregation of tones on the first beat of m. 2 of that example looks like a IV^6_4 chord, but, because of the bass note, the listener hears this as a delayed I. The implication here of an intervening IV can be openly manifested (Ex. 2–8c). It is this elaboration of the authentic cadence that Wagner employs on a large scale in the final bars (m. 25 ff from end) of *Tristan und Isolde*.

From these examples we conclude that a cadential progression is elaborated by delaying one or more of its chords through the introduction of <u>nonharmonic tones</u> which comprise in themselves an <u>intervening chord.</u>

THE HALF CADENCE The half cadence (semicadence) is one which can close a phrase within a composition but is not conclusive. It can take various forms, the most common being one in which the chord progression ends with V (Ex. 2–9a). Other types of half cadence occasionally appear, such as that which ends with IV (as in "never brought to mind" in *Auld Lang Syne*). Occasionally, especially in music of the late nineteenth century, another chord, such as the transposed augmented six-five-three chord ("German sixth"), acts as a dominant substitute (Ex. 2–9b).

Example 2–9

Half cadences

The deceptive cadence, in which the V is followed not by the expected I but by some other chord, often vi, is actually no more than a type of semicadence.

Not infrequently a phrase cadences with harmonies producing an effect midway between a half cadence and an authentic cadence. Such a "three-quarter" cadence could result from the use of an augmented sixth chord which, containing a secondary leading tone, produces a mildly conclusive effect (Ex. 2–9c). In cases such as these and similar ones, there can be no cut-and-dried rule regarding which harmonies produce cadences that can reasonably be called "conclusive." The same chord progression may sound conclusive in one context and not in another, for the effect of a particular cadence is to a large extent dependent on its relation to the other cadences of the same piece.

<h2 style="text-align:center">2–D.
SPECIAL TREATMENT OF THE
CADENCE</h2>

The phrases in a good composition do not normally give the impression of having been baldly juxtaposed with obvious gaps between them. Rather, the composer treats the cadences in ways designed to create a flow throughout a number of phrases. This continuity often tends to obviate the conclusive quality of an otherwise strong cadence. The means by which this continuity is achieved can be grouped into several categories.

CONTINUED RHYTHMIC MOVEMENT IN THE ACCOMPANIMENT

A simple and extremely common method of linking two phrases is to provide rhythmic motion in the accompaniment. Example 1–1 illustrates this method (mm. 4 and 12).

CONTINUATION OF THE MELODIC LINE

The motion linking the two phrases may take place in the main melodic line itself.

LINK.

Example 2–10

HINDEMITH: *Quintet, Op. 24 No. 2*, Waltz

© Copyright 1922, B. Schott's Soehne, Mainz. Reprinted by permission of the original copyright owner and Associated Music Publishers, Inc., New York.

ELISION OF THE CADENCE

Example 2–11

BIZET: *Carmen*, Second Entr'acte

In Ex. 2–11 Bizet achieves a particularly smooth effect by causing the cadence of one phrase to occur simultaneously with the beginning of the next. In such cases, which occur frequently, we speak of elision, or the elided cadence. (See also Beethoven's *Symphony No. 8*, First Movement, mm. 11–12.)

OVERLAPPING   **Example 2–12**

WOLF: *Gebet, Mörike-lieder No. 28*

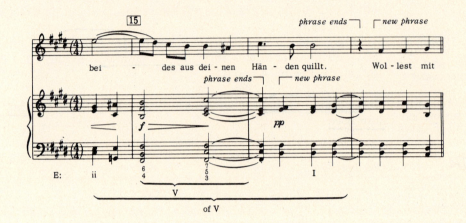

In Ex. 2–12 the new phrase begins in the piano on the second beat of the second bar while the voice continues the old phrase until the end of that bar. This is an illustration of the overlapping of phrases, a device most frequently found in music with a contrapuntal texture. [See also Bach, *The Well-Tempered Clavier (WTC), Vol. 2, Prelude No. 19,* mm. 8–9.]

EXERCISES

1. Terms to define:
   Conclusive cadence   Deceptive cadence
   Half cadence   Full cadence
   Authentic cadence   Link
   Plagal cadence   Elision

2. Contrast:
   Strong-beat and weak-beat endings
   Overlapping and elision

3. Answer the questions in reference to each of the passages listed.
   (1) How many phrases does the passage comprise?
   (2) Do these phrases exhibit caesuras in the melody?
   (3) Identify cadences as to type. Which is strongest? Why?
   (4) Are the phrases connected by any special means? If so, what are these means?

16

It is suggested that the exercises be done in the order given below. The least ambiguous phrases are listed first, the more problematic ones later.

a. Schumann, *Album for the Young*, No. 8 (entire)
b. Anon., *Aria* (entire)
c. Anon., *Menuet*, mm. 1–16.
d. Bach, *Chaconne*, mm. 1–8 and 17–24.
e. Mozart, *Sonata, K. 333*, second movement, mm. 1–8.
f. Corelli, *Sonata No. 8*, Preludio, mm. 1–14.
g. Schubert, *Who Is Sylvia?*, mm. 5–10.
h. Chopin, *Nocturne, Op. 27 No. 2*, mm. 2–9.
i. Wolf, *Das verlassene Mägdlein*, mm. 5–12.
j. Bach, *English Suite in G minor*, Gavotte I, mm. 1–8.
k. Bach, *Suite for Violoncello Solo in G major*, Menuet II (entire).
l. Schumann, *Album for the Young*, No. 31, mm. 1–12.

2–E.
THE HARMONIC ORGANIZATION
OF THE PHRASE

The question of the organization of the harmony within a phrase is an exceedingly important one. To a large extent, phrases present in miniature the same basic tonal structures exhibited on a larger scale by entire sections and, indeed, by complete compositions.

How does the composer arrive at the series of harmonies which connects the first chord of his phrase with the first chord of the cadence? The ensuing discussion should not be taken as implying that the composer is necessarily conscious of the process during the act of composition. It seems likely that the creative artist who has mastered his craft will grasp intuitively what is "right" in a composition without having to plod through the intervening steps.

Example 2–13

Melodic motions

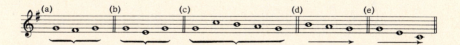

A comparison of the first three melodic motions (Ex. 2–13a, b, c) with the last two (d, e) reveals that the former conclude by returning to the first note, whereas the latter move to a different note. The first three may be described as motions *within* an area, the last two as motion *from* one area *to* another.

In Ex. 2–13a, the middle tone, a neighbor note, provides motion that simply returns to its starting place. Its function is decorative but, more than that, the movement it engenders serves to prolong the main tone. In d, on the other hand, the middle tone is a passing note that serves to fill up the space between the first tone and the third. Its function is to lead from one tone to another. The middle tones of b and c have a function essentially the same as that of a: prolongation of the main tone. The function of the middle tone of e is to divide in half the distance from the first note to the third, thus leading from one to the other.

Example 2–14 illustrates in the harmonic sphere the same types of motion exemplified by the melodic fragments of Ex. 2–13.

Example 2–14

Harmonic motions

Example 2–14a, b, and d show extremely simple harmonic motions within an area, c a more complex one. A series of chords moving within an area is called a *chord succession*. Example 2–24e and f show harmonic motion from one area to another, illustrations of the *chord progression*. Although Ex. 2–14d and e have identical melodies, the former is harmonized as a succession, the latter as a progression. Progression to a chord whose bass lies a fifth away is often accomplished by means of a chord whose bass cuts this distance into two equal parts (Ex. 2–14f).

Example 2–15

a.   Chord succession
b.   BACH: *Christmas Oratorio,* Part VI

The opening chord of Ex. 2–15a changes from root position to first inversion. Although the bass seems to "progress" from G to B, the fact that the first and third chords comprise the same harmony results essentially in movement within an area. We have, then, a chord prolongation: a succession, not a progression. The same is true of Ex. 2–15b. In spite of the longer bass movement down a sixth, the end result is a prolongation of the tonic triad followed by the full cadence.

If one bears in mind these distinctions of chord succession and chord progression, the chief ways of organizing a phrase harmonically can be set forth under seven headings.

HARMONIC
SCHEME OF THE
PHRASE
EQUIVALENT TO
THE CADENCE

Example 2–16

a. BEETHOVEN: *Sonata, Op. 31, No. 3,* First Movement
b. SCHOENBERG: *Gurrelieder,* Part One

Copyright 1914 by Universal Edition A. G., Vienna. Reprinted by permission of original copyright owner and Mrs. Arnold Schoenberg.

By means of cadential elaboration it is possible for the harmonic scheme of a phrase to consist of no more than the chords of a cadential formula. Example 2–16a shows cadential elaboration by means of chromatic passing tones (pt) in the manner illustrated by Ex. 2–8a. Example 2–16b allows a IV to intervene between the vii and its resolution on I (see Ex. 2–8c, wherein the first cadential chord was V, not vii).

CADENCE PRECEDED BY SINGLE CHORD

Example 2–17

VERDI: *La Traviata*, Act I

By permission of G. Ricordi & C., Milan.

Example 2–17 is a ten-bar phrase ending with an authentic cadence. The first six bars consist, harmonically speaking, of nothing more than a tonic chord. (See also Chopin, *Nocturne in D Major, Op. 27, No. 2*, and Ex. 1–1, first phrases.)

CHORD SUCCESSION WITHIN THE CADENCE

Not infrequently the first chord of a cadence is preceded by only a single chord and, at the same time, the phrase makes an impression of greater harmonic complexity than that of Ex. 2–17. This impression comes about through the use of a chord succession within the cadence, a form of cadential elaboration (see section 2–c).

Example 2–18

PURCELL: *Dido and Aeneas*, Act III

Example 2–18a shows a lengthy extension of the penultimate cadential chord by approaching it through a secondary dominant (m. 2) and prolonging it by chord succession (mm. 3–4). Ex. 2–18b summarizes the harmonic content of the phrase by showing the essential melodic movement of the two outer voices. (Stemless notes in this representation are used to indicate passing tones.) Example 2–19 is similar. In both the Purcell and the Mendelssohn phrases the iv is prolonged by a move from root position to first inversion via a passing chord. Diagonal lines show that this move to first inversion is accomplished by exchange of voices.

Example 2–19

MENDELSSOHN: *Symphony No. 3 in A Minor* ("Scotch"), First Movement

b.

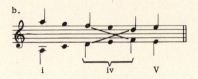

i   iv   V

**CADENCE
PRECEDED BY
CHORD
SUCCESSION**

The harmony of much music of a light character, such as the waltzes of Johann Strauss, often merely alternates between I and V. This back and forth motion, extending until the cadence is reached, is actually no more than motion within an area. Alternation between I and vii characterizes the chord succession that makes up most of the first part of the phrase in Ex. 2–20.

Example 2–20

D. SCARLATTI: *Sonata, K. 446*

F: I   vii° I   IV   I₆ vii°₆ I   vii°   I   II₆   V

In Ex. 2–21 the cadence is preceded by a series of harmonies overlying a tonic pedal point. The continual sounding of the tonic note in the bass tends to cause these harmonies to be heard as a prolongation of I.

Example 2–21

C. P. E. BACH: *Sonata, Wq 57,* Second Movement

F: I   V₇   I   vi₆   IV   V   I

In the chord succession in Ex. 2–22 the tonic triad (with added sixth) makes its final appearance at the lower octave, the interval being filled in by a series of seventh chords descending stepwise.

Example 2–22

DEBUSSY: *Suite Bergamasque, Clair de lune* (Harmonic outline)

Example 2–23

SCHUBERT: *Ständchen*

The distance from the bass of the first chord of the phrase (m. 1) to the bass of the first chord of the semicadence (m. 3) is a perfect fifth. By using a chord whose bass note falls in the middle of this interval, Schubert divides a large leap into two smaller ones, the same principle we have seen used melodically in Ex. 2–13e and harmonically in 2–14f. We have here, then, a chord progression, for the VI of m. 2 leads from i to ii$_5^6$, motion not within an area, but from one area to another.

It is important to note that we concern ourselves here not so much with harmonic roots as with the bass. A listener's orientation comes from the bass line as it is actually sounded rather than from a theoretical knowledge of the root of each chord.

Example 2–24

FAURÉ: *Requiem*, Part VI

Used by permission of Hamelle et Cie, Paris, copyright owner.

The distance from the low note D which opens the phrase to the G with which the bass of the cadence begins (m. 5) is a perfect fourth. Here the progression moves not by two small leaps as in the former example, but stepwise.

Both preceding illustrations have shown bass lines that aimed at their goals and went there directly. Often the progression makes a slight detour. In Ex. 2–25 the bass line in m. 2 passes over its goal, then returns to it in m. 3. Compare Handel's bass line with that of the reduction on the lowest staff.

Example 2–25

HANDEL: *Concerto Grosso, Op. 6, No. 6,* First Movement

(reduction)

Not infrequently a series of harmonies will progress by means of descending or, more rarely, ascending fifths.

Example 2–26

VIVALDI: *Concerto for Four Violins, Op. 3, No. 10,* Third Movement

24

Example 2–27

RAVEL: *String Quartet*, Third Movement

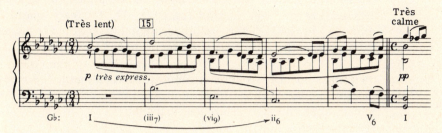

Example 2–27 shows a movement from a tonic g♭, expressed at the upper octave, downwards to a c♭ (m. 17). The implied interval of a perfect fifth is cut in half by the note e♭ of m. 16, much as in Ex. 2–23. The e♭ itself, however, is prepared by means of the chord at its upper fifth b♭ (m. 15). Again it must be stressed that analysis of harmonic progression is concerned more with the bass line than with root movements. If we considered only the roots of the chords, we should assume that the progression in Ex. 2–27 was arrived at by means of descending fifths (iii–vi–ii–V–I), a reading belied by the ear.

Example 2–28

ZIPOLI: *Suite No. 4 in D Minor*, Minuet

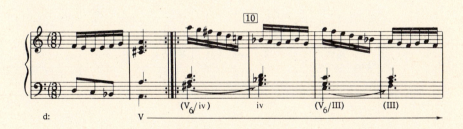

25

Example 2–28 is another illustration of a progression which, judged by roots, moves by descending fifths. The ear, on the contrary, hears a progression from the V that closes the preceding phrase (m. 8) to I (m. 18) via descending stepwise motion (mm. 10, 12, 14), each chord being emphasized by its secondary dominant in first inversion. (The harmony of m. 13 serves as the secondary dominant of m. 14 by analogy.)

CADENCE PRECEDED BY COMBINATION OF SUCCESSION AND PROGRESSION

Perhaps a majority of phrases combine the two methods so far discussed, beginning with a chord succession, then progressing to the cadence. The illustrations in Ex. 2–29 are self-explanatory.

Example 2–29

a. MENDELSSOHN: *Symphony No. 3 in A Minor ("Scotch")*
b. BACH: *WTC, Vol. 1, Prelude No. 1*
c. COUPERIN: *Messe à l'Usage des Couvents, Quoniam Tu Solus*

CADENCE
PRECEDED BY
PARALLEL
MOTION IN
OUTER VOICES

Rather than constructing independent bass lines, composers have not infrequently written a bass which, up until the first cadential chord, moves in parallel tenths or (less often) parallel sixths with the melody. The result may be a succession or a progression depending on the nature of the melodic line which the bass doubles in tenths or sixths.

Several examples of this type of bass are included in Burkhart's *Anthology for Musical Analysis*. In Bach's harmonization, the bass of the chorale "O Haupt voll Blut und Wunden" (in Appendix) moves through m. 1 in parallel tenths with the melody and results in a progression to the first cadential chord, first beat of m. 2. In Schubert's *Moment Musical in A-flat Major*, mm. 93–100 present a chord succession on an A-flat sixth chord (V⁶ in D♭ major) brought about by parallel motion in tenths with the uppermost voice. Schumann's "Melodie," *Album for the Young No. 1*, moves in parallel sixths in m. 5, then in tenths from m. 6 to m. 8, the whole phrase being a prolongation of a dominant seventh chord.

EXERCISES

4. Terms to define:
    Chord succession   Chord progression

5. Consider the passages for Exercise 3 of this chapter. Studying the harmonic organization with special attention to the bass line, describe the harmonic movement of each phrase.

2–F.
SUMMARY

Although the phrase is not always easy to pinpoint, there are certain criteria that can be of aid to the student.

1. A change of chords, harmonic action, helps give the impression of a measure of completeness, a characteristic of the phrase.

2. Common to all phrases is the feeling of comparative repose reached at the end. This is often brought about through either or both of the following:
    a. A pause, or caesura, in the flow of the music accomplished through held notes or rests.
    b. The movement of the harmonies from dissonance to consonance or from greater to lesser dissonance.

    An important aspect of the phrase is its cadence, the chords that bring it to a close. Cadences have differing effects and are of varying strengths. A conclusive cadence carries with it a definite conviction of finality lacking in the half cadence. The strongest conclusive cadence is the strong-beat perfect authentic (V_7–I, root in soprano of I), especially when it has been broadened into a full cadence by the use of a prefix as dominant preparation.

For the sake of continuity, composers have generally made a practice of tying a number of phrases together by one of the following cadential treatments:

Linking

1. Filling in the gap between two phrases by continued rhythmic movement in the accompaniment
2. Directing the melodic line over the gap between two phrases
3. Avoiding a gap between two phrases by causing the last moment of one phrase to occur simultaneously with the first moment of the next; that is, elision of the cadence

Elision

4. Avoiding a gap between phrases by the process of overlapping, in which the various voices of a contrapuntal or semicontrapuntal texture may cadence at different times

An understanding of the harmonic organization of the phrase depends upon distinguishing succession and progression in a chordal sequence. The former refers to harmonic movement within the area of a single chord. The latter refers to movement from one chordal area to another.

The phrase, as a rule, is organized harmonically by the use of

1. Chord succession followed by the cadence
2. Chord progression leading to the cadence
3. Chord succession followed by progression leading to the cadence

Sometimes, on the other hand, the phrase consists harmonically of no more than a single cadential formula, such as ii–V–I or vii⁰–I, or of a single chord followed by a cadence.

3

MELODIC STRUCTURE
OF THE PHRASE

3–A.
INDIVISIBLE PHRASES

Some musical phrases are not susceptible to subdivision. They consist simply of one steady flow of sound with no break, real or implied. Phrases with melodies of the *perpetuum mobile* type often fall into this category (Ex. 3–1a), but there are a number of other examples as well (Ex. 3–1b).

Example 3–1

a. BACH: *Cantata 147*, Part One, No. 6
b. BEETHOVEN: *Symphony No. 4*, Second Movement

3–B.
SUBDIVISION OF THE PHRASE

Example 3–2 is the beginning of the famous English horn melody in the second movement of Franck's *Symphony in D Minor*.

Example 3–2

FRANCK: *Symphony in D Minor*, Second Movement

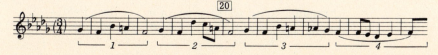

The first five notes comprise a short melodic unit that is twice repeated, each time in a different version. Another melodic fragment brings the phrase to a close. Although no actual rests exist in the score, the presence of a caesura is clearly felt after the first fragment and after the second. In spite of the composer's slurs, a caesura after the third fragment is much less in evidence, for the final note of this third fragment (g′♭) is not a half note but a quarter. The music pushes on into the fourth fragment. As heard, then, the eight-bar phrase contains three *phrase members*, two bars plus two bars plus four bars (2 + 2 + 4).

Franck's melody shows, to some extent, symmetrical subdivisions, and it typifies the melodic structure of a large number of melodies of the late eighteenth and nineteenth centuries. Divisions of other eight-bar phrases may be even more rigidly symmetrical (2 + 2 + 2 + 2). Not infrequently a phrase is unevenly subdivided. In the following excerpt, for instance, the first phrase member consists of three bars and the second of five. This division shows a different kind of symmetry, the symmetry of the "golden mean," wherein the smaller portion is (approximately) to the larger as the larger is to the whole (3 is to 5 as 5 is to 8). The larger phrase member is further subdivided (1 + 1 + 3).

Example 3–3

MOZART: *Quartet, K. 458*, Second Movement

EXERCISE

1. Consider the following passages of music, deciding whether each phrase melody is indivisible or whether it consists of several phrase members. In the latter case, mark and number the phrase members, comparing their lengths.
   a. Haydn, *Symphony No. 101* ("Clock"), Menuetto, mm. 1–8; Finale, mm. 1–4; 5–8.
   b. Mozart, *Concerto, K. 491*, mm. 1–12.
   c. Mendelssohn, *Song Without Words, Op. 62 No. 1*, mm. 1–4; mm. 35 (beat 3)—41.
   d. Schumann, *Album for the Young, No. 17*, mm. 1–4; mm. 12 (last beat)—20.
   e. Schumann, *Vogel als Prophet*, mm. 18 (last beat)—22.
   f. Brahms, *Intermezzo, Op. 76 No. 4*, mm. 20–32.

g. Bartók, *Mikrokosmos, No. 115*, mm. 1–4.
h. Hindemith, *Un Cygne*, mm. 1–5.
i. Dallapiccola, *Quartina*, mm. 1–5; mm. 10–13.

3–C.
THE MOTIVE

Example 3–4

BACH: *Brandenburg Concerto No. 3*, First Movement

The melody in Ex. 3–4 is built almost entirely from a three-note melodic fragment called a motive. The motive is a short melodic fragment used as a constructional element. However, not every short melodic figure is a motive. In order to act as a constructional element and thus constitute a motive, a melodic fragment must appear at least twice, though reappearances need not be in the original form. A motive can be as short as two notes, as in the opening theme of Brahms' *Symphony No. 4*. It is rarely longer than six or seven notes (Ex. 3–6).

The motive is characterized by its melodic contour, with its harmonic implication, and especially by its rhythm.

Some melodies, such as Ex. 3–4, are built out of one motive only. More often the melody contains two or even three motives. Example 3–5 is a melody constructed from two motives (marked a and b).

Example 3–5

GOUNOD: *Faust*, Duet, *"Il se fait tard"*

31

3–D.
MOTIVIC CONSTRUCTION OF THE
PHRASE MELODY

REPETITION AND
SEQUENCE

Example 3–6

BEETHOVEN: *Sonata, Op. 14, No. 2,* First Movement

G: I   ii *(tonic pedal point)*

The phrase excerpt in Ex. 3–6 is built entirely of a single six-note motive, a melodic fragment with a definite harmonic implication: the first, second, fourth, and sixth notes outline a triad, the third and fifth notes embellishing the fourth and sixth respectively. The first appearance of the motive expresses the tonic triad. After an exact repetition the motive again appears, this time at a new pitch level, expressing the supertonic triad. When a motive is thus repeated in the same voice at a new pitch level, we speak of sequence. Repetition and sequence comprise the two simplest ways of using the motive in building a phrase melody.

The fact that the I is a major triad while the ii is minor necessitates in Ex. 3–6 slight changes within the motive in the sequence. The interval between the second and third notes is, in the first appearance, a diminished fourth, and that between the fourth and fifth notes a perfect fourth. In the corresponding places of the sequence these intervals are reversed. Sequences involving such slight changes due to transposition are extremely common—they are called *tonal sequences*—and are not to be considered actual variations of the motive. Motivic variation, as we shall see, involves much more than this.

MOTIVIC
VARIATION

An examination of Ex. 3–5 will reveal some of the methods of motivic variation.

Variation by Ornamentation The first motive of Ex. 3–5, marked a, outlines a tonic triad in the key of D♭ major. At its second appearance (a′) it is somewhat changed, not due to transposition as in the case of the sequence, but due to the addition of an appoggiatura to its final note. Its third appearance (a″) is similar to the second in that the final note is ornamented by an appoggiatura, but it differs from both preceding versions in that this final note is changed from the fifth degree of the scale to the fourth degree.

Variation by Intervallic Change A comparison of the second motive of Ex. 3–5, marked b, with the version in which it makes its final appearance (b′)

32

shows an even more radical change of its melodic intervals. In spite of the great difference in melodic contour between b and b', the motive is recognizable due to its characteristic rhythm. Even though the melodic intervals are altered, if the rhythm is maintained the listener will generally be aware of the presence of the motive. Brahms' *Symphony No. 4* opens with a melody made up of a two-note motive that takes various melodic guises (descending third, ascending sixth, descending octave, ascending third) but persists in the same rhythmic pattern. Example 3–7 is another phrase made up of a motive the intervals of which are constantly altered, while the rhythm is only slightly altered.

Example 3–7

SCHUBERT: *Sonata, Op. 53,* Second Movement

Variation by Inversion

Example 3–8

STRAVINSKY: *L'Oiseau de feu, Berceuse*

Reprinted by permission of B. Schott's Soehne, Mainz.

Interval changes in the melody sometimes occur by systematic change of direction. In Ex. 3–8 an upward leap of a third becomes a downward leap of a third, a descending fourth becomes an ascending fourth. (See also the beginning of the Second Movement of Brahms' *Symphony No. 4*.) A motive can be freely, rather than strictly, inverted. A general upward movement becomes a general downward movement, and vice versa, with no attempt to retain the precise intervals involved.

Example 3–9

BRAHMS: *Symphony No. 3,* Third Movement

(See also the beginning of Puccini's *La Bohème*.)

Variation by Retrogression When the notes of a passage recur in reverse order, we speak of retrograde motion or retrogression.

Example 3–10

DEBUSSY: *Prelude No. 10* ("The Engulfed Cathedral")

When a passage of music recurs in retrograde motion, the rhythm may or may not participate in the exact reversal. In the examples below (Ex. 3–11) Bach reverses the pitches only, whereas Haydn reverses all elements (pitches, rhythm, dynamics, articulation, and—not shown—the other instrumental parts as well).[1]

Example 3–11

a. BACH: *Art of the Fugue, Contrapunctus No. 19*
b. HAYDN: *Symphony No. 47*, Third Movement

[1] Since all aspects are to be played exactly as notated, but in reverse order, Haydn did not write out the retrograde. The performers are merely instructed to play the music backwards.

Since motives are most easily perceptible by means of their rhythms, it is unlikely that many listeners notice the retrograde aspect of Bach's fugue subject. If Bach had considered the pitch reversal an important feature of his theme, he would probably have composed it in such a way that the retrograde of the rhythm, as well as of the pitches, would have produced an acceptable melody.

Although in the past retrograde motion has been used only sporadically, many twentieth-century composers have come to include it among their means of organization.

Variation by Augmentation or Diminution Another method of motivic variation involves an alteration in the rhythm while the intervallic structure of the melody is retained. Since a rhythmic change is apt to destroy the identity of the motive, this method is not common. However, if the rhythm is varied systematically, such as by augmentation or diminution, the motive is readily perceived.

Example 3–12

a. BEETHOVEN: *Sonata, Op. 90,* First Movement
b. BRAHMS: *Sonata, Op. 120, No. 2,* First Movement
c. BRAHMS: *Intermezzo, Op. 118, No. 6*

By augmentation the durational value of each note is multiplied, usually by two. By diminution it is divided. The change by augmentation or diminution may be general rather than exact. Measures 9–10 of Ex. 3–9 include augmentations of the main motive, and Ex. 3–12 provides further illustrations.

Variation by Combination of Means Any of the foregoing methods may be used in combination. In illustration let us examine Ex. 3–13. The devices used are intervallic variation and ornamentation. The melody is built up out of a single motive. Example 3–13a represents a conjectural version of the theme before being ornamented. Each pair of bars consists of the original motive with rhythm maintained but melodic intervals varied. Example 3–13b shows the theme as Brahms left it, each motive further varied by means of ornamentation.

Example 3–13

BRAHMS: *Sonata, Op. 38,* First Movement

Another possible combination of methods is that of both rhythmic and intervallic variation.

Example 3–14

HAYDN: *Symphony No. 104,* Third Movement

The chief methods of variation can be summarized under three headings:

1. Change of intervals with retention of rhythm (intervallic, inversion)
2. Change of rhythm with retention of intervals (augmentation, diminution)
3. Ornamentation of the motive

3–E.
THE COMPOUND MOTIVE

In the first four bars of Beethoven's *Sonata, Op. 14, No. 2* (see Ex. 3–6) we noted the presence, with repetition and sequence, of a six-note motive. If we listen to the entire first movement, we will notice that this six-note motive is fragmented, each bit playing a part separate from the other. For instance, the development section begins as shown in Ex. 3–15.

Example 3–15

BEETHOVEN: *Sonata, Op. 14, No. 2,* First Movement

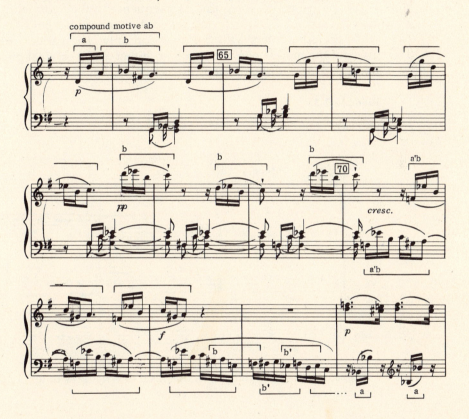

The right hand part of mm. 67–69 makes use of only the last four notes of the motive, the left hand part of mm. 74–75 the first two notes. Although Beethoven, at the beginning of the piece, presents the six notes as a single motive, he separates them in the course of the piece into two segments which are then treated independently. For convenience we can label the first two notes a, the last four notes b, and speak of the complete six-note figure as "compound motive ab." The over- and underlying brackets in Ex. 3–15 indicate how the compound motive is employed. Special note should be taken of the way the right hand imitates the left in mm. 70–71 (imitation will be discussed in the next section of this chapter), and of how segment b is made to overlap itself in mm. 72–73.

3–F.
MOTIVIC CONSTRUCTION IN
PHRASE TEXTURE

So far we have limited ourselves to a discussion of motivic construction of the phrase melody only. Example 3–16 illustrates motivic interplay among all the parts of a phrase, not only the uppermost voice.

The motive is presented first as a sequence in the first violin. Immediately the second violin and viola invert it, then turn it right side up again, while the cello enters with the inversion only. The various instruments give out the motive one after another, either at the original pitch level or transposed to a different one.

Example 3–16

MOZART: *Quartet, K. 387,* First Movement

The technique of imitation, as this kind of writing is called, occurs quite commonly in any of its various types.

1. *Real,* or *exact imitation* exists when the motive is unchanged by the imitating voice, except perhaps for transposition to a new pitch level (Ex. 3–12, left hand imitating right hand).
2. *Imitation by inversion* is illustrated in Ex. 3–16.
3. *Tonal imitation* is present in Ex. 2–29c (mm. 1–3). Here the imitating voice presents the motive in a version corresponding to that of a fugal answer, explained in Chapter 14 (section 14–C).
4. *Imitation by augmentation* or by *diminution* is occasionally found as well. In Ex. 3–17, with one exception, each note of the imitating voice is six times the length of its corresponding note in the original motive. This motive is itself a diminution of the fugue subject that had appeared earlier in the movement.

Example 3–17

BEETHOVEN: *Sonata, Op. 110,* Third Movement

5. *Free imitation* occurs when the imitating voice changes the motive rhythmically (but not systematically as in augmentation and diminution) or by intervallic change and/or ornamentation.

6. *Imitation of rhythm only* is the appropriation of the motive's rhythm for the accompaniment without any attempt at imitating its melodic contour.

Example 3–18

a. ROSSINI: *Stabat Mater,* Second Movement
b. RAVEL: *Trio pour violon, violoncelle, et piano*

EXERCISES

2. Terms to define:

Motive	Retrograde motion
Compound motive	Diminution
Sequence	Augmentation
Tonal sequence	Real imitation
Inversion	Free imitation

3. Contrast:
   a. Imitation and sequence
   b. Inversion and retrograde motion

4 Consider the passages for Exercise 1 of this chapter (pp. 30–31). Decide whether each phrase melody is motivically constructed. If it is, mark the various appearances of each motive and point out the relationships among them.

5. Examine the following passages for evidence of the use of compound motives.
   a. Bach, *WTC*, Prelude No. 22, mm. 1–7. (*WTC = Well-Tempered Clavier*)
   b. Beethoven, *Sonata, Op. 2, No. 1,* mm. 1–14.
   c. Schubert, *Who is Sylvia?* (entire bass line)
   d. Schubert, *Erlkönig,* mm. 1–57.
   e. Wagner, *Tristan,* Prelude, mm. 1–17.
   f. Webern, *Wie bin ich froh!* (entire piano part)

6. Decide whether motivic construction exists within the texture of each of the passages listed below. If so, mark the various appearances of each motive and point out the type of imitation used.
   a. Bach, *Invention No. 4,* mm. 44–52.
   b. Bach, *WTC,* Fugue No. 8, mm. 52–67.
   c. Bach, *WTC,* Fugue No. 16, mm. 1–3.
   d. Beethoven, *Sonata Op. 2, No. 3,* Scherzo, mm. 1–28.
   e. Beethoven, *Quartet, Op. 135,* Fourth Movement, mm. 1–4.
   f. Brahms, *Intermezzo, Op. 118, No. 2,* mm. 34–38.
   g. Bartók, *Mikrokosmos, No. 133,* mm. 1–8.

3–G.
SUMMARY

From the melodic point of view, the phrase may exhibit a single unbroken line. More often it subdivides itself into smaller sections, the phrase members. These are often built up of very short melodic fragments called motives. The motive can, by repetition, sequence, and variation, become the primary melodic factor of a phrase, appearing as a constructional element not only in the phrase melody but also, through imitation, in the bass line and inner voices. Sometimes a motive, during the course of a piece, is divided into segments which then may act independently. A motive separated in this manner is referred to as a *compound motive.*

4

DEVELOPMENT
OF THE PHRASE

A phrase is developed by expanding it at one or more points. Expansion at the beginning of the phrase is an *introduction*; during the phrase, an *interpolation*; and at the end, an *extension*.

4–A.
INTRODUCTION TO THE PHRASE

There are four common methods of introducing a phrase:

1. By a bar or two of the accompaniment

Example 4–1

SCHUBERT: *Quartet, Op. 29,* First Movement

(See also Mozart, *Symphony No. 40,* mm. 1–3.)

2. By one or more chords

41

Example 4–2

IVES: *The Greatest Man*

(See also Beethoven, *Symphony No. 3*, mm. 1–4.)

3. By one or more tones

Example 4–3

BEETHOVEN: *Sonata, Op. 106*, Third Movement

(See also Ex. 6–1, first phrase.)

4. By anticipation of the opening motive of the phrase

Example 4–4

BARTÓK: *Quartet No. 2*, First Movement

(See also Schubert, *Sonata, Op. 147*, Finale, mm. 1–3.)

While there are additional ways of introducing a phrase, it would be impractical to attempt to enumerate every possible method which the imagination of a gifted composer might conceive. The student's attention is, nevertheless, directed to the opening of Beethoven's *Symphony No. 5* and Brahms' *Symphony No. 2.*

4–B.
INTERPOLATION DURING THE PHRASE

MOTIVIC INTERPOLATION

Example 4–5

BEETHOVEN: *Symphony No. 5*, Third Movement

Example 4–5 shows a phrase and its repetition. While the original phrase is eight bars long, the repetition has been expanded to a length of ten bars, accomplished by means of a two-bar interpolation. This interpolation begins with a sequence of the final motive of the first phrase member (m. 11). The method employed here is called, then, phrase expansion by motivic interpolation.

PROLONGATION OF A NOTE OR CHORD

Example 4–6

BEETHOVEN: *Sonata, Op. 57*

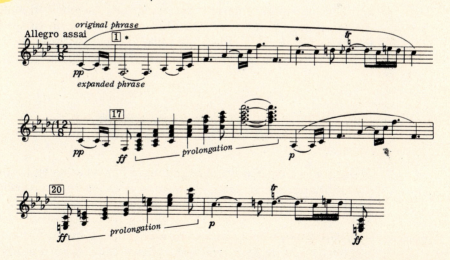

In Ex. 4–6, the second phrase expands the first by a prolongation of a chord. Asterisks in the original phrase mark the points that are prolonged in the second.

Unless the phrase with the interpolation has appeared previously in its original form, one cannot speak confidently of an interpolation. Without the original phrase for comparison, there can be no certainty whether the assumed interpolation is really such, or is an integral part of the phrase.

Example 4–7

HAYDN: *Quartet, Op. 76, No. 5*

In Ex. 4–7, the two phrases begin in an identical manner. Since they are so similar, the listener might well expect them to be of the same length, and hence he might interpret the rising scale fragment in mm. 7–8 as an interpolation. However, similar phrases are under no compulsion to be the same length. It is at least as valid to consider the scale fragment an integral part of the phrase as to deem it an interpolation.

4–C.
EXTENSION OF THE PHRASE

There are two chief ways of extending a phrase at its end. The first is to add to it after the cadence; the second is to evade a conclusive cadence until after the extension has been made.

EXTENSION ADDED AFTER THE CADENCE

Prolongation of Final Note or Chord A common method of lengthening a phrase by adding to it after the cadence consists in repeating the final chord or chords, or in prolonging the final chord by means of succession. Many compositions end with such extensions of the final phrase. Phrases within the piece may also be extended in the same manner.

Example 4–8

BRAHMS: *Rhapsody, Op. 119, No. 4*

prolongation of cadence

Repetition of Final Phrase Member

Example 4–9

SCHUBERT: *Ständchen*

Often the phrase is extended by a simple repetition of the final phrase member. In vocal music and music for a solo instrument with accompaniment, such extensions frequently take the form of interludes, as in Ex. 4–9. Still, one must not assume that each time the soloist is silent and the accompaniment becomes prominent, the resulting interlude is an extension of the phrase. A regular phrase member or motive may be taken up by the accompaniment while the soloist rests.

Example 4–10

SCHUMANN: *Der Nussbaum*

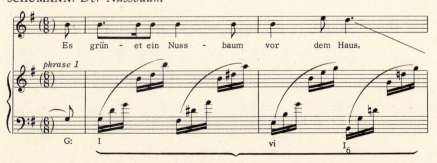

Schumann, in Ex. 4–10, has given the first phrase member to the voice, and the second (the cadence) to the piano. There is no question here of an interlude formed by any device of phrase expansion. Only if the interlude is clearly an addition to the phrase, considering the whole complex of sound and not only the soloist's part, should it be attributed to phrase development.

Sequence of Final Phrase Member

Example 4–11

HAYDN: *Symphony No. 88*

In the excerpt in Ex. 4–11 the phrase cadences regularly on the tonic, the subsequent extension, a modified sequence, establishing V as a secondary tonic.

EXTENSION BY
EVADED
CADENCE **Example 4–12**

SCHUBERT: *Winterreise, Wasserfluth (No. 6)*

In the foregoing examples the extensions occurred *after* the phrases' cadences. An extension may also be the result of an evaded cadence. In Ex. 4–12 the melodic line and the harmony of m. 11 imply a cadence in m. 12, but by means of a deceptive progression this cadence is postponed two bars. Motivically the extension is derived by free inversion from the preceding phrase member. At other times the extension is a repetition or sequence of a previous phrase member, or it may be entirely new.

4–D.
PHRASE DEVELOPMENT BY A
COMBINATION OF METHODS

The methods of phrase expansion used in combination with themselves and also with those of motivic construction may result in phrases of considerable length.

Example 4–13

SCHUBERT: *Trio, Op. 99,* Third Movement

In Ex. 4–13 a two-bar phrase member is greatly expanded by sequences, repetitions, and imitations before coming to a cadence. In addition, the phrase is preceded by an introduction and closed with two extensions following the cadence. What could have been a four-bar phrase has thus been worked up to twenty-one bars.

EXERCISE

1. Locate, identify, and describe all phrase developments to be found in the following passages.

   a. Beethoven, *Quartet Op. 135*, Third Movement, mm. 1–6; and mm. 7–12.

   b. Schubert, *Who Is Sylvia?* (entire).

   c. Schubert, *Der Doppelgänger*, mm. 1–14.

   d. Schumann: *Album for the Young, No. 31*, mm. 21–28.

   e. Chopin, *Mazurka No. 5*, mm. 1–12.

   f. Chopin, *Nocturne, Op. 27 No. 2*, mm. 1–9.

   g. Wagner, *Tristan und Isolde*, Prelude, mm. 1–17.

   h. Brahms, *Intermezzo, Op. 119, No. 2*, mm. 3–6 (compare mm. 1–2).

   i. Wolf, *Das verlassene Mägdlein*, mm. 38–47 (compare mm. 5–12).

   j. Debussy, *Prélude à "L'après-midi d'un faune,"* mm. 55–74.

   k. Bartók, *Mikrokosmos, No. 133*, mm. 18–24 (compare mm. 3–4).

5

PHRASES IN COMBINATION

Just as motives may combine to become a phrase member and phrase members become a phrase, so may a number of phrases combine to become a larger unit. When we hear two or more phrases as a larger unit, we may describe the result in one of three ways. These are the *period*, the *phrase group*, and *phrase chain*.

In order to distinguish among the three types of larger unit it is essential that we first consider the differences in meaning among the following terms: *repetition*, *varied repetition*, *similar*, and *dissimilar*. When we say a certain phrase is a varied repetition of another phrase, we mean something quite different from what we mean when we say that a certain phrase is similar to another phrase. When an idea is repeated, even in a varied form, the repetition is essentially the same idea stated again. When two ideas are similar, they are essentially different, but with certain features in common. And, of course, when an idea is dissimilar to another, it is essentially contrasting to it.

5–A.
VARIED AND SIMILAR PHRASES

CADENCES
DIFFERING
RADICALLY

Example 5–1

SCHUBERT:
a. *Die Nebensonnen*
b. *Am Meer*

50

Each excerpt of Ex. 5–1 consists of two phrases greatly resembling each other in melody. Those of *Am Meer* carry out this resemblance in the harmony as well, while the second phrase of *Die Nebensonnen* is harmonized quite differently from the first phrase. But in the cadences the situation is reversed. In spite of the difference in harmonies of the two phrases of Ex. 5–1a, the cadences are identical. Although the phrase melody is supported in the second phrase by a new harmonization, the difference between the two phrases is superficial, for the goal of both harmonic sequences is the same: V_7–I. The second phrase is a varied repetition of the first.

In Ex. 5–1b the cadences are radically different, the first being a semicadence ending on V, the second a perfect cadence, V_7–I. Regardless of the fact that the two phrases, up to the cadences, exhibit identical harmonies, the second is not a repetition but a different phrase similar to the first, for the two harmonic sequences have different goals.

The plan of a house is altered if a wall is moved, but not if the wall is only painted. Phrases are varied if unessential, but not essential, changes have been made between them. Altered harmony, transfer of the melody to a higher or lower octave, melodic embellishment—these are decorative changes, not structural ones.

The crux of the question of whether an essential or an unessential change has been made lies in the cadence.

If the harmonic movement of the two phrases leads to the same goal, the second is a varied phrase. If the cadences are radically different, then an essential change has been made, and the second is a similar phrase.

A wall can be both moved and painted. It need hardly be pointed out that if both decorative and structural changes have been made in the second of two phrases, from the point of view of the study of form it is the structural change which is the more noteworthy.

CADENTIAL STRENGTH DETERMINED BY GOAL OF MELODIC LINE The nursery song *Mary Had a Little Lamb* consists of two phrases which illustrate an important point. Although each phrase closes with an authentic cadence, the two cadences exhibit very different degrees of strength. The first (the third "little lamb") is an imperfect cadence, as the third and the fifth of the tonic triad are in the melody. The second ("white as snow") is a perfect cadence, the root of the tonic triad in the melody. Since both use the progression V–I, the two cadences cannot be considered radically different. Nevertheless, the greater strength of the perfect cadence does give the listener the impression of an essential change in the second phrase, for it is in the second phrase that the melodic line completes its descent to the final tonic note. In this case then, and in others which exhibit decided differences in cadential strength, the second phrase is not to be considered a varied repetition of the first, but a different phrase, similar to the first—the difference lying not necessarily in the harmony but in the melodic line of the cadences. (Another familiar example of the same phenomenon is to be found in the first two phrases of *Believe Me If All Those Endearing Young Charms.*)

REPETITION OF PHRASES It is common for a speaker to make a statement and repeat it at once, either exactly or in different words. This device emphasizes, or clarifies, the original statement but does not cause the argument to progress. Similarly, in music a phrase may be sounded, then immediately repeated, either exactly or with some variation. The repetition does not contribute to the growth of the musical form, but exists, if repeated exactly, for emphasis. It exists as a means of elaboration or clarification if repeated in a variation— the composer is saying, "In other words. . . ." Identification of the larger unit depends upon the distinction between varied and similar phrases. A series of phrases, each one of which is no more than a repetition, varied or exact, of the other, remains a series of repeated phrases. They do not form a larger unit. The period, phrase group, and phrase chain must each comprise at least two *different* phrases.

EXERCISE

1. Each of the following passages consists of two phrases. Locate these, then compare the second with the first. Is it a similar phrase, a varied repetition, or neither? Why?
    a. Couperin, *La Bandoline*, mm. 1–8.
    b. Anon., *Aria*, mm. 1–8 and 9–16.
    c. Bach, *English Suite in G minor*, Gavotte I, mm. 1–8.
    d. Bach, *Suite for Violoncello Solo in G major*, Menuett II, mm. 25–32.
    e. Beethoven, *Sonata, Op. 13*, Third Movement, mm. 5–12.
    f. Chopin, *Prelude No. 20*, mm. 1–8.
    g. Chopin, *Mazurka No. 45*, mm. 1–16.
    h. Brahms, *Intermezzo, Op. 118, No. 2*, mm. 1–8 and 57–64.
    i. Wolf, *Das verlassene Mägdlein*, mm. 5–12.
    j. Debussy, *Prélude à ''L'après-midi d'un faune''*, mm. 55–74.
    k. Bartók, *Mikrokosmos No. 144*, m. 1–5 (beat 1).

5–B.
PHRASE CHAIN

Example 5–2

MOZART: *Don Giovanni*, Overture

Example 5–2, found between the principal and secondary themes of Mozart's Overture to *Don Giovanni,* consists of three phrases which do not resemble each other. True, they are not completely contrasting, for they show singleness of meter and tempo with unity of key and general style. For instance, the accompanimental figure of repeated eighth notes plays a role in each phrase. Still, the contrasts inherent in the three phrases are more readily apparent than their similarities. Such phrases are spoken of as *dissimilar.* Several dissimilar phrases sometimes appear consecutively in a composition and may be referred to as a phrase chain. The phrase chain ends with an inconclusive cadence, in this case vii°$_7$/V–V.

5–C.
PHRASE GROUP

Example 5–3

CHOPIN: *Prelude, Op. 28, No. 22*

Example 5–3 consists of two different phrases that are similar. Their similarity links them together in the mind of the listener and we therefore speak of them as forming a group rather than a chain of phrases. Some phrase groups contain a number of phrases. To qualify as a group it is necessary for at least two of these phrases to be similar.

Special note should be taken of the fact that neither phrase group nor phrase chain ends with a conclusive cadence.

5–D.
PERIOD

From the melodic standpoint the period may resemble either the phrase chain or the phrase group. It consists of similar phrases, dissimilar phrases, or a combination of both. But it is distinguished from the others in a different way. The period consists of a series of phrases which, aside from the question of resemblances in design, are related by virtue of harmonic organization or *tonal structure* (see section 1–c).

Example 5–4

BEETHOVEN: *Symphony No. 7*

Phrase 1 of Ex. 5–4 presents a chord succession prolonging the i, then cadences on III, treated as a secondary tonic. Phrase 2 begins with III, progresses to i, prolonged by chord succession, and closes with a perfect authentic cadence. There are two important observations to be made in connection with this harmonic movement.

SINGLENESS OF TONAL STRUCTURE The tonal structures of both phrases can be considered as comprising a single harmonic movement. Phrase 1 moves from i to III, phrase 2 from III to i, brought to a close with V–i. The first fourteen measures of the example can be understood in the light of the whole passage as an extended chord succession, i–III–i, preceding the final cadence V–i.

The harmonic organization of the phrase was pointed out (section 2–E) as particularly important, since it exhibits on a small scale the same type of structures that the larger sections show magnified. We have just witnessed a simple case, still on rather a small scale, of the resemblance between the tonal structure of the phrase and that of a larger unit. As we concern ourselves more and more with forms of greater dimensions, we shall continue to note this striking phenomenon.

STRENGTH OF FINAL CADENCE The second observation to be made is concerned with the relative strength of the cadences of Ex. 5–4. The cadence of phrase 2 is stronger than that of phrase 1, for the latter is an imperfect cadence, the former a perfect one.

These two observations combine to point to an essential characteristic of the period:

> The final phrase of the period completes a harmonic movement that the preceding phrase or phrases had left incomplete.

The final cadence, exhibiting greater strength than any previous one, helps to bring about the conclusive quality requisite to the completion of the entire harmonic movement. The total impression of the period is not unlike that of question and answer. Some theorists do speak of the phrases in these terms, but in common usage they are called *antecedent* and *consequent*.

Example 5–4 is a two-phrase period consisting of one antecedent and one consequent. The consequent is, in fact, repeated, this pianissimo echo providing an exquisite conclusion. But a repeated consequent does not change a two-phrase period into one of three phrases. Only when three different phrases are present, as in *Silent Night*, does one speak of a three-phrase period. Occasionally periods consist of even more than three phrases.

5–E.
TYPES OF HARMONIC MOVEMENT
IN THE PERIOD

COMPLETE HARMONIC MOVEMENT **Example 5–5**

BRAHMS: *Wie Melodien zieht es mir*

The final section of Brahms' song, *Wie Melodien zieht es mir, Op. 105, No. 1*, is made up of three phrases which show such slight motivic resemblances that they must be considered virtually dissimilar. Being dissimilar, they are not to be thought of as a phrase group. An examination of the tonal structure will reveal whether they are a phrase chain or a period. If the final phrase fulfills a harmonic movement left unfulfilled by the previous phrases, the passage is a period.

Phrase 1 moves from I through IV to the imperfect cadence $\flat II_6$–I. Phrase 2 progresses from I to an imperfect authentic cadence on $\flat VI$. Phrase 3 leads through $\flat II$ (prepared by the $\flat II_6$ in phrase 1) back to I where it closes with a perfect full cadence. The essential harmonic movement of the whole excerpt may be summarized as:

$$
\begin{array}{ccc}
\text{phrase I} & \text{phrase 2} & \text{phrase 3} \\
\text{I} \rightarrow \flat II_6\text{–I} & \text{I} \rightarrow \underbrace{V_7\text{–I}}_{\text{of } \flat VI} & \underbrace{V_7\text{–I}}_{\text{of } \flat II} \rightarrow ii_6\text{–}V_7\text{–I}
\end{array}
$$

The three phrases of the period embody a series of harmonies which establish I, move to $\flat VI$ and $\flat II$, then return to I with a perfect full cadence: A complete harmonic movement, expressed succinctly as I–$\flat VI$–$\flat II$–ii_6–V_7–I. It is this completion, this rounding off of the tonal structure, that creates the most significant relationship among the three phrases of this period.

Re-examination of Ex. 5–2 and Ex. 5–3 will reveal no such completion in the final phrase of a harmonic movement begun by the preceding phrases. On the contrary, in each of these examples the final phrase ends with a half cadence.

INTERRUPTION OF THE HARMONIC MOVEMENT

Referring back to Ex. 5–1b, we now realize that its two similar phrases form a period, for the authentic cadence that closes the second phrase concludes a harmonic movement that was left inconclusive by the semicadence of phrase 1. Nevertheless, the tonal structure of this period is quite unlike that of the periods illustrated in Ex. 5–4 and Ex. 5–5. These periods consisted of a complete harmonic movement begun by the antecedent, continued (in Ex. 5–5) by the second antecedent, and further continued and concluded by the consequent. In Ex. 5–1b, however, the consequent does not merely continue and conclude a harmonic movement begun by the antecedent—it first repeats this movement from the beginning, both in harmony and in melody, then brings it to a close with the authentic cadence. In other words, the antecedent, initiating the harmonic movement, brings it as far as the cadential V which, instead of going on to a final I, is left unresolved. At this point the harmonic movement is interrupted. The consequent begins the movement again, traverses the same harmonic and melodic path, and this time reaches a conclusion.

Example 5–6

SCHUBERT: *Am Meer* (reduction)

Interruption of the harmonic movement will be indicated in this book by two vertical lines. Thus the tonal structure of Ex. 5–1b can be outlined as:

$$\underbrace{\text{I–V–I–IV}^6_4\text{–I–V}}_{\text{I}} \, \| \, \underbrace{\text{I–V–I–IV}^6_4\text{–I–V}_7\text{–I}}_{\text{I}}$$

or, I → V ‖ I → V₇–I.

The harmonic and melodic pattern of the consequent in Ex. 5–1b is, up to the cadence, identical to that of the antecedent. Example 5–7 is an illustration of another possibility.

Example 5–7

BERLIOZ: *The Damnation of Faust*, Part IV, Romance

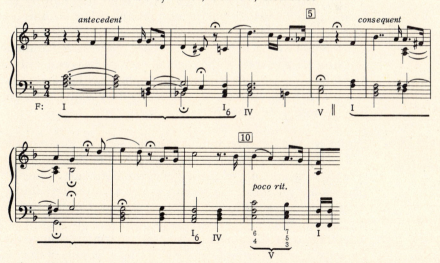

Both antecedent and consequent precede their respective cadences with chord successions prolonging the tonic chord, first in root position, then in first inversion (see Ex. 2–15). However, the two harmonic sequences of which these successions are comprised are decidedly different, in spite of melodic similarity. The consequent in this case travels from the starting point of the antecedent to its goal, but not via the same route.

PROGRESSIVE HARMONIC MOVEMENT

Example 5–8

SCHUMANN: *Kinderscenen No. 7*

The antecedent of the period in Ex. 5–8 ends with a half cadence on V. The consequent also ends with V, not as a half cadence, but as a secondary tonic. The harmonic movement here differs from that of the previous examples, for it progresses from the tonic area to that of the dominant. The full cadence at the end of the second phrase closes the movement, even though this movement has led away from the starting place without returning to it. Periods making up portions of larger forms often establish such secondary tonics at their close.

It should be especially noted here that progressive harmonic movement is taking place in spite of the fact that both phrases end with a V. Since the first V (m. 4) is part of a half cadence in the tonic key and the second V (m. 8) is part of a perfect authentic cadence with V acting as a secondary tonic, they represent different harmonic areas.

REPETITION OF THE HARMONIC MOVEMENT

Earlier we had occasion to note that the second phrase of the song *Mary Had a Little Lamb* is different from, though similar to, the first phrase (see section 5–A). In spite of the fact that the harmonic sequences of the two phrases are identical, the second is not a varied repetition of the first. Attention was called to the differing strengths of the two cadences, the first being imperfect, the second perfect. The question now arises as to whether two similar phrases, identical in harmony even to their cadences, can form a period. In spite of the differing strengths of the cadences, both phrases have the same harmonic goal, hence the second phrase cannot complete a harmonic movement left incomplete by the first phrase. The two phrases of Ex. 5–9 show a parallel situation.

Example 5–9

GOUNOD: *Faust*, Act I

The ear hears phrase 1 as incomplete, phrase 2 as complete. The reason for this phenomenon is that although the harmonic movement completes itself in both antecedent and consequent, the melodic movement is such that at the end of phrase 1 the uppermost voice has not reached the tonic note but the mediant or the dominant note. When, then, in phrase 2 the melody as well as the harmony arrives at the tonic, the listener is given a definite impression that something incomplete has now been completed. This is, however, merely an impression. The imperfect cadence is actually a conclusive cadence, not an inconclusive one, as many compositions ending with the third or fifth of the tonic triad in the soprano testify (for instance, *Chorale No. 74* or the first and last pieces of Schumann's *Kinder-*

scenen). It is only after the listener has heard the perfect cadence and compared it ex post facto with the imperfect, that the latter seems inconclusive. This strong, universal impression is the probable cause of the general recognition that two phrases with identical harmonic goals can, under the circumstances just described, form a period.

SUMMARY OF TYPES OF HARMONIC MOVEMENT FOUND IN THE PERIOD

1. *Complete harmonic movement* refers to a move away from a tonic with a return to that tonic via a conclusive cadence.

2. *Interrupted harmonic movement* occurs when a passage makes its way as far as the cadential V but does not reach the final I. Instead, it returns immediately to the beginning and repeats both the melodic and harmonic movement, exactly or with variation, altering the ending so that it concludes with a final tonic.

3. *Progressive harmonic movement* refers to a move away from a tonic without an immediate return. Such a move may embody a real modulation or the establishment of only a brief secondary tonic.

4. *Repeated harmonic movement* occurs in a period when the harmonic goal of the consequent is reached by the antecedent (or, in a multiphrase period, by one or more of the antecedents). In this case it is the melodic goal that remains for the consequent to fulfill, and in so doing the harmonic movement takes place twice.

    Complete, interrupted, and progressive are all single harmonic movements. When the harmonic movement is repeated, it is a double harmonic movement.

EXERCISES

2. Terms to define:

    Phrase chain   Complete harmonic movement
    Phrase group   Interrupted harmonic movement
    Period   Progressive harmonic movement
    Antecedent   Repeated harmonic movement
    Consequent

3. Consider the passages of Exercise 1 of this chapter. Which type of harmonic movement is represented by each?

5–F.
DESIGN OF THE PERIOD

A number of two-phrase periods have been illustrated in previous examples (Ex. 4–7, Ex. 5–1b, Ex. 5–4, Ex. 5–7, and Ex. 5–8). The two-phrase period, consisting of a single antecedent balanced by a single consequent, is considered to be a symmetrical period. Whether or not the consequent is of precisely the same length as the antecedent is immaterial here. Usually they are the same, but the consequent of Ex. 4–7 is one bar longer than the antecedent; in Ex. 5–7 it is two bars longer. These "irregularities" do not destroy the basic symmetry created when a single antecedent is answered by a single consequent.

Example 5–10

MENDELSSOHN: *Song without Words, Op. 85, No. 1*

Example 5–10 illustrates a ==symmetrical period== in which both the antecedent and the consequent have been extended to two phrases. Since each component part of this symmetrical period consists of two phrases, we refer to this type of larger unit as a ==double period==. Similarly, one occasionally comes across triple periods (three phrases in the antecedent and three in the consequent) and even quadruple periods.

A comparison of Ex. 5–10 with Ex. 6–5 (Brahms' *Cradle Song*) will point up the essential difference between a ==double period and two symmetrical periods== of two phrases each. In Ex. 5–9, the second phrase ends with a weaker cadence than that of the fourth phrase. The four phrases comprise one double period because the last two phrases (the consequent) complete a harmonic motion left incomplete by the first two phrases (the antecedent). In Ex. 6–5, on the other hand, the cadence of the second phrase has the same strength as that of the fourth. The harmonic motion completes itself in the first two phrases, the last two phrases constituting a second harmonic motion.[1]

THE ==ASYMMETRICAL PERIOD==

Silent Night and Ex. 5–5 are three-phrase periods. Example 5–11 is one of five phrases. (The complete piece is in Burkhart's *Anthology*.)

Example 5–11

BRAHMS: *Intermezzo, Op. 118, No. 6*

[1] The fact that the second period nevertheless does seem more conclusive than the first can be attributed to (1) the effect of the subdominant harmony in the second period, and (2) the descent of the voice line from the high tonic to the low.

In the above cases we have a series of antecedents, an *antecedent group*, followed by a consequent.

Example 5–12

MOZART: *Die Zufriedenheit, K. 349*

The melodic resemblance between the last two phrases of the preceding period causes them to be associated together in the mind of the listener. It would be proper, then, to speak here of an antecedent followed by a *consequent group*.

PARALLEL CONSTRUCTION

By returning once again to the symmetrical period by Haydn (Ex. 4–7), we notice that the first bar of the antecedent is restated by the first bar of the consequent, the second of the antecedent by the second of the consequent. This kind of correspondence between the opening bars of two similar phrases is termed *parallel construction* and results in a *parallel period*. Other parallel periods have been Exx. 5–1b, 5–7, and 5–8. Ex. 5–9 shows parallel construction in a double period. It must not be assumed that every period consisting of similar phrases necessarily exhibits parallel construction. Exx. 5–4 and 5–6, for instance, are made up of similar phrases but the requisite correspondence between measures is lacking.

A two-phrase period consisting of dissimilar phrases is referred to as a *contrasting period*. (See the first eight bars of Ex. 6–3.)

EXERCISE

4. Contrast:
    a. Symmetrical and asymmetrical periods
    b. Two-phrase symmetrical period and double period
    c. Double period and two adjacent symmetrical periods
    d. Parallel and contrasting periods

5–G.
IDENTIFICATION OF THE LARGER UNIT

The six steps outlined below are offered as an aid to the student. After acquiring a certain amount of practice, one may find it unnecessary to employ these steps methodically. The experienced musician is often able to grasp the essence of a passage of music without having to resort to a slow, painstaking process. But until students have acquired the requisite experience, they would do well to use consciously and carefully the method presented here.

Step 1. Locate each phrase and note its cadence, discovering whether the phrases are different or merely repetitions of a single phrase.

Step 2. Consider the phrase melodies, taking note of any varied or exact phrase repetitions, and identifying similar and dissimilar phrases.

Step 3. In the light of steps 1 and 2, decide whether the phrase series forms a larger unit or not, and if so, in which general category—period, phrase group, or phrase chain—it belongs. (Remember that the larger unit must consist of at least two *different* phrases and that only the period comes to a conclusive cadence.)

Step 4. Locate the phrase which seems to close the larger unit, then examine the phrases which immediately follow it to make certain they do not belong with those in question. It is possible that a subsequent phrase might conclude with a cadence stronger than that of the presumed final phrase, or it might be a repetition of the final phrase.

Once the ending of the larger unit has been definitely located, one can proceed with confidence. If step 3 has led to the conclusion that what is being dealt with is only a series of repeated phrases, there is no more to be done, for no larger unit is present. If a decision in favor of a phrase group or phrase chain has been reached, the identification is complete at this point. But if a period exists, steps 5 and 6 must be taken.

Step 5. Examine the phrases again for harmonic content, noting whether the period exhibits:

a. A complete harmonic movement (as in Ex. 5–4, 5–5, and 5–12)
b. Interrupted harmonic movement (as in Ex. 5–1b and Ex. 5–7)
c. Progressive harmonic movement (as in Ex. 5–8, 5–10, and 5–11)
d. Repetition of harmonic movement (as in Ex. 5–9)

Step 6. Come to a conclusion regarding the symmetry of the period. If symmetrical, is it a single or double period? If asymmetrical, does it exhibit an antecedent group or a consequent group? (In an asymmetrical period, all phrases except the last are antecedents unless the last shows a close and exclusive relationship to the phrase or phrases immediately preceding it.)

5–H.
APPLICATION OF THE SIX STEPS

For demonstration purposes we shall consider the beginning of César Franck's *Violin Sonata in A Major* following the six steps (see Ex. 5–13). Admittedly, this passage is somewhat difficult. It has purposely been chosen to illustrate the length and complexity which some periods attain to. The student who works through the explanation with care will find that, by comparison, other periods appearing in this study will be apt to seem simple.

Step 1. Measures 1–4 consist of dominant harmony, played by the piano alone, and anticipate the opening two notes of the violin's melody. Clearly these four bars are an introduction to the first phrase. We begin, then, at m. 5, the harmony moving from a succession on V_9 to an imperfect cadence on I (m. 8), the melody dividing itself into two halves of two bars each. This would seem to be a phrase of two phrase members. Its cadence is somewhat conclusive, but as this is still phrase 1 we can hardly have reached the end of a larger unit. The next melodic caesura is at m. 12, supported by the half cadence on V^7/III. These four bars (mm. 9–12) form phrase 2. Another melodic caesura appears in m. 16 accompanied by the half cadence on V^7/V, and we recognize phrase 3. In m. 20 the melody again shows a clear caesura, indicating the end of phrase 4, although only a very slight harmonic movement has taken place (V/V → vii$^6_5$, with no change of bass). Phrase 5 begins with m. 21 and continues like the others for four bars, semicadencing similarly to phrase 4 on vii$^6_5$/II. Phrase 6, unlike the preceding phrases, is not a four-bar phrase but is extended to seven, closing with an imperfect authentic cadence on V. Although this is not the strongest possible cadence with which a period can end, the different character of the music taken up at this point by the piano gives us a hint that we should, at least for the time being, stop here. Whether we have really reached the end of a period remains to be seen. Meanwhile, we go on to step 2.

Step 2. It is a universal practice in formal analysis to employ symbols that stand for the various members of a composition. A phrase, for example, could be symbolized by the letter A. Its repetition, whether varied or exact, would also be dubbed A, while a similar phrase would be represented by A′ (A prime). Should there be a third phrase similar to the others it would be called A″ (A double prime). When dissimilar phrases appear they are labeled B, C, D, and so on, and each of these might carry with it a similar phrase of its own: B′, C′, D′, and so on.

Example 5–13

FRANCK: *Violin Sonata in A Major*

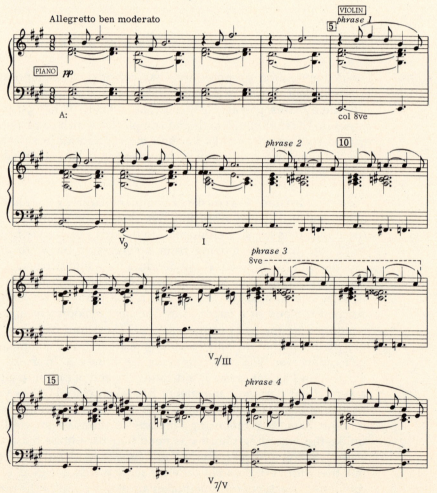

In applying step 2 to Ex. 5–13, then, the pattern of similar and dissimilar phrases could be represented by the symbols ABB'CC'A'.

Step 3. Step 1 has shown that the cadences of the six phrases are all radically different. We are, therefore, dealing with six different phrases combined into a larger unit. Since phrase 6 ends with a conclusive cadence the general category of this larger unit is the period.

Step 4. The phrase that follows phrase 6 ends with a semicadence and therefore cannot act as a final phrase to the previous six, for to do so it would have to be stronger than the cadence of phrase 6. Phrase 6 is therefore the end of the period. A number of other factors combine to separate the seventh phrase from the previous six, factors having to do with design:

a. The cadence of phrase 6 carried the direction *molto ritard.*, the first *ritardando* so far and indicative of a conclusion
b. Phrase 7 is for piano alone, an important change in timbre
c. Phrase 7 shows a new figure in the accompaniment
d. Phrase 7 carries with it a different dynamic and emotional quality

These additional factors can do no more than confirm what the cadential relationships have already established.

Step 5. It frequently happens that step 5 can be much simplified by making an outline of the essential harmonic movement of each phrase, for an outline readily shows the cadential relationships.

Example 5–14

FRANCK: *Violin Sonata in A Major* (harmonic outline)

In the harmonic outline (Ex. 5–14a), we perceive at once that the period closes with V treated as a secondary tonic. The seventh chord on B which acts as V_7/V had already made its appearance at the close of phrase 3 and was retained throughout most of phrase 4. The harmonies, then, which intervene between the V_7/V in phrase 3 and the V_7/V in the cadence of phrase 6 are part of a chord succession prolonging this V_7/V. These harmonies themselves point to II (that is, V/V) as a secondary tonic and throughout phrases 5 and 6 proceed by descending fifths (= ascending fourths).

Another interpretation of the harmonic events of this period is equally plausible. The bass outline (Ex. 5–14b) is self-explanatory.

By either reading, this period is based on a single harmonic movement of the progressive type, moving from I through III to V (Ex. 5–14c).

Step 6. The design, as symbolically represented in step 2, is clearly not an ordinary symmetrical period. Yet it shows a certain symmetry in that the first phrase is balanced by a similar phrase acting as a consequent.

The application of the six steps has led to the conclusion that Franck's *Violin Sonata* opens with a six-phrase period (a five-phrase antecedent group, a single phrase consequent) based on a progressive harmonic movement that passes from I through III to V. The phrases in the antecedent group are of a uniform length of four bars, while the consequent is extended to seven. Phrase 1 is preceded by four bars of introduction. The design of the period (ABB'CC'A') is symmetrical to the extent that the first antecedent is balanced by a consequent which is similar.

EXERCISES

5. Consider the passages of Exercise 1 of this chapter. Following the six-step method, identify those which comprise a larger unit and the type (period, phrase group, phrase chain). Give further identifying labels to all the periods.

6. Do the same for the following passages, some of which comprise more than two phrases.
   a. Haydn, "Clock Symphony," Finale, mm. 1–8
   b. Schumann, *Album for the Young*, No. 17, mm. 1–8
   c. Chopin, *Mazurka No. 24*, mm. 1–16; and 17–32
   d. Wagner, *Tristan*, mm. 1–24
   e. Brahms, *Intermezzo*, Op. 119, No. 2, mm. 1–12
   f. Ravel, *Le jardin féerique*, mm. 1–22

APPROACHES TOWARD MUSICAL UNDERSTANDING When we speak of music as a temporal art, we do not mean simply that sound takes place in time, for every aspect of our lives takes place in time. We mean, rather, that time, as well as sound, is one of the basic "ingredients" of music. When a composer organizes his sounds in time, he is also organizing time by means of his sounds. It is due to this interaction between sound and time that, when we hear a piece of music, it seems to be taking shape, in a sense *growing*, before us. And so music is often spoken of as "sound in motion." We can chart the growth of a piece only by listening to it from the beginning and keeping track of it as it emerges. Thus we often hear a melody being built up by a succession of motives or by a single motive succeeding itself with repetitions, variations, and sequences. Phrases following upon one another give rise to impressions of chains, groups, or periods.

The growth of a piece may also be considered from the point of view of the resulting shape or contour. The shape of a piece, as was pointed out in Section 1–B, has to do with matters of tension and relaxation, thinness or complexity of texture, qualities of movement, harmonic consonance and dissonance, matters of instrumentation and orchestration, types of figuration, and so forth. Often, as phrase follows phrase, these various aspects of the music produce a gradually increasing tenseness, mounting to a climax which then subsides. Very often such a build-up to a climax occurs more than once, with one climax, placed from about two-thirds to four-fifths of the way through, being broader and stronger than the others. A case in point is Chopin's *Prelude No. 4 in E Minor* (in the Burkhart *Anthology for Musical Analysis*). The tension builds from the beginning of the piece through m. 9, then subsides only to build again to a greater climax in m. 17. (Measure 17 is two-thirds of the way through this twenty-five bar piece.) Each build-up of tension with its subsequent relaxation is clearly felt, although it is difficult to pinpoint a single reason for it. Rather, the cause is a combination of the harmonies, constantly changing beneath the repeated b's and a's of the melodic line, the descent of the bass line, the smaller note values in mm. 7, 9, and 16–18, and, to some extent, increases in loudness (mm. 9, 16, and 17).

As we listen to the gradual growth of the music we cannot feel that any point of arrival or repose has been reached until the half cadence of m. 12. There is no second point of arrival until the end, for the chord and silence of m. 23 are felt as an interruption within the motion toward a goal, not as goals in themselves. Thus we have heard only two very long phrases in the entire piece. And these phrases stand in a periodic relationship to each other: antecedent and consequent.

In learning to recognize the phrase and its component parts, as we have done so far in this study, and in considering the larger unit created by the juxtaposition of several phrases, we have been considering the music from the point of view of the listener who hears the music from the start and follows its progress as it gradually takes shape from its opening to its closing sounds. For the most part we have not been *analyzing* the music in the literal sense of the word, but have instead been *synthesizing* it. It has not been so much a matter of taking the music apart, as of recognizing and identifying the way in which the motives and/or phrase members and phrases have forged themselves together into larger units.

There are those who argue that this is the only valid approach to understanding music: since music is a temporal art, one must discuss it only in the terms one might use while hearing the piece for the first time. On the other hand, committed listeners do not cease their musical experience with the fading away of the last note of the composition. To a lesser or greater extent, depending on their musical capabilities, they retain the piece in their memories. They can think back over it (or refresh memory by referring to a score), recalling points of arrival strong enough to divide the piece into two or more parts, or perhaps an area so different in character from the rest that it stands alone as a contrasting part.

Such an approach depends on having heard the entire piece through, then thinking back to find how the whole divides into parts, the parts into sections, and so on, and how these divisions are related to each other. This is the procedure to which we refer when we speak of *analysis*. The next chapter outlines a method by which the student can acquire the necessary skill to perform this kind of analysis.

6

THE ANALYTICAL
METHOD: SMALL FORMS

6–A.
FORM AND ANALYSIS

Analysis is the separation of a whole into its parts and the exploration of the relationship of these parts to the whole and to each other. In this study we have so far done the opposite: We have begun with the basic unit of music, the phrase, and concerned ourselves with the various methods of developing it and combining it with other phrases to form phrase chains, phrase groups, and periods.

We are now prepared to begin the process of analysis, either of complete one-movement compositions or of isolated movements from larger works, such as symphonies, concertos, quartets, sonatas, operas, oratorios, and so forth.

The works of the great composers rarely seem to have been created by pouring musical ideas into a preconceived mold. On the contrary, great music shapes itself into whatever form is most fitting to make explicit the particular concept in the mind of the composer. Consequently it is a mistake to think of the study of form as a process by which we familiarize ourselves with a certain number of standard "blueprints," then proceed to label each composition accordingly. To approach a composition with an open mind, ready to discover what the composer has in store for us, is a safer procedure than to assume in advance that any particular pattern will be in evidence.

This does not mean that we cannot attempt a systematization of forms. A perusal of the great musical literature of the past shows that certain broad formal categories tend to appear again and again. Thus we speak of "standard forms" and give them names. Such an undertaking is advantageous only if at the same time it is clearly realized that these names are applied to the music by theorists. The composer does not adapt his music to the form. Indeed, if it were otherwise, two compositions with precisely the same form would not be such a rarity.

6–B.
DIVISION INTO PARTS

Most compositions divide themselves into two or more parts, and the first goal of analysis is the discovery of the number of these parts. We have seen that Ex. 1–1 is a continuous binary form (section 1–D). It also consists of two periods. These labels do not conflict with each other for they move in different spheres. The former is an analytic term indicating that the piece divides itself into two parts. The latter is a descriptive term indicating the particular relationships exhibited by its various phrases. In the case of Ex. 1–1 part one of the composition is made up of a pair of phrases in a periodic relationship; part two is similarly disposed. In other binary compositions part one may be a single phrase, a phrase group, a series of repeated phrases, several periods, or anything else, and part two may show similar or entirely different constructions.

A part may be further divided into sections, and a section into subsections. Lengthy works usually exhibit these subdivisions, but many short compositions do not.

Often compositions are found that show none of the characteristics of division. These are the *one-part forms*.

6–C.
NAMING THE FORMS

BINARY AND TERNARY Some standard forms have names which are, and which have been for many years, in common use. We shall retain many of these names. "Binary" and "ternary," for instance, standing for forms in two and three parts respectively, are compact and useful. They are somewhat imprecise, however, in that they give no indication as to which of the several types of two- and three-part forms they refer. In this book we shall attempt to convey some idea of the tonal structure of the piece by employing in addition either the word "continuous" or the word "sectional."

CONTINUOUS AND SECTIONAL An "open" part of a composition is harmonically incomplete. The listener expects a continuation. A "closed" part contains within itself a complete harmonic movement. A tonal structure that causes the listener to expect a continuation after the first part gives rise to a continuous form. Thus any form with an "open" first part is continuous. A form with a "closed" first part grows by the addition of sections and hence is called a sectional form. Additional words of definition added to the names of some forms will be introduced later.

UNIQUE Certain forms are observed in very few compositions, sometimes in only one. These scarcely need to be given names and can be considered nonstandard or unique forms (see Chapter 15). At the same time it is important to remember that the so-called "standard forms" are standard only in their broadest outlines, almost never in details.

EXERCISE

1. Terms to define:
    Binary   Continuous forms
    Ternary   Sectional forms
    "Open" part   Standard forms
    "Closed" part   Unique forms

6–D.
TWO-PART FORMS

THE
CONTINUOUS
BINARY FORM:
DIVISION BY
DESIGN

Continuous forms in two parts are referred to as continuous binary forms. There are three standard types: (1) simple, (2) rounded, and (3) balanced.

Simple Continuous Binary

Example 6–1

HANDEL: *Suite No. 5 in E Major*, Air ("The Harmonious Blacksmith")

The Air from Handel's *Suite in E Major* for harpsichord consists of a three-phrase period. The first phrase moves from I to a strongly conclusive (strong-beat perfect authentic) cadence on V. The second phrase ends with a semicadence on V, while the third returns to I with another strong conclusive cadence. The basic tonal structure, then, comprises a single harmonic movement: I–V–I. Nevertheless, the listener feels a definite division take place at the close of the first phrase due to the strength of the strong-beat perfect authentic cadence on V. Only the final cadence surpasses its strength. Further, in comparing the cadence at the end of the first phrase with that which concludes the second, we observe that the eighth-note motion stops with the first B major chord, increasing the feeling of strong punctuation, while the less conclusive ending of the second phrase is partly due to the continuing rhythmic movement in the bass. The piece, then, is in two parts: Part one consists of the first phrase, part two of the two remaining phrases.

The repetition of each part is a by-product, not a cause, of the division. Nor is the tonal structure responsible for the separation into two parts. Example 6–1 illustrates the fact that a composition with a single harmonic movement can divide itself into two parts by means of an emphatic conclusive cadence on a nontonic chord, that is, by an aspect of design. It is the design of the piece as manifested in the relative strength of the cadences that has brought about the division. Division into two results in a binary form. The first part is harmonically "open": it is, therefore, continuous. Its form is referred to as continuous binary and the design symbolized by the letters AB, or, as in Ex. 1–1, AA'.

Rounded Continuous Binary In the description of the technique of interruption in the preceding chapter, the examples of this technique were alike in that, *as soon as* the cadential V was reached, the harmonic and melodic movement returned to the beginning (Exs. 5–1b and 5–6). It often happens, however, that this V is prolonged by means of chord succession before the actual interruption takes place. In Ex. 6–2, for instance, the V is reached in m. 2, then prolonged by succession (iv₆–V–iv₆–V) before the interruption occurs in bar 3 followed by the return to the opening.

Example 6–2

PERGOLESI: *Lo frate 'nnamorato,* Act I

Used by permission of Gli Amici Della Musica Da Camera, Rome.

b. *(reduction)*

g: i   V ____ *extension* ‖ i   V   i

The prolongation of V in Ex. 6–2 took the form of a short extension, repeated, to the phrase. Example 6–3 is a piece in which the chord succession prolonging V becomes a phrase of its own.

Example 6–3

MOZART: *Symphony, K. 183* ("Little G Minor"), Third Movement

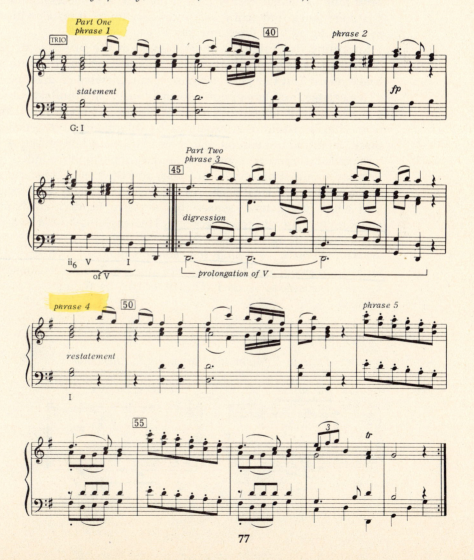

Let us examine Ex. 6–3 first from the point of view of its tonal structure. The opening period (phrases 1 and 2, mm. 37–44) comprises a progressive harmonic movement from I to V. The ensuing chord succession making up phrase 3 (mm. 45–48) prolongs this V. Interruption now occurs. The harmonic and melodic movement returns to the beginning, this time cadencing on the tonic. The tonal structure can be summarized as follows:

$$I \rightarrow \frac{V\text{–}I}{\text{of } V} \ldots V_7 \parallel I \rightarrow V\text{–}I$$

Special notice should be taken of the fact that the interrupting V which is prolonged by means of the chord succession plays a different role at the beginning of the succession than at the end. The succession begins with this dominant chord acting as a secondary tonic; it closes with the same chord acting as V of the home key.

Regarding its design, Ex. 6–3 exemplifies the principle of statement, digression, restatement. Part one is a two-phrase period. Phrase 3, though based on the first two bars of phrase 1, is somewhat contrasting by virtue of the change from homophonic to an almost contrapuntal texture. Phrase 4 is a literal restatement of phrase 1; phrase 5 is a variation (transposed from V to I) of phrase 2, expanded by interpolation. The design of the piece, then, can be symbolically expressed by the letters AB ‖ A′, and the form called a rounded continuous binary, or simply rounded binary.

In the rounded binary the cadential and the melodic aspects of design are in conflict. The two conclusive cadences mark the ends of the two parts into which the listener senses the music to be divided. Nonetheless, melodically there are three sections. This explains how a two-part form can have the design AB ‖ A′.

Balanced Binary Very often the cadences that end each part of a simple binary movement are identical except in pitch. The first is usually on III or V while the second is on I. The result can be thought of as a musical "rhyme."

Example 6–4

HANDEL: *Suite in E Minor for Harpsichord, Allemande*

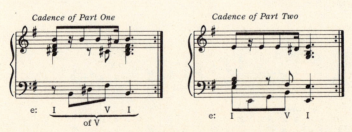

78

When these resemblances are, as in this case, no more than a bar or two in length, they can hardly be thought of as greatly influencing the listener's perception of form in the work. But sometimes the similarity in the endings of each part goes further than the final bar or two. For instance, in the *Courante* of Handel's *Suite in E Minor* (from which Ex. 6–4 was taken), the last eight bars of the first part, in the dominant key, appear in an almost exact transposition to the tonic as the last eight bars of the second part. Since the entire closing section of part one reappears as the close of part two, a piece so constructed is called a balanced binary. A parallel case is the well-known *Invention No. 8 in F Major* of J. S. Bach.

HISTORICAL NOTE Neither Bach nor Handel wrote balanced binary forms so often as they did simple binaries. Domenico Scarlatti, on the other hand, made very frequent use of the form. While his hundreds of sonatas show much variety in other ways, the great majority of them conclude part two with a transposed restatement of the final bars of part one. Scarlatti, however, did not care much for exact transpositions. Instead, he liked to end the two halves with a somewhat varied form of the same material.[1]

EXERCISES

2. Contrast:
   a. Simple continuous binary and rounded binary
   b. Simple continuous binary and balanced binary
   c. Rounded binary and balanced binary

3. Examine the compositions in continuous binary form listed below, answering the following questions:
   (1) Which measure marks the end of part one?
   (2) How is division into two brought about in each case?
   (3) What is the design of the composition?
   (4) Which type of continuous binary (simple, rounded, balanced) is represented by each piece?
   a. Chorale, *Ach Gott und Herr* (in Appendix)
   b. Chorale, *Schaut, ihr Sünder* (in Appendix)
   c. Anon., *Aria*
   d. Anon., *March*
   e. Haydn, *Symphony No. 101* ("Clock"), Third Movement, Trio only
   f. Beethoven, *Sonata Op. 2 No. 1*, Menuetto only
   g. Beethoven, *Sonata Op. 2 No. 1*, Trio only

[1] See No. 274 in Davidson and Apel, *Historical Anthology of Music*. Cambridge, Mass.: Harvard University Press, 1956. For a detailed study of form in Scarlatti's sonatas, see R. Kirkpatrick's *Domenico Scarlatti*. Princeton, N. J.: Princeton University Press, 1953, Chapter XI.

h. Beethoven, *Sonata, Op. 28,* Scherzo only
i. Schumann, *Album for the Young,* No. 1
j. Chopin, *Prelude No. 20*
k. Brahms, *Feldeinsamkeit,* mm. 1–17 (first stanza only)

THE SECTIONAL
BINARY FORM:
DIVISION BY
DOUBLE
HARMONIC
MOVEMENT

Sectional forms in two parts are referred to as sectional binary forms. There are three standard types: (a) simple, (b) rounded, and (c) barform. *Simple Sectional Binary*

Example 6–5

BRAHMS: *Wiegenlied*

Phrases 1 and 2 form a symmetrical period ending with the strongly conclusive perfect authentic cadence on I. The harmonic movement can in no sense be considered incomplete. Phrases 3 and 4 form another symmetrical period ending with a cadence as strong as the former. We have here, then, two periods (not a double period), each manifesting a complete harmonic movement. On the basis of this tonal structure the piece divides into two parts. The design follows suit: each period consists of two similar phrases, but the periods contrast with each other. Brahms' *Cradle Song* is a two-part form because of the double harmonic movement. The song's design, two symmetrical, parallel periods which contrast with each other, reinforces and confirms the division brought about by the tonal structure. The design is represented by the letters A–B, the hyphen indicating that A comprises a complete harmonic movement.

Example 6–5 illustrates the fact that a composition may divide itself into two parts by means of a tonal structure which consists of two complete harmonic movements. Division into two results in a binary form. The first part is harmonically "closed": It is therefore sectional. Its form is referred to as sectional binary, and the design is symbolized by the letters A–B. When the second part of a sectional binary form is constructed from the same material as is the first part, the design, of course, is A–A'.

On the other hand, when double harmonic movement results in a period, as in "Mary Had a Little Lamb," "Believe Me, If All Those Endearing Young Charms," and Example 5–9, the result is not perceived as a binary form in spite of the double harmonic movement. The effect of the melodic line which descends at the end of the antecedent to the third or fifth degree of the scale, and only at the end of the consequent to the first degree, is enough to offset the feeling of division into two parts. In these cases, the resulting piece is a one-part form (see Section 6–G).

Rounded Sectional Binary Example 6–6 illustrates a design frequently found in the sectional binary form. This design will be recognized as the counterpart of the rounded continuous binary. It differs from that form only in that its first part completes a harmonic movement. It may be spoken of as the rounded sectional binary.

Example 6–6

HAYDN: *Symphony No. 100 ("Military"), Third Movement*
Barform

Example 6–7

CRÜGER-BACH: *Schmücke dich, o liebe Seele*

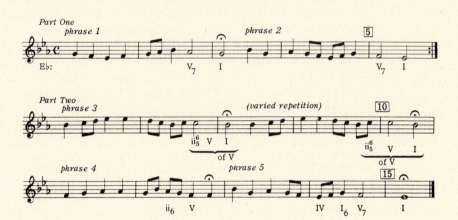

The chorale (Ex. 6–7) consists of five phrases, the third of which is repeated with varied harmony (not shown in the example). Phrases 1 and 2 comprise a symmetrical period which, concluding with a divisive perfect authentic cadence on the tonic, is readily recognized as part one, the remaining phrases forming part two. The tonal structure, like that of all sectional binaries, consists of two complete harmonic movements. The feature that distinguishes the form of this piece from the ordinary sectional binary is simply the fact that part one is repeated. Rather than A–B, the design is A–A–B. It is referred to as the barform.[2]

The two parts of the form exemplify a pattern of repetition followed by contrast. In some barforms the repetition is varied rather than exact. In Ex. 6–7 it will be noted that phrase 5 is a restatement of phrase 2. Thus the same phrase is used to close each of the two parts. While such "musical rhymes" are not an inevitable characteristic of barform, they are quite commonly found. A parallel case is the Lutheran hymn *A Mighty Fortress Is Our God* (in Appendix of Burkhart's *Anthology*).

HISTORICAL NOTE Ordinarily the repetition of a part is of little significance in formal analysis. If we make an exception here it is only because barform has for centuries been recognized as a distinct entity. Indeed it has a longer history than any other single form. It appeared during the early Middle Ages in the music of the Eastern Church, having been foreshadowed in the ancient Greek odes. Later it became the basis of the *canzo* of the troubadours in Provence and from there it moved to

---

[2] We retain the name because it is in common use although it is actually a misnomer (see Manfred Bukofzer, *Music of the Baroque Era*. New York: Norton, 1947, p. 356.)

northern France to become the trouvères' *ballade*. The German Minne-singer, and after them the Meistersinger, cultivated this form above all others and it is from these that the name "barform" derives. In medieval German nomenclature the first part and its repetition were called the *Stollen* ("stanzas"), the second part *Abgesang* ("aftersong"). These terms are often used today, in English as well as German, but some writers prefer to adopt the names of the parts of the ancient Greek odes: Part one is called the strophe, its repetition the antistrophe, and part two the epode.

After the decline of the Meistersinger the form continued to appear in Protestant chorales and folk songs. Barforms familiar to all are *Dixie* and *The Star-Spangled Banner*. Barform is not of particularly frequent occurrence in the art music of the eighteenth and nineteenth centuries,[3] but Wagner made much of it in his opera *Die Meistersinger von Nürnberg*, the *Trial Song* in Act I and the *Prize Song* in Act III both being highly developed, if somewhat irregular, examples.[4]

EXERCISES

4. Contrast:
   a. Continuous binary form with sectional binary form
   b. Simple sectional binary with rounded sectional binary
   c. Simple sectional binary with barform

5. Examine the compositions in sectional binary form listed below, answering the following questions:
   (1) Which measure marks the end of part one?
   (2) How is division into two brought about in each case?
   (3) What is the design of the composition?
   (4) Which type of sectional binary (simple, rounded, barform) is represented by each piece?
   a. Chorales (in Appendix) *Aus tiefer Not, Ermuntre dich,* and *Jesu, meine Freude*
   b. Anon., *Minuet*
   c. Anon., *Polonaise*
   d. Haydn, *Symphony No. 101* ("Clock"), Finale, mm. 1–28
   e. Schumann, *Album for the Young,* No. 6
   f. Hindemith, *Un Cygne*

[3] On the other hand, A. Lorenz, in his *Das Geheimnis der Form bei Richard Wagner* (1924–1933) claimed that the barform was the basic formal principle of Wagner's operas and Dr. S. Levarie has interpreted parts of Mozart's *Marriage of Figaro* as barforms (in *Mozart's Le Nozze di Figaro*. Chicago: University of Chicago Press, 1952)

[4] When Walther concludes the antistrophe on V rather than on I, Hans Sachs comments that to do so is painful to the mastersingers ("*das macht der Meistern Pein.*" Act III, Scene 2).

6–E.
THREE-PART FORMS

Example 6–8

MENOTTI: *The Medium*, Act I

Copyright, 1947, by G. Schirmer, Inc. Reprinted by permission.

Measures 1–12 comprise a three-phrase period completing a harmonic movement in the area of the tonic, forming part one. Phrases 4, 5, and 6 (mm. 13–25) have a special quality of their own contrasting with that of the previous phrases: the melody is made up almost entirely of new motives; the rhythmic character and instrumentation, though not clearly indicated here, are in the original completely changed. With phrase 7 (m. 26 and ff) a return to the beginning is effected. The chief characteristic of the design, then, is statement, digression, restatement.

Because of their contrasting quality, phrases 4–6 strike the listener as a part in themselves. The result is a three-part form, the first division being accomplished by the completion of a harmonic movement, and the second by contrast in the melody, texture, rhythm, and so forth—that is, contrast in design. The three parts constitute a ternary form. The first part is harmonically "closed": it is therefore sectional. The form is referred to as a sectional ternary, the design indicated by the letters A–BA.

The sectional ternary is probably the most common of all three-part forms, occurring again and again in folk songs, hymns, familiar community songs, and popular tunes (for example, *Drink to Me Only with Thine Eyes* and *The Bluebells of Scotland*). This form is a near relation of the rounded sectional binary, which is similar in both tonal structure and design (see Ex. 6–6). The distinction between the two lies in the relationship of the digression to the rest of the piece. In Ex. 6–8 the digression (B) is clearly and strikingly contrasting in character to A. This contrast is strong enough to set B apart in the mind of the listener as distinct in itself. Even if B can be related motivically to A (as it can in mm. 21, 24, and 25 of Ex. 6–8), it will form a part in itself if it is strongly contrasting in character. Examination of Brahms' *Intermezzo in E Minor, Op. 119, No. 2* (in Burkhart's *Anthology*), will provide ample evidence for this point. Still, even if B is not strikingly contrasting in character to A, it will be heard as a part in itself if its material is not based on that of A.

Only if B is derived melodically or motivically from A and only if it continues in the same general character (as in Ex. 6–6) does it merge with the return of A into a single part and result in a binary form.

THE FULL
SECTIONAL
TERNARY FORM:
DIVISION BY
THREE COMPLETE
HARMONIC
MOVEMENTS

Example 6–9

SCHUMANN: *Kinderscenen No. 6*

Two very short phrases combine to form a symmetrical period (mm. 1–4), completing a harmonic movement with a weak-beat perfect authentic cadence. The subsequent eight bars (mm. 5–12) are a symmetrical period in the subdominant key, completing a harmonic movement and ending with a strong-beat perfect authentic cadence. Measures 13–16, not included in the illustration, are exactly like part one. On the basis of the three complete harmonic movements, Ex. 6–9 divides itself into three parts. The design coincides with this division.

Part One (A)	Part Two (B)	Part Three (A)
I → ii₆–V–I	V–I → ii⁶₅–V–I	I → ii₆–V–I
	of IV	

When a composition consists of three complete harmonic movements, the third part is as a rule either exactly like, or a varied repetition of, the first part. The middle may or may not be of a contrasting character. The symbolic designation is A–B–A. Since all parts are harmonically "closed," the form is called a full sectional ternary.

THE
CONTINUOUS
TERNARY FORM:
DIVISION INTO
THREE PARTS BY
DESIGN ALONE

Example 6–10

MOZART: *Im Frühlingsanfang, K. 597*

Phrases 1 and 2 (mm. 1–8) are a symmetrical period with a progressive harmonic movement ending with a strong cadence on V (m. 8). Phrase 3 (mm. 8–12) exhibits a chord succession prolonging V and supporting a melody of a contrasting nature. Interruption now occurs. The harmonic and melodic movement returns to the beginning, this time cadencing on the tonic. The tonal structure, then, consists of a single harmonic movement interrupted at m. 12. The design, on the other hand, divides the piece into three parts. Measures 1–8 become part one due to the divisive strength of the strong-beat perfect authentic cadence in m. 8. Measures 9–12 become part two due to the contrasting nature of the phrase melody. The remainder is part three.

To acknowledge the continuity of the harmonic movement, the form is called a continuous ternary. The design is graphically represented as AB ‖ A'.

FORMAL AMBIGUITY The basic tonal structure of the continuous ternary is identical to that of the continuous rounded binary (see Ex. 6–3):

$$I \rightarrow \underbrace{V_7\text{–}I}_{\text{of } V} \ldots V_7 \| I \rightarrow V\text{–}I$$

The designs of the two forms are also very similar, both being expressed as AB ‖ A'. As with the sectional ternary and sectional rounded binary, the difference between the two forms lies in the nature of the material that makes up section B. In the continuous binary form the melodic and motivic material of B is clearly taken from A, so that unless there is a striking contrast in character between them, B will not be heard as a distinct part in itself. In the continuous ternary, on the other hand, B is made up of new material or contrasts strikingly in some other way and hence becomes the middle part of a three-part form.

Since the only clear distinction between the continuous rounded binary and the continuous ternary lies in the nature of the material used for the digression (section B), from time to time one comes across a composition for which it is difficult to make a definite decision. Fauré's charming song *Nell, Op. 18, No. 1,* is a case in point. The vocal melody of the digression, beginning with m. 19, is contrasting to that previously heard but not strikingly so, and certain motives are vaguely suggestive of motives in part one. The accompaniment, though at first slightly more complicated than previously, continues with the identical pianistic figure. It is easy to work out a plausible argument in favor of either form. Such ambiguous cases should not annoy the student. On the contrary they serve to reinforce the contention presented earlier that, however numerous the formal similarities among a number of works, the good composer does not create a piece of music by forcing his ideas to fit a stereotyped pattern. Often his labor results in a work which falls neatly into one of our categories; often it will fit none. And sometimes it seems to hover indecisively between two of them.

For other examples of continuous ternary form using the basic tonal structure of Ex. 6–10, the student is directed to Brahms' piano *Intermezzi, Op. 118, No. 6, Op. 119, No. 1,* and Mendelssohn's *Song without Words, Op. 19, No. 2.* Some continuous ternary forms use a different tonal structure. Rather than establishing V as a secondary tonic, part one may progress to the dominant of whichever chord begins part two. For instance, part one of Schubert's *Moments Musicaux, Op. 94, No. 2,* progresses from I to IV. This IV is taken to be V/♭vii, ♭vii (enharmonically expressed) being the key of part two.

Other continuous ternary forms mark the end of part one with a strong cadence on III. Rather than a chord succession prolonging V, part two then becomes a progressive movement, leading from this III to the interrupting V which immediately precedes part three. Such a movement is to be found in Mendelssohn's *Song without Words, Op. 85, No. 1,* in F major (see Ex. 5–10) though it is more characteristic of compositions in the minor mode.

Still other tonal structures are to be found among the continuous ternary forms of the great composers. We will consider some of these in more detail in Chapter 8. For now it is enough to emphasize that the usual tonal structure is that of Ex. 6–10 and the fact that

> the division into three is brought about entirely by design: the first division due to a strong conclusive cadence marking the end of part one, and the second due to the contrasting nature of part two.

EXERCISES

6. Contrast:
   a. Sectional ternary and full sectional ternary
   b. Sectional ternary and continuous ternary
   c. Continuous ternary and rounded continuous binary
   d. Sectional ternary and rounded sectional binary

7. Examine the compositions in ternary form listed below, answering the following questions:
   (1) Which measure marks the end of part one and which the end of part two?
   (2) How is division into three brought about in each case?
   (3) What is the design of the composition?
   (4) Which type of ternary (sectional, full sectional, continuous) is represented by each piece? Is any one of them formally ambiguous?
   a. Plainchant, *Mass XI*, Kyrie.
   b. Schumann, *Album for the Young*, No. 3.
   c. Schumann, *Album for the Young*, No. 8.
   d. Chopin, *Mazurka No. 24*.
   e. Chopin, *Etude in A flat major*.
   f. Ravel, *Le jardin féerique*.

6–F.
COMPOSITIONS IN MORE THAN THREE PARTS

Example 6–11

SCHUMANN: *Nachtstücke, Op. 23, No. 4*

After a brief introductory figure part one, a symmetrical period, presents a complete harmonic movement based on interruption. Part two is a complete harmonic movement in the key of the mediant. Part three is a slightly varied restatement of part one. So far the form is like the full sectional ternary, A–B–A. The subsequent passage is a progressive harmonic movement leading through ♭III and ♭VI to V_7, cleverly semicadencing with the introductory figure. Contrasting in melody and texture it

89

becomes part four. Part five is another restatement of part one, with further changes. The design of the piece is A–B–A–CA and the form can be called a sectional five part. The derivation of this five-part form is clearly from the (full) sectional ternary. The basic idea of repetition after contrast has simply been applied twice rather than once, as in the ternary.

The design of A–BA–BA, as in Chopin's *Nocturne in E♭ Major, Op. 9, No. 2*, does not result in a true five-part form. It is, rather, a ternary with repetition, exact or varied, of the last two parts (A–BA–BA equals A–‖: BA : ‖).

The four-part form, such as Schubert's *Impromptu in E♭ Major, Op. 90, No. 2*, is also derived from the ternary, in this case the sectional ternary, form. The contrasting middle part of the ternary A–BA returns as the fourth and final part, resulting in the design A–BA–B'.

Pieces in more than five parts occur from time to time, particularly in the piano works of Schumann. As a rule these multipartite pieces are assembled by several applications of the principle of contrast and restatement as found in the ternary forms. There is no need to discuss them here, for those who have followed this study so far will have no trouble in discovering their forms for themselves.

6–G.
THE ONE-PART FORM

THE ONE-PART
FORM WITH
COMPLETE
HARMONIC
MOVEMENT

Example 6–12

BACH: *WTC*, Vol. 1, *Prelude No. 2* (harmonic skeleton)

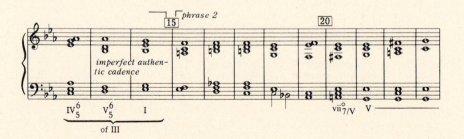

Bach's *Prelude No. 2* in C minor from the *Well-Tempered Clavier*, Vol. 1 (Ex. 6–12) shows none of the devices that we have enumerated as divisive. Its four phrases are clear enough, but none of these except the last ends with a strong conclusive cadence. The cadenzalike six measures marked "presto" and the single bar marked "adagio" notwithstanding, the design exhibits no contrasts which could separate the single harmonic movement into more than one part. The piece, a four-phrase asymmetrical period, is divided by neither design nor tonal structure. It is a one-part form.

THE ONE-PART FORM WITH PROGRESSIVE HARMONIC MOVEMENT

Example 6–13

CHOPIN: *Prelude, Op. 28, No. 2*

Some of Chopin's preludes have only a single part. Example 6–13 gives a skeletal outline of one of these. This piece is remarkable in many ways, not least of which is the tonal structure. The vast majority of tonal music establishes the tonic key at or very near the beginning of the piece. Here no tonality is unequivocally established until the third and last phrase is sounding. Once the piece is over the listener realizes that the goal of the preceding harmonic movement is an authentic cadence on an A minor triad. It is then simple enough, by applying hindsight, to label all the preceding harmony as expressing the tonality of A minor. This is what has been done in Ex. 6–13. But until the whole piece has been played through, it is impossible to know for certain what tonality the opening phrases express. For the first phrase, either E minor or G major is as plausible, or even more so, than A minor. The piece, then, actually shows a progressive harmonic movement and is a period consisting of three similar phrases. None of these phrases reaches a strong conclusive cadence except the last and no contrasts in design occur. It is therefore a one-part form in three sections with the design AA'A".

THE ONE-PART FORM WITH INTERRUPTED HARMONIC MOVEMENT

A more common type of one-part form is that based on an interrupted harmonic movement. Chopin's *Preludes No. 1* and *No. 4* are so constructed. These are both symmetrical periods, the interruption occurring at the end of the antecedent phrase, with extended consequents, especially so in the case of the first prelude. Their design is A ‖ A'. They cannot be considered two-part forms because an interrupted harmonic movement does not have the requisite divisive strength to separate a composition into two real parts. Instead, they are to be considered one-part forms in two sections.

THE ONE-PART FORM WITH TWICE INTERRUPTED HARMONIC MOVEMENT

Example 6–14

CHOPIN: *Prelude, Op. 28, No. 9*

92

Table of Standard Small Forms	*Form*	*Description*
	1. One part	Single harmonic movement (complete, progressive, or interrupted); no divisive aspect in design either through strongly conclusive cadences or striking contrasts. Double harmonic movement providing the result is a single period.
	2. Continuous binary	Single harmonic movement divided by design (conclusive cadence).
	a. simple	Design: AB or AA'.
	b. rounded	Design: AB ‖ A'.
	c. balanced	Design: AA'. Part two closes with a transposed restatement of the passage that ends part one.
	3. Sectional binary	Double harmonic movement, that is, two complete or interrupted harmonic movements.
	a. simple	Design: A–B or A–A'.
	b. rounded	Design: A–BA.
	c. barform	Design: A–A–B. Part one repeated, part two not repeated.
	4. Sectional ternary	Double harmonic movement the second of which is further divided by design (contrast). Design: A–BA.
	5. Full sectional ternary	Triple harmonic movement, that is, three complete or interrupted harmonic movements. Design: A–B–A.
	6. Continuous ternary	Single interrupted harmonic movement divided by design (conclusive cadence and contrast). Design: AB ‖ A'.
	7. Sectional four part	Same as sectional ternary plus transposed restatement of part two as part four. Design: A–BA–B'.
	8. Sectional five part	Same as sectional ternary plus new part four and restatement of part one as part five. Design: A–BA–CA.

The *Prelude in E Major* shows a harmonic movement twice interrupted, the harmonic sequence each time taking a different course toward the interrupting V. Like Ex. 6–13 it is a one-part form in three similar sections but is to be distinguished from that work by its two interruptions of the harmonic movement. The design is therefore represented as A ‖ A' ‖ A". The *Prelude in F Major, No. 23*, is similarly constructed as is, on a much larger scale, the *Nocturne in D♭ Major, Op. 27, No. 2* (in Burkhart's *Anthology*).

6–H.
THE SIX-STEP METHOD OF ANALYSIS

As with the six steps leading to identification of the larger unit outlined in section 5–G, students are urged to follow the systematic method presented below until they have gained experience in analytical techniques.

Step. 1. Consider the successive phrases, note their cadences, and come to a conclusion regarding the tonal structure of the piece, deciding whether it exhibits a single, double, triple, or other harmonic movement.

If single, is the harmonic movement complete, interrupted, or progressive? In a double harmonic movement, of which type is each?

Step 2. Consider the design from the cadential point of view, noting the presence or absence of any divisive conclusive cadence.

Step 3. Consider the design from the motivic and melodic point of view, noting the presence or absence of contrasting phrases and phrases that are restatements of other phrases. (A restatement differs from a repetition in that the former is a recurrence after contrast while the latter is an immediate recurrence. Restatements are important elements of form; repetitions are not.) Represent the design graphically by means of letter: A–BA, A–B–A, A ‖ A', and so on.

Step 4. In the light of steps 1, 2, and 3 come to a conclusion regarding the number of parts into which the piece will separate.

Step 5. Considering steps 1 and 4, decide whether the form is continuous, sectional, or (if there are three or more parts) full sectional.

Step 6. Decide whether or not the piece coincides in a general way with any of the commonly used standard forms listed in the table.

6–I.
APPLICATION OF THE SIX-STEP
METHOD OF ANALYSIS

Example 6–15

FAURÉ: *Lydia, Op. 4, No. 2*

Used by permission of Hamelle et Cie, Paris, copyright owner.

For the purpose of demonstration Gabriel Fauré's *Lydia*, a song for voice and piano, will be analyzed. Example 6–15 presents the song reduced for piano alone. The original has two stanzas that are not, as in our example, indicated by repetition signs but are written out completely. Comparison of the original second stanza with the first will show certain slight changes in the voice part not reproduced here. These changes occur only to accommodate the words of the second stanza to the music of the first. Such slight changes, often necessary in strophic songs, have nothing to do with form and can therefore be disregarded.

Step 1. After two introductory bars played by the piano alone, the voice enters with four successive phrases (mm. 3–19); each consists of four bars except the last, which has five. The piano introduction recurs, this time as an interlude, and stanza two is sung, after which a fifth phrase, for piano, concludes the song. The cadences are: phrase 1, imperfect authentic on iii; phrase 2, "three-quarter" on V (see Section 2–C); phrase 3, perfect authentic on ii; phrase 4, perfect authentic on I; phrase 5, imperfect authentic on I.

Before going further we must pause to consider phrase 5. It indubitably presents a complete harmonic movement, $I \rightarrow IV_2^4\ V_4^6\ I$. Are we then faced with the necessity of considering this a piece with double harmonic movement, the first covering the first four phrases with their repetition, and the second only this final phrase? Before answering this question, let us consider the relative strength of the cadences. The strongest cadence of the piece is the strong-beat perfect authentic on I which concludes phrase 4, and it is this cadence which completes the harmonic movement that began with the first phrase. The final phrase, beginning and ending with the tonic chord, is a chord succession whose purpose seems to be not to add to the "argument" of the piece, but only to reinforce the conclusion. The harmonic movement has been from I through iii, V, and ii, back to I. The final chord succession, prolonging and emphasizing this I, is therefore not a new harmonic movement but merely an appendage to the other. As such, it is, appropriately enough, called a *coda* (Italian: "tail"). The fact that the voice is silent during the coda confirms our interpretation but does not influence it. Even if the voice had taken part, phrase 5 could only have been interpreted as a coda.

Discounting the coda, the tonal structure is that of a single harmonic movement, complete.

Step 2. Although the cadence of phrase 3 is a perfect authentic, it is comparatively inconclusive: (1) it is a weak-beat cadence, the i being in a weaker rhythmic position than the V, and (2) the accompaniment moves with no slowing of pace into the link which connects it to the next phrase. Therefore no divisive conclusive cadence is present, the only cadence possessing the requisite strength being that which closes phrase 4.

Step 3. Although motive a (marked by overhanging brackets) reappears either direct or inverted in each phrase except the coda, the phrase melodies are not enough alike to warrant calling them similar phrases. The rising thirds in the lower staff of the coda are related to the similar rising thirds of phrase 3 (m. 11), but the right hand plays a new melody, an elaboration of a descending F major scale. In graphically representing the design of a composition, a convenient indication of the coda is to place its letter or letters in parentheses. Thus the design of Fauré's *Lydia* is

$$ABCD- \left({}^{E}_{C} \right)$$

the two letters arranged vertically denoting simultaneity.

Step 4. Steps 1 and 2 provide no basis for separation into parts. The result of step 3 is the realization that, though the melody is partially unified motivically, it provides continuous contrast. In the absence of any restatement, this contrast is not divisive, particularly since it is not far reaching. Tempo, meter, and the general style and mood remain unified. The song is therefore in one part.

Step 5. Since we are dealing with a one-part form this step is unnecessary. All one-part forms are by nature continuous.

Step 6. The form coincides generally with the standard uninterrupted one-part form. The existence of a coda plays no part in this decision. Any musical form is likely to be provided with a coda.

A full consideration of a given piece of music undertakes, among other things, both a formal analysis and identification of its larger units. Example 6–15, which is in genre a strophic song of two stanzas, is a four-phrase asymmetrical period (the song proper) plus a single phrase (the coda); it is a one-part form with coda, the design of which is:

$$ABCD- \left(\tfrac{E}{C}\right)$$

EXERCISE

8. The following pieces are listed in approximate order of difficulty. Analyze some or all of them, following the six-step method.
   a. Couperin, *La Bandoline*, mm. 1–8.
   b. Brahms, *Minnelied.*
   c. Chopin, *Mazurka No. 5.*
   d. Ives, *The Cage.*
   e. Chopin, *Prelude No. 6.*
   f. Chopin, *Prelude No. 1.*
   g. Schumann, *Album for the Young*, No. 14.
   h. Schumann, *Album for the Young*, No. 17.
   i. Schubert, *Who Is Sylvia?*
   j. Schumann, *Ich grolle nicht.*
   k. Wolf, *Das verlassene Mägdlein.*
   l. Scriabin, *Prelude, Op. 74, No. 3.*
   m. Scriabin, *Prelude, Op. 74, No. 1.*

7

THEME AND VARIATIONS

Having familiarized ourselves with the forms most commonly found in short pieces, we are in a position to undertake a consideration of larger works. The theme and variations is an advantageous starting point, for here we will be dealing with the small forms studied in the last chapter expanded into longer pieces by the principle of varied repetition. A theme is stated, then repeated a number of times, each time in a new guise. The theme and variations does not lack contrast, but the contrast is not juxtaposed to the restatement, as in the rounded binary and the ternary forms. Rather, the contrast is merged with the restatement.

7–A.
SECTIONAL AND CONTINUOUS VARIATIONS

There are two chief categories of the theme and variations. *Sectional variations* are those based on a theme that consists of one or more periods with, usually, a pause or clear caesura at the end of the theme and each variation. *Continuous variations* are those based on a theme comprising only a phrase or two (usually covering a total of from four to eight bars), the variations following each other uninterruptedly. The former are represented by the theme and variations (or variations on a theme) and the eighteenth-century doubles; the latter by the ground bass (*basso ostinato*), *chaconne*, and *passacaglia*.

HISTORICAL NOTE ON SECTIONAL VARIATIONS Sectional variations are one of the oldest instrumental practices, having been in continuous use since their appearance in the early sixteenth century in the lute and keyboard music of Spain and England [see Nos. 122, 124, and 134 in *Historical Anthology of Music (HAM)*].

Often the theme and variations form part of a larger work, a movement in a sonata or suite, but they appear frequently as independent compositions. In all periods it has been common practice for a composer to borrow the theme which he sets out to vary, either from folk song or from the work of another composer, as in Brahms' *Variations and Fugue on a Theme by Handel, Op. 24*, or Dohnanyi's *Variations on a Nursery Song*. But when the set of variations occurs as part of a larger work, the theme is usually an original creation of the composer.

In the eighteenth-century keyboard suite (see Chapter 10, Historical Note), particularly those of French origin, certain dance movements were provided with a very simple type of variation. The movement was played through, then repeated with new ornaments in the melody. The second version was called the double. Sometimes more than one double was written, as in the second Courante of Bach's *English Suite No. 1*, which has two. Sometimes the composer went further than merely to provide new ornaments for the double of a dance. In the doubles of Bach's courante just referred to, the bass lines as well as the melodies are varied.

In addition to the use of the term described above, the name "double" sometimes occurs in the eighteenth century as a synonym for "variation." Thus, the airs in Handel's *Suites No. 4* and *No. 5* for harpsichord are provided with doubles which in no way differ from his works expressly entitled "variations."

7–B.
FIXED AND VARIABLE ELEMENTS OF A THEME

It is obvious that a varied repetition of a theme will change some aspects of the original and retain others. To change everything would destroy the element of repetition; to retain everything would leave the original unvaried. We shall examine the air known as "The Harmonious Blacksmith" chosen by Handel for the variations that close his *Suite No. 5* for harpsichord. Reference to this air (Ex. 6–1) reveals certain features which might be changed or which might be maintained.

1. Key: E
2. Mode: major
3. Form: simple continuous binary
4. Length: part one, two bars, repeated; part two, four bars, repeated
5. Basic tonal structure:

$$\| : I \to \frac{V-I}{\text{of } V} : \| \; \| : I \to V-I : \|$$

6. Precise harmonic sequence:

$$\| : I\ V\ I \mid V_6\ vi_6\ vii_6^{\circ}\ iii\ \frac{ii_6\ V\ I}{of\ V} : \|$$

$$\| : I_6\ IV\ I_6\ I \mid IV\ I_6\ IV\ I_6\ vii_6^{\circ}\ I \mid V\ I_6\ ii_6\ I_6 \mid ii_6\ I_6\ vii_6^{\circ}\ I\ V_7 \mid I : \|$$

7. Tempo: not indicated; presumably *moderato*
8. Melody
9. Bass
10. Texture: homophonic, mostly four-part chordal style

Example 7–1 is part one of each of the doubles.

Example 7–1

HANDEL: *Suite No. 5 in E Major*

Examination of the five doubles which follow the air reveals that of the features listed above, six remain fixed throughout. These are key, mode, form, length, basic tonal structure, and tempo. Changes in the precise harmonic sequence take place, though these are few and unimportant. The only features subjected to real variation are the melody, the bass, and the texture.

The fixed and variable elements of Handel's "Harmonious Blacksmith" variations are not those of every set of variations. In his *Aria with Thirty Variations*, commonly called the "Goldberg Variations," Bach sometimes varies the mode and the (presumable) tempo in addition to melody, bass, precise harmonic sequence, and texture. Other sets of variations sometimes go further and vary the basic tonal structure and the key. In his *Piano Variations in F Major, Op. 34,* Beethoven changes key with each variation, though such a procedure is very exceptional. Normally both the form and length of the theme remain fixed throughout the variations. Exceptions to this observation will be discussed later.

To sum up, it is usual for the composer to retain as fixed the length and form of the theme throughout his variations. The other elements—key, mode, basic tonal structure, precise harmonic sequence, tempo, melody, bass line, and texture—may or may not be subjected to variation during the course of the work. Of these the most commonly varied features are the melody, the bass, the texture, and the precise harmonic sequence.[1]

7–C.
PROCEDURES IN SECTIONAL
VARIATIONS

Reference to Ex. 7–1 will reveal the various procedures used by Handel in constructing his variations on "The Harmonious Blacksmith."

ORNAMENTAL VARIATION The melody of the theme is made up for the most part in eighth notes. Double 1 turns these into sixteenth notes, ornamenting the melody in a simple manner (Ex. 7–1a).

---

[1] In the light of this discussion it will be clear that the term "theme" does not refer, as is sometimes assumed, to the melody alone, but to the entire passage in all its dimensions. It is important to maintain this distinction not only for this chapter but for the remainder of the book.

SIMPLIFYING VARIATION

Double 2 continues the sixteenth-note motion but transfers it to the left hand as an accompaniment to a simplified version of the melody in eighth notes (Ex. 7–1b).

FIGURAL VARIATIONS

Doubles 3 and 4 are constructed from a three-note triplet motive (marked by overhanging brackets in Ex. 7–1c and d). When a variation is thus built from a particular figure or motive—which may or may not be derived from a part of the theme—it is spoken of as a figural variation. Sometimes more than one motive is employed. Double 5 is another figural variation in which the motive employed is a scale through an octave, sometimes ascending and sometimes descending.

The theme of Bach's "Goldberg Variations" has a bass consisting of slow-moving notes mainly constructed from segments of the downward scale. This bass is simple and easily grasped by the listener. The melody, on the other hand, is so elaborate and laden with ornamentation that only after repeated hearings is one able to keep it in mind. This matters not the least to Bach, for he builds these variations on the bass of the theme rather than on the melody. He makes use of the principle of the ornamental variation, but applies it to the bass.

Example 7–2

BACH: "Goldberg Variations" (some bass lines)

MELODIC VARIATION

Once the aria has been played, its melody is virtually abandoned until the variations are completed, after which it returns *da capo* to bring the work to a close. In this piece many variations, then, provide new melodies while retaining the same bass and general harmonic scheme, a procedure known as the melodic variation. (See also Beethoven's *Sonata, Op. 109,* Third Movement, Variation 1.)

CONTRAPUNTAL
VARIATION

In the "Goldberg Variations" counterpoint is prominently exhibited in several ways. These can be grouped under four headings.

Example 7–3

BACH: "Goldberg Variations"

Imitative Example 7–3a illustrates a type of contrapuntal variation in which motivic imitation plays an important role.

Canonic When two voices are written in canon, the second is a strict imitation of the first. Every third variation of the "Goldberg Variations" is so written, nine canonic variations in all. Variation 3 is a canon at the unison, that is, the second voice imitates at the pitch of the first voice. Variation 6 is a canon at the second, the imitating voice being placed a second higher than the leading voice. Variation 9 is at the third (see Ex. 7–3b), Variation 12 at the fourth, and so on.

Fugal Example 7–3c illustrates a variation which proceeds along the lines of a fugue. The fugue will be explained in Chapter 14. Here we can only point out its presence. (This is the only variation that bears a definite relationship to the melodic line of the theme. The first two bars of the fugue subject are derived from the first two bars of the original tune.)

Additive Example 7–3d shows the beginning of variation 30, the final variation of the work. This variation has been constructed by Bach as a contrapuntal *quodlibet* (Latin for "what you please"), a piece which combines various tunes or fragments of tunes. Bach uses two songs popular in his day, *Ich bin so lang nich bei dir gewest* ("It's been so long since I've been with you") and *Kraut und Rüben haben mich vertrieben* ("Cabbage and turnips have driven me away") which he combines with each other and superimposes over the bass of the theme. Since the fragments have been added to the pre-existing bass, this type of contrapuntal variation is called "additive." In other music the additive variation does not ordinarily make use of borrowed melodies, but combines newly invented counterpoints with the melody of the theme (see Ex. 7–4).

CHARACTERISTIC VARIATION

Bach has introduced into the "Goldberg Variations" many characteristic variations, so called because each one takes on a special character, such as a march or dance of some kind. Variation 7, for instance, has the quality of a *gigue*,[2] and Variation 19 is a minuet. Variation 16 is particularly interesting in that its two halves are utilized to imitate first the slow, dignified opening and then the fast fugal section of a French overture (see Section 14–J).

The sets of variations by Bach and Handel discussed so far have yielded up the commonly used procedures to be found in the variations of the great composers. But no pretense is made of having exhausted all possibilities. The variations of certain composers—Beethoven and Brahms in particular—contain many isolated procedures invented for particular pieces which do not readily form themselves into groups or categories. The student is urged to study the variations of these composers, especially Beethoven's *Diabelli Variations, Op. 120,* and to make his own discoveries.

The list of variation procedures given before can be misleading if one supposes that every variation must fall into one and only one category. It is not uncommon for variations to partake of features of two or even three types. For instance, double 3 of the "Harmonious Blacksmith" variations is listed as a figural variation. Nevertheless, the perpetual fast-moving triplets give it the nature of a *gigue*. It is at once a figural and a characteristic variation. In the Finale of Mozart's *Quartet in D Minor, K. 421,* the second variation alternates every four bars between the figural and the melodic types.

[2] In Bach's own copy he wrote "al tempo di Giga" before this variation (C. Wolff, "Bach's *Handexemplar* of the Goldberg Variations: A New Source," *Journal of the American Musicological Society,* Vol. XXIX, No. 2 (1976), p. 227).

7–D.
FORM IN SECTIONAL VARIATIONS

FORM OF THE
THEME

A glance through a great number of the sectional variations of the composers of the last two centuries reveals that most themes contain a double bar with repetition signs somewhere near their middle, the so-called "two-reprise form." But one must avoid the hasty conclusion that two repeated halves inevitably indicate one of the binary forms. It is true, of course, that the first part of the binary form is often repeated before the statement and repetition of the second part. But a one-part or ternary form can also be subjected to a similar repetition scheme. For instance, the theme of the *Allegretto con Variazioni* from Mozart's *Clarinet Quintet, K. 581*, is a sectional ternary form with a repetition scheme as follows: ‖: A– : ‖ ‖ : BA : ‖. The theme of the Allegretto con Variazioni from Beethoven's *Quartet in E♭ Major, Op. 74* ("Harp") is a one-part form, a period with repeated antecedent and repeated consequent, as is the theme of Brahms' *Handel Variations, Op. 24.* It is necessary, then, to disregard the repetition scheme and to focus one's attention on the tonal structure of the theme and its design before coming to a conclusion regarding the form of the theme.

FORM OF EACH
VARIATION

It has been pointed out that one of the aspects of the theme that is usually maintained throughout the variations is its form. Not infrequently variations occur which seemingly change the form of the theme in that they do not retain the double bar and repetition marks which appear at the presentation of the theme. Often this change is only an apparent one, the repetition of each half of the theme having been written out rather than indicated by the repetition sign. The composer does this in order to incorporate certain changes the second time. Sometimes only small changes appear in the repetition (as in double 2 of the "Harmonious Blacksmith" variations), sometimes important ones (as in the Finales of Beethoven's *Sonatas, Op. 109* and *Op. 111*). In variations for two instruments, such as violin and piano, the material first given to the violin might be given to the piano in the repetition or vice versa (for example, Mozart, *Violin Sonata, K. 305,* Second Movement, Variation 6). When the repetition itself is thus varied, one speaks of a double variation.

Nevertheless, variations which really do change the form of the theme occur occasionally. In the latter half of the nineteenth century this device became common and was used along with changes of key and length. Indeed, almost none of the original features of the theme were regularly maintained, each variation being more in the nature of an independent development on some motive or other distinctive feature of the theme. Richard Strauss's *Don Quixote* (1897) is a theme with variations of this kind. Some maintain that this species should not be called "Variations on a Theme" at all, but "Developments on a Theme." When the form of the theme is abandoned, the resulting variation is termed "free" in contrast to the regular strict type.

Elgar's *Variations on an Original Theme, Op. 35,* known as the "Enigma Variations" (1899), represents a mid-point between strict and free variations. All elements of the theme are subjected to variation throughout the piece. Its sectional ternary form, however, though not rigidly adhered to, exerts a definite influence on the form of each variation. All manner of varied repetitions of different passages, introductions, extensions, and codettas are brought in, creating differences in length and outward appearance of the form. Yet through it all the ternary form can be traced in each variation.

THE FINALE The problem of finding a satisfactory means of concluding a set of variations is one which has admitted a great number of solutions. Handel, in his "Harmonious Blacksmith" variations, provides no special finale, simply ending with the last and most brilliant variation. In the "Goldberg Variations," Bach concludes by repeating the theme *da capo*. Not infrequently the last variation gives place to a fugue which concludes the work, as in Brahms' *Variations and Fugue on a Theme by Handel, Op. 24,* or Benjamin Britten's *Young Person's Guide to the Orchestra (Variations and Fugue on a Theme by Henry Purcell)*. In his *Variations on a Theme by Haydn, Op. 56,* Brahms concludes with a ground bass (see Section 7–H). Occurring more often than any other type, however, is the addition of a coda. Sometimes the coda is quite short, as in the variations on the "Austrian Hymn" from Haydn's *Quartet, Op. 76, No. 3,* but not infrequently it is lengthy and devotes itself to a free development of all or part of the theme. Beethoven's *Twenty-Four Variations on Vieni Amore* conclude with a developing coda which is exactly four times the length of the theme.

EXERCISE

1. Examine the following sectional variations and answer the questions listed below.
    a. Mozart, *Theme with Variations from Sonata, K. 284* or either of the following (not in Burkhart's *Anthology*):
    b. Beethoven, *Op. 14, No. 2,* Second Movement
    c. Beethoven, *Op. 26,* First Movement

    (1) Compare the theme with each variation. Indicate which of the following elements are fixed and which are varied in each variation: key, mode, form, length, basic tonal structure, precise harmonic sequence, tempo, melody, bass, texture.
    (2) In what way are the varied elements of the variations changed?
    (3) Which procedure is used for each variation? Does any variation fail to

fall neatly into one of the categories listed in Section 7–C? If so, describe the procedure used.

(4) How is the problem of the finale dealt with?

7–E.
SHAPE IN SECTIONAL VARIATIONS

A good composer will not be satisfied to string together a number of variations at random with no attention to the order in which they appear, for to do so would result in a lack of coherence despite the unity of material. Common ways of achieving a coherent arrangement of the variations can be summarized under four headings.

RHYTHMIC CRESCENDO A glance back at Ex. 6–1 and Ex. 7–1 will show that the rhythmic movement of Handel's "Harmonious Blacksmith" variations gradually increases from eighth notes in the air itself to thirty-second notes in the final variation. The consistent use of notes of smaller and smaller value is known as a "rhythmic crescendo" and imparts to the work as a whole a unity over and above that of the separate variations. A particular double is thus more than just an interesting variant of the theme, for it has an integral part in the whole work, helping along the gradual increase of intensity that builds steadily from the beginning to the end.

The rhythmic crescendo often occurs in works in variation form, not usually throughout the whole work as is the case here, but extending over several of the variations.

GROUPING The five variations in Handel's work actually make up only three groups: doubles 1 and 2 belong together due to their sixteenth-note motion and doubles 3 and 4 belong together because of the similarity of their triplet figure; at one end double 5 stands alone, balancing the theme which stands alone at the other. Grouping of the variations into larger parts is a second road toward unity.

SCHEMATIC ORDER In Bach's "Goldberg Variations," every third variation is constructed as a two-voice canon at a different interval. Here we encounter a schematic order used as one means of organizing the entire set of variations (see Table).

Following are some observations regarding Bach's schematic order:

1. All groups except the first and last follow a single plan:
   (a) a characteristic variation playable on one keyboard.
   (b) a brilliant variation written in the manner of an etude, or technical study, with an indication that it is for both keyboards.
   (c) a canon for one keyboard

Table of
Schematic
Order in
the
Goldberg
Variations

Part One		
	Aria	
	Var. 1	Characteristic (two-part invention, *corrente*)
Group 1	Var. 2	Characteristic (trio sonata)
	Var. 3	Canon at unison
	Var. 4	Characteristic (*passepied*)
Group 2	Var. 5	Brilliant, 2 keyboards
	Var. 6	Canon at second above
	Var. 7	Characteristic (*gigue*)
Group 3	Var. 8	Brilliant, 2 keyboards
	Var. 9	Canon at third below
	Var. 10	Characteristic (fughetta)
Group 4	Var. 11	Brilliant, 2 keyboards
	Var. 12	Canon at fourth below
	Var. 13	Characteristic (violin concerto slow movement)
Group 5	Var. 14	Brilliant, 2 keyboards
	Var. 15	Canon at fifth above in contrary motion, minor mode
Part Two		
	Var. 16	Characteristic (French overture)
Group 1	Var. 17	Brilliant, 2 keyboards
	Var. 18	Canon at sixth above
	Var. 19	Characteristic (*minuet*)
Group 2	Var. 20	Brilliant, 2 keyboards
	Var. 21	Canon at seventh above, minor mode
	Var. 22	Characteristic (Alla Breve, *stile antico*)
Group 3	Var. 23	Brilliant, 2 keyboards
	Var. 24	Canon at octave below
	Var. 25	Characteristic (ornamented aria), minor mode
Group 4	Var. 26	Brilliant, 2 keyboards
	Var. 27	Canon at ninth above
	Var. 28	Brilliant, 2 keyboards
Group 5	Var. 29	Brilliant, 1 or 2 keyboards
	Var. 30	Quodlibet
	Aria da capo	

2. The first and last groups differ but complement each other. One might guess that this arrangement recommended itself to Bach on the grounds that it reserves extra brilliance for the end of the piece.

3. The Quodlibet replaces the expected canon at the tenth and acts as an amusing bridge (with rhythmic decrescendo) between the most brilliant variation and the return of the sedate Aria.

4. Part Two is set off by beginning with a typical French Overture.

5. The arrangement is essentially symmetrical:

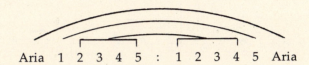

Aria 1 2 3 4 5 : 1 2 3 4 5 Aria

In his *Quartet, Op. 76, No. 3,* Haydn has written a set of additive variations on the "Austrian Hymn." The melody is left intact throughout the four variations (see Ex. 7–4), but passes from the first violin (theme) to the second violin (Variation 1), to the cello (Variation 2), to the viola (Variation 3), and back to the first violin (Variation 4).

Benjamin Britten's scheme in his *Young Person's Guide to the Orchestra* is to construct the successive variations in such a way as to emphasize and demonstrate the various orchestral instruments, beginning with those at the top of the orchestral score (flutes and piccolo) and continuing systematically through the string basses.

Beethoven devised a rather unusual plan for the slow variations in his *Piano Sonata in F Minor, Op. 57* ("Appassionata"). The theme uses only the low register of the piano. Variation 1 continues in this register but includes a few notes of higher pitch. Variation 2 is set in the middle register of the piano and Variation 3 in the highest. Its final measures bring about a quick descent into the original low register, at which point the theme is restated. This restatement of the theme closely resembles the original version except that it is presented in two-bar segments which alternately employ the three registers exploited in the variations themselves. Thus the overall effect of the variations is that of a gradual rise from the depths to the heights, a quick descent, and then a final reminiscence of the three registers.

In none of these cases is the schematic order the only means of over-all organization, but it serves as one factor making a definite contribution to a unified whole.

INCREASING COMPLEXITY In the case of the variations on the "Austrian Hymn," the effect of the schematic order is aided by a gradually increasing complexity.

Example 7–4

HAYDN: *Quartet, Op. 76, No. 3,* Second Movement

The theme first appears with straightforward four-part harmony. Variation 1 is a contrapuntal duet between the two violins, violin II playing the melody and violin I adding a counterpoint above it (Ex. 7–4a). Variation 2 stresses the violins and cello while the viola plays only occasional bass notes. The melody is given to the cello (Ex. 7–4b). Variation 3 is still mostly in three voices, but the voices are divided up among the four instruments, each voice having greater independence than previously, and the element of chromaticism heightens the sense of urgency (Ex. 7–4c). Finally, in the last variation, the four instruments play continually and in their upper registers, providing an elaborate contrapuntal texture to support the melody. To this last variation is appended a five-bar coda in which the texture is gradually simplified and the music descends to a normal playing register.

The following diagram, admittedly oversimplified, is meant to show the total shape of the piece regarding the degree of textural complexity. It has nothing to do with dynamics, for the theme and all the variations are to be played softly.

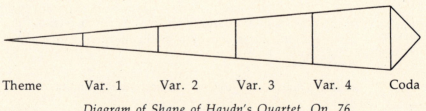

Theme   Var. 1   Var. 2   Var. 3   Var. 4   Coda

Diagram of Shape of Haydn's Quartet, Op. 76,
No. 3, Second Movement

The device of gradually increasing the complexity of the successive variations is somewhat akin to that of the rhythmic crescendo, for in both cases the variations tend to become steadily more engaging, more intense, though not necessarily louder. It is also possible to reverse either procedure by a rhythmic diminuendo or a gradual decrease in complexity.

Arnold Schoenberg's *Variations on a Recitative for Organ, Op. 40,* has a rather complex shape. The work consists of a theme, ten variations, a cadenza, and a finale which bears some resemblance to a fugue.[3] The theme and the first three variations group themselves together by a steady increase in tension achieved through a rhythmic and dynamic crescendo. Variation 4 brings in a quieter, slower movement; Variation 5 is fast and light; Variation 6 returns to the serene character of Variation 4. These three, then, form a second group: Two calm variations surrounding a scherzo. With Variations 7, 8, and 9 a rhythmic and dynamic crescendo combine with increasing complexity to build toward a second climax. This tapers off for Variation 10, a very slow, extremely quiet movement. A brilliant cadenza introduces the finale, the over-all effect of which is of increasing complexity and rhythmic crescendo to a point of climax (m. 14 from the end). The music then seems to crouch down within itself and gather up its energy for the grandiose outburst of the last few bars (see Ex. 2–6).

A simplified diagram illustrates the shape of Schoenberg's organ variations:

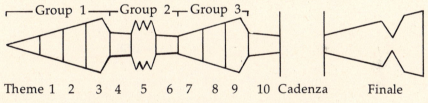

Diagram of Schoenberg's Organ Variations

In summary, the chief methods by which a coherent shape in sectional variations is attained are as follows. Any of these methods may be used in combination.

1. *Grouping.* If each variation is a self-contained unit unrelated to the other variations, the work is apt to be sprawling and disconnected. But if two or more variations are constructed with enough similarity to be perceived as a group, the total number of parts in the work can be considerably reduced. Fewer parts will greatly increase comprehensibility.

2. *Schematic order.* A systematic plan imposed on the variations can do much

[3] Although the score does not expressly call it so, in conversation Schoenberg referred to this finale as a fugue.

in the way of tying them together. Bach's series of groups of three variations (characteristic-study-canon) and Haydn's passage of the theme from instrument to instrument are examples of such ordering.

3. *Rhythmic crescendo or diminuendo.* A gradual build-up of intensity or excitement can sometimes be achieved by introducing into successive variations notes of smaller and smaller value. Or, conversely, a gradual relaxation by the systematic use of notes of larger value can be effected. In this way, each variation becomes an integral part of a larger unit.

4. *Increase or decrease in complexity.* Similar in effect to 3 above is the gradual increase in complexity of texture—two-voice counterpoint moving to three voice, then to four voice, is a means of achieving greater complexity. A more subtle method would be a greater degree of independence in the voice parts within the texture of a fixed number of voices. A gradual decrease in complexity is to be had by reverse methods.

CONTRAST Sometimes variations are juxtaposed not to obtain maximum unity, but to achieve the greatest possible variety. For instance, in Beethoven's *Diabelli Variations, Op. 120,* Variations 29, 30, and 31 are clearly a part in themselves, grouped together to achieve coherence, with the preceding Variation 28 acting almost like a transition to this section. Earlier, however, many adjacent variations exhibit a high degree of contrast, for example, Variations 13, 14, and 15, or Variations 18, 19, and 20.

EXERCISE

2. Re-examine Mozart's *Theme with Variations* or the variations from Beethoven's *Op. 14, No. 2,* or *Op. 26.* Do they exhibit a coherent shape? By what method or methods is coherence attained? Make a diagram.

7–F.
MODIFICATIONS OF SECTIONAL VARIATIONS

VARIATIONS ON TWO THEMES Some works present not one, but two themes as subjects for variation. The themes are sometimes contrasting, but not infrequently they are motivically related and share the same key, though often they differ in mode. Since it takes so much longer to get through two themes than one, composers generally write only a very few variations for each theme. Haydn's exquisite *Piano Variations in F Minor* are a notable example. Here theme B, called Trio by Haydn, is in the same key as theme A, but the opposite mode. Each theme is presented, then alternately twice varied, a lengthy coda concluding the piece. A twentieth-century example of variations on two themes occurs as the second movement of Schoenberg's *Quartet No. 3, Op. 30.*

Variations on two themes are sometimes referred to as "double variations." It is preferable to reserve this term for variations in which the repetition of each part is itself varied (see Section 7–D).

VARIATION RONDO

From time to time composers have contrived to write movements that combine essential features of different forms. The basic principle of the rondo (see Chapter 9) is the regular recurrence of a *refrain* which contrasts with interspersed *episodes.* One occasionally comes across sets of variations that include insertions in the form of episodes, either between each variation or between a group of variations. There is no term universally applied to this type of hybrid form. For convenience we shall refer to it as the variation rondo.

A well-known example of the variation rondo is the *Andante* of Haydn's *Piano Trio in G Major* which is a theme and two variations separated by episodes.

Refrain 1	*Episode 1*	*Refrain 2*	*Episode 2*	*Refrain 3*
Theme I A	New (related to theme) B	Var. 1 I A	New C	Var. 2 I A
10 + 11 bars	8 + 13 bars	10 + 11 bars	7 + 8 bars	10 + 11 bars

The refrains and episodes are all in two repeated halves, though the episodes have lengths different from each other and from the refrains. In the last movement of Mozart's *Piano Concerto in C Minor, K. 491*, the episodes have almost the same length and basic form as the theme itself. It is therefore possible to construe them as further variations. Nevertheless they are so different in quality from the other variations that the listener has the impression of hearing a variation rondo rather than an ordinary theme and variations. The first episode, in the submediant key, is inserted between Variation 3 and Variation 4. The second, in the major mode of the tonic, occurs between Variations 4 and 5. An extension at the end of Variation 5 leads to an improvised cadenza followed by Variation 6 and a lengthy coda.

ISOLATED MODIFICATIONS BY BEETHOVEN

On several occasions Beethoven invented special modifications of the variation form to suit his purpose for a particular work. These forms are interesting and instructive, but as they do not appear again in other works, it is not necessary to go into more than one in detail here. Students are nevertheless urged to study the scores and discover for themselves what Beethoven has done in the slow movements of *Symphony No. 5, No. 7,* and *No. 9,* and in the slow movement of the *Quartet in A Minor, Op. 132.*

The particular work to be discussed here is the Finale to the *Symphony No. 3* ("Eroica"). This movement is unique in a number of ways. First, it makes use of both "strict" and "free" variations; second, the theme is preceded by an introduction; and third, perhaps most striking of all, the melody of the theme is not introduced until the third variation.

The movement opens with a stormy unison passage in the strings, emphasizing iii which soon settles down to a V_7. This constitutes the introduction and occupies eleven bars. We then hear the theme—or what we presume to be the theme—played in unison (mm. 12–43). It is a symmetrical period with both antecedent and consequent repeated, but although this is its first presentation, the repetition of each phrase is varied. Variations 1, 2, and 3 are strict in that they keep to the form and key of the theme. They are of the additive type and at the same time gradually increase in complexity, creating a rhythmic crescendo that goes from eighth notes to triplets to sixteenth notes. Variation 3, along with the added sixteenth-note counterpoint in the first violins, introduces in the woodwinds the actual melody of the theme (mm. 75–107), for what we have heard previously turns out to be only its bass.

Example 7–5

BEETHOVEN: *Symphony No. 3*

The gradual increase in complexity that occurs from the original presentation of the bass of the theme through Variation 3, in addition to the rhythmic crescendo, ties together this portion of the movement, so that it plainly forms a part in itself. Moreover, all the variations have been strict ones and have expressed the main tonality of E♭ major. As the third variation closes (m. 107), a new and different part begins. The new part is devoted to free variations. Except for Variation 5 the form of the theme is disregarded, new keys appear, and the variations are sometimes separated from each other by passages called *transitions* which lead from one to another. One of these transitions does, in fact, open the new part and leads into the submediant key, C minor. Variation 4 (mm. 117–174), expressing vi, is like a fugue, using as its subject the first four notes of the bass theme, to which a new ending is appended. Its counterpoint is taken from Variation 1. The variation ends with a semicadence (V$_7$/vi). The fifth variation (mm. 175–210) expresses VII (D major). It is an ornamental variation on the melody of the theme. D major acts as the dominant of G minor (VII = V/iii) and Variation 6 (mm. 211–256) expresses the latter key. It is a melodic variation: a new melody, with a dancelike Hungarian quality, is superimposed over a recurring bass figure made up of the first four notes of the bass of the theme. The seventh variation (mm. 257–277) is short and might almost be considered a transition. It begins with a statement of the theme—bass and melody—in the major mode of VI, then treats the first phrase in sequence through the minor mode of vi and so through ii to V$_5^6$ and thence to I$_6$. From this point until the end of the movement, the main key of E♭ major is maintained.

Variation 8 (mm. 277–348) corresponds to Variation 4 in that it is like the beginning of a fugue. This time, however, the bass subject is inverted and appears with a new counterpoint in the manner of a double fugue (see Section 14–G). The melody also makes its appearance in this section in a rhythmically altered version. Gradually the bass of the theme becomes less and less prominent, being reduced to a three-note motive and treated in diminution, and before the variation is completed it disappears entirely.

With Variation 9 (mm. 348–380), an abrupt change occurs and the third part begins. The tempo slows from *allegro molto* to *poco andante* and the melody of the theme, with new harmonies and a new bass, is played expressively by the woodwinds, then taken up by the strings. An accompaniment of triplets is added, and the variation rises to a climax ushering in Variation 10 (mm. 380–396), which continues Variation 9 more broadly and fully, with the melody in the bass instruments. With 9 and 10 the "strict" type of variation returns except that the repetitions are omitted for Variation 10. The final coda (mm. 396–473), based on the melody of the theme, is in several sections, the fourth of which brings back the introduction and the quick tempo so that the movement ends brilliantly and triumphantly.

Particularly remarkable is Beethoven's treatment of the bass of the theme. At the beginning of the movement it is the most prominent

Outline
Summary
of
Beethoven's
Symphony
No. 3,
Finale

Bars	Section	Material	Description	Tonal Structure
1–11	Intro.	Independent	Unison flourish, slowing to halt on V_7.	V_7–I $\longrightarrow V_7$ of iii
Part One				
12–43	Theme	Bass only	Varied repetitions	I → V I
44–59	Var. 1	Bass & counterpoint	Additive var., eighths	I → V I
60–75	Var. 2	Bass & new counterpoints	Additive var., triplets	I → V I
75–107	Var. 3	Bass & new counterpoints, plus melody	Additive double var., sixteenths	I → V I
Part Two				
107–116	Trans.	Motive from melody	Sequential	I → V/vi
117–174	Var. 4	Motive from bass & counterpoint from Var. 1	Fugue	I → V_7 of vi
175–210	Var. 5	Melody	Ornamental double var. with 4-bar extension	VI V_7 I → V_7 I of VII
211–256	Var. 6	Motive from bass	Melodic var. over recurring bass figure	I → IV → I of iii
257–277	Var. 7	Melody, antecedent only	Sequential, quasi-transition	VI–vi → ii V_2^4 I_6
277–348	Var. 8	Bass motive inverted; new counterpoint; melody, antecedent	Double fugue; bass motive in diminution	I → V_7
Part Three				
348–380	Var. 9	Melody	Ornamental double var., new bass; slow tempo.	I → V_7 I
380–396	Var. 10	Melody	Additive var., repetitions omitted, melody becomes bass	I → V_7 I
Coda				
396–404	Sec. 1	Melody, antecedent	Melody hidden in uppermost voice	I → V_7/IV
404–420	Sec. 2	Melody, antecedent	Melody hidden in uppermost voice	IV → V I of iii
420–430	Sec. 3	Melody, antecedent	Melody hidden in uppermost voice	iii
431–435	Sec. 4	Introduction	Intro. flourish transposed; fast tempo	iii → V_7
435–473	Sec. 5	Motive from melody; new	Brilliant conclusion	I → V_7 I

feature, first played alone; later in the movement it dominates many of the variations, even acting as the subject of the two fugal portions. Gradually disappearing during the second fugue (Variation 8) it remains absent during the rest of the movement, which is completely given over to the melody. In the final variation the melody itself becomes the bass.

Variations 1 through 3 are characterized by dependence on the formal structure of the theme and remain in the home key. Variations 9 and 10 do likewise. Variations 4 through 8, on the other hand, display the "free" type of variation and express vi, VII, and iii, only the final fugue emphasizing the tonic. Thus the variations group themselves into three parts as a kind of sectional ternary form.

Bass Outline of Essential Tonal Structure

EXERCISES

3. Contrast:
   a. Double variations and variations on two themes
   b. Variations on two themes and variation rondo

4. Examine at least one of the following works (not included in Burkhart's *Anthology*):
   a. Haydn, *Piano Variations in F Minor*
   b. Haydn, *Piano Trio in G Major*, First Movement
   c. Mozart, *Concert Rondo, K. 382*
   d. Mozart, *Piano Concerto in C Minor, K. 491*, Third Movement
   e. Beethoven, *Symphony No. 5*, Second Movement
   f. Beethoven, *Symphony No. 7*, Second Movement
   g. Beethoven, *Symphony No. 9*, Third Movement
   h. Beethoven, *Quartet in A Minor, Op. 132*, Third Movement

7–G.
SUMMARY OF SECTIONAL
VARIATIONS

We speak of sectional variations when the theme and each variation is a complete little piece in itself. Whether the theme is one part, binary, or ternary it will in many cases be laid out in two repeated halves. Usually there will be a distinct stop between variations.

"Strict" variations keep the form of the theme and, normally, the key and length as fixed elements. Other elements may or may not be modified in the course of the variations. In "free" variations the form and length of the theme are as variable as the other elements.

An attempt to list all the possible procedures used by the great composers in constructing different types of variations would result in a cumbersome list of mammoth proportions and be of little use to the student. Some common procedures are the (1) ornamental, (2) simplifying, (3) melodic, (4) figural, (5) contrapuntal (imitative, canonic, fugal, additive), and (6) characteristic, but no variation is necessarily limited to only one category.

Composers have often attempted to achieve an over-all coherence to their sets of variations by means of (1) grouping certain ones together, (2) setting in motion a rhythmic crescendo or diminuendo which operates over some or all of the successive variations, (3) devising a series of variations which evince steadily increasing or decreasing complexity, and (4) imposing some kind of schematic order which permeates the whole set.

HISTORICAL NOTE ON CONTINUOUS VARIATIONS Since the early seventeenth century continuous variations have tended to group themselves into two types. In one the fixed element is a persistently recurring bass melody, in the other it is a series of harmonies.

The idea of the constantly repeating bass melody, called a ground bass or *basso ostinato* (Italian: "obstinate bass"), can be traced back to the thirteenth century. The well-known canon *Sumer Is Icumen In* is one of the earliest extant compositions to make use of this technique. In the sixteenth century the ground bass is to be found in connection with the dance (see *HAM No. 103*) and during the seventeenth century it came into prominent use not only in dance music but in vocal music as well. Monteverdi, for example, composed continuous variations for voices. Often the groundbass melody was not repeated in its original form but was constantly varied. In spite of the different versions in which it appeared, its skeletal outline would engender the same series of harmonies at each repetition. Thus the continuous variations in which the fixed element is a persistently recurring series of harmonies comes about. Such a procedure will be referred to as *variations on ostinato harmonies.*

During the seventeenth century there appeared a type of continuous variation that used a standard bass pattern of moderately slow tempo in triple meter, moving stepwise through the interval of a descending fourth, either diatonically or chromatically, sometimes concluding with a drop to the lower octave. Compositions of this type were sometimes called *chaconne* or *passacaglia*. Seventeenth-century composers used the terms indiscriminately. The terms might also be applied to variations on *ostinato* harmonies in which the standard bass pattern is absent or only hinted at.

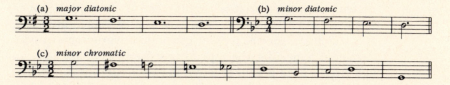

The major diatonic form was used by Monteverdi in the duet *Pur ti miro* that concludes his *L'Incoronazione di Poppea* (1642) and the minor chromatic one by Purcell as the bass of the song *When I Am Laid in Earth* from *Dido and Aeneas* (1689). Both diatonic and chromatic versions of the descending scale fragment, or slight variations of them, occur commonly in the works of composers of the seventeenth and early eighteenth centuries. Many *bassi ostinati*, on the other hand, are more elaborate melodies, although the descending scale fragment can often be detected as the basis of these as well.

While it is true that most seventeenth-century composers seem to have considered the terms chaconne and passacaglia as musically synonymous (the actual dance steps may have been different), during the second half of the century in France the chaconne took on a special rhythmic quality of its own. In the operas of Lully, as well as in those of his successor Campra, the chaconne made great use of the "sarabande rhythm": triple meter with the accent on the second beat, often expressed as a quarter note, a dotted quarter, and an eighth. Compositions making conspicuous use of this rhythm, perhaps along with the standard bass pattern, were sometimes called *chaconnes* even when not written as continuous variations or, as in Lully, when the succession of variations is not rigidly adhered to. Such chaconnes were often in the form of a rondeau (see Chapter 9), as in Chambonnières' *Chaconne in F major* (in *HAM, No. 212*). Association of the chaconne with rhythms based on triple meter with accented second beat occurred even outside France (as in Purcell's *Chacony* for three instruments and continuo), and continued into the eighteenth century. No doubt it was this association which is the reason for Bach's choice of that title for his great *Chaconne* for solo violin which acts as finale to his *Partita in D Minor*, as well as Handel's 21-variation *Chaconne in G Major* for keyboard. Another keyboard work, the *Chaconne in F Major* (published in Volume II of the Handel Gesellschaft Edition, though perhaps not composed by Handel), points up even more clearly that in the eighteenth century the term "chaconne" could designate a stylistic rather than a formal attribute, for it is neither a set of variations nor a rondeau.

During the late eighteenth century interest in continuous variations of either type was negligible, but it revived again in the nineteenth century with Beethoven's *Thirty-Two Variations in C Minor* for piano (WoO 80). Beethoven's successor in this field was Brahms, whose two most celebrated continuous variations occur as the finales to his *Variations on a Theme by Haydn* and his *Symphony No. 4 in E Minor*. The former is a ground bass. The latter is a special type of continuous variations in which the fixed element is a melodic line appearing sometimes in the bass, but frequently in a middle or upper voice, often in varied form. It is of some interest that both Beethoven and Brahms (in the *Symphony No. 4*) make conspicuous use of the "sarabande rhythm." It would be valid, then, to think of these compositions as nineteenth-century chaconnes. In addition, Beethoven's bass line conforms to the minor chromatic version of the standard chaconne-passacaglia bass.

In this century the continuous variation is of very common occurrence, two notable examples being the passacaglias in Berg's opera *Wozzeck* (Act I Scene 4) and in Britten's *Peter Grimes*.

7–H.
PROCEDURES OF CONTINUOUS
VARIATIONS

THE GROUND BASS

Example 7–6

RAISON: *Organ Mass on the Second Tone, Trio en Passacaille*

120

Beginning on the last beat of m. 2, the bass presents a melody[4] four bars in length that is repeated five times. In two of these statements (mm. 11 ff and mm. 23 ff), the theme undergoes striking variation. Otherwise it remains virtually in its original form. This bass melody supports two contrapuntal voices which at each statement continue their melodic motion beyond the final note of the theme in order to cadence with the first or second note of the subsequent statement. Thus the movement flows uninterruptedly.

As in Ex. 7–6, the ground bass normally remains in the lowest voice throughout and is not transposed to a different pitch. But in his *Passacaglia in D Minor* Buxtehude transposes the middle statements first to III, the relative major key, then to v. In his continuous variations Bach does not transpose ground-bass melodies to different keys. In the organ *Passacaglia*, however, he does transfer the theme in two variations from the bass to the uppermost voice and, immediately after, places it in a middle voice (mm. 89–113).

With the foregoing observations in mind we can attempt to list the characteristics of a set of continuous variations of the ground-bass (*basso ostinato*) type.

---

[4] Taken from the Gregorian chant *Acceptabis sacrificium*, the communion antiphon for the tenth Sunday after Pentecost. This melody, extended to double its length, was also used by J. S. Bach as the ground bass for his great organ *Passacaglia*.

1.   A melody, normally in the lowest voice, is repeated a number of times.

2.   Ornamentation of this bass melody may or may not be introduced during the course of its repetitions.

3.   The melody is fairly short, usually a single phrase, and normally no more than eight bars in length.

4.   The bass melody is not ordinarily transposed to a different pitch, though on occasion transpositions take place.

5.   The recurring melody supports other voices that supply a changing fabric above it by added melodic counterpoints, motivic figuration, chordal harmonies, or any other means the imagination of the composer has devised.

6.   The supporting voices often cadence at a point different from the ground-bass melody in order to keep up a continuous flow.

VARIATIONS ON OSTINATO HARMONIES

Example 7–7

HANDEL: *Suite No. 7 in G Minor, Passacaille*

Example 7–7 presents the theme and three of the fifteen variations of the *Passacaglia* which closes Handel's *Suite No. 7 in G Minor* for keyboard. Comparison of the basses will show that it is possible to trace the original bass line in the lowest voice of each variation. (It should be noticed that in every variation the bass note on the first beat of each bar produces the minor diatonic form of the standard chaconne-passacaglia bass line, as illustrated on p. 119.) Since the actual bass line is different in virtually every variation, it does not have the effect of a recurring melody as the ground bass does. Rather it is the repetition of the precise harmonic sequence that shapes each variation.

The characteristics of a set of continuous variations on *ostinato* harmonies include the following:

1. A theme, usually comprising a single phrase, is sounded.
2. While the theme has a distinct melody and bass line, these are not necessarily fixed elements of the successive variations. Rather, the precise harmonic sequence constitutes the fixed element. On occasion slight changes in the precise harmonic sequence occur.
3. Successive variations normally follow each other without a perceptible break, thus insuring a continuous flow.
4. Any of the types of sectional variations (see Section 7–C) are likely to occur here, but emphasis is on those of homophonic texture rather than the contrapuntal types.

7–I.
SHAPE IN CONTINUOUS
VARIATIONS

Since the themes of continuous variations are short (eight bars or less), they are generally provided with many variations. In a piece with a short theme varied a great number of times it is extremely important—perhaps more so than in the case of sectional variations—to utilize shape to gather the variations into groups which can give a unified impression to the movement as a whole. In continuous variations a particular group is generally even more coherent than in sectional variations, for here there is no pause between the end of one variation and the beginning of the next.

The twenty variations of Bach's *Passacaglia* are grouped together into three parts. The variations of part one cohere by virtue of their gradually increasing intensity and excitement. There is a rhythmic crescendo operating until the establishment of continuous movement in sixteenth notes at Variation 6. The principle of increasing complexity is then applied through the next three variations. Variation 9 introduces a new and vigorous motive which leads into the brilliant runs of Variation 10, continued in Variation 11 with the bass melody leaping to the uppermost voice. Variation 12 is the most brilliant of all, with rapid pedal figures imitated in the manual parts.

The variations of part two (Variations 13–15) are all without pedal and should therefore presumably be played on a different manual with a decrease in volume. The musical texture bears out this assumption, for it becomes less and less complex, Variation 15 consisting only of delicate arpeggio figuration.

Part three (Variations 16–20) enters abruptly with the return of the ground bass in the pedals and introduces majestic organ figuration in the manuals. Variation 17 is a whirlwind of rapid sixteenth-note triplets which are slowed down to regular sixteenths for the passionate final variations. For a finale Bach treats the first four bars of the *Passacaglia* theme as the subject and, with the addition of a new theme, presents a double fugue which brings the work to a mighty and solemn close.

A diagram of the shape of the *Passacaglia* might look something like this:

Part One   Part Two   Part Three
(Theme, Var. 1–12)   (Var. 13–15)   (Var. 16–20)

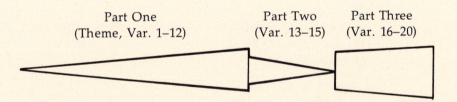

The grouping of these variations manifests on a large scale the symmetry of the "golden mean," a type of symmetry we saw working on a small scale in Ex. 3–3. The theme appears a total of twenty-one times. The largest group consists of thirteen appearances. The remaining eight are divided into two groups, one of three, the other of five. In length part two is to part three as part three is to their sum (approximately, 3 is to 5 as 5 is to 8); and the sum of parts two and three is to part one as part one is to the whole (8 is to 13 as 13 is to 21).

7–J.
SPECIAL APPLICATIONS OF THE
GROUND-BASS PRINCIPLE

THE OSTINATO FIGURE

Example 7–8

STRAVINSKY: *Symphony of Psalms,* Third Movement (trumpet and cello parts omitted)

In Ex. 7–8 the ground bass is not a complete melody but only a motive. It is referred to either as a ground motive or an *ostinato* figure.

The *ostinato* figure is too short to serve as a bass for a series of variations superimposed over it, as the regular ground bass does. Therefore it cannot act as the structural basis for a composition. Rather, it occurs as a technical procedure for certain sections within a composition of another form. For instance, the third movement of Stravinsky's *Symphony of Psalms* uses the *ostinato* figure of Ex. 7–8 only for the final section. Beethoven's *Symphony No. 9* uses an *ostinato* figure in one section of the coda to the first movement (see Section 12–B). Brahms uses the *ostinato* figure a number of times, one of the most prominent being as the bass to the second theme in the Finale of his *Symphony No. 1*. Chopin uses the idea for the rocking left-hand accompaniment of his *Berceuse, Op. 57*, and in the middle section of the grandiose *Polonaise in A flat Major, Op. 53*.

Example 7–9

BACH: *Partita on "O Gott, du frommer Gott"*

Bach's *Partita on "O Gott, du frommer Gott"* for organ comprises nine different settings of the hymn tune. The excerpt in Ex. 7–9 presents the first twelve measures of the second setting.

In mm. 1–2 a bass melody is heard alone, then repeated in mm. 3–5 as support for a modified version of the chorale. A third statement of this bass melody begins in m. 5 but is lengthened and modified in mm. 6–7. Measures 7–8 are derived motivically from the bass theme, yet they constitute an essentially different melody, as does m. 9. The melody returns in mm. 10 and 11, but again its ending is altered in order to cadence on III rather than on I. Throughout the rest of the piece various other changes take place in the melody.

It cannot be denied that this piece is constructed over a recurring bass melody, but the melody is treated freely. It is lengthened, separated by interludes, transposed in part or in its entirety. We speak of such irregular bass melodies as free ground basses. The procedure is not at all uncommon during the Baroque period. Many of the slow movements of Vivaldi's concertos consist of a *cantabile* melody over a free ground bass and Bach, in the slow movements of his *Italian Concerto* for harpsichord and his *Violin Concerto in E Major*—to name only two cases among many—has imitated Vivaldi's practice.

THE SOPRANO OSTINATO   Occasionally the concept of the persistently recurring melody is applied to the uppermost voice rather than to the bass of a composition. A striking case is the exquisite *Agnus Dei* from Verdi's *Requiem Mass*. A two-phrase melody, constructed as a thirteen-bar double period, recurs five times, alternating between presentations by soprano and mezzo-soprano soloists, who sing it in octaves, and the full chorus.

The melody is first sung without accompaniment by the soloists, then repeated, as Variation 1, by the chorus and orchestra. Variation 2, in the minor mode, brings in a harmonized orchestral accompaniment. Variation 3, sung by the full chorus in three parts (sopranos and altos moving in octaves), is abridged to consist of only the consequent of the double period. Variation 4, for soloists, is given a flowing accompaniment in the orchestra which continues in Variation 5, the latter abbreviated in the manner of Variation 3. A short coda concludes the piece.

A contemporary use of the soprano *ostinato* is the *Dirge* from Benjamin Britten's *Serenade for Tenor, Horn, and Strings*.

EXERCISES

5. Contrast:
   a. Continuous variations and sectional variations
   b. Variations on a ground bass and variations on *ostinato* harmonies
   c. Ground bass and *ostinato* figure
   d. Ground bass and free ground bass
   e. *Basso ostinato* and *soprano ostinato*

6. Analyze the following compositions in detail:
   a. Purcell, *Dido's Lament*, beginning at m. 9.
   b. Beethoven, *Quartet, Op. 135*, Third Movement.
   c. Schubert, *Der Doppelgänger*.

7. Examine and describe the following compositions:
   a. Handel, *Chaconne*.
   b. Bach, *Chaconne*.

8. Locate and describe the *ostinato* aspects of the following passages:
   a. Beethoven, *Quartet, Op. 135*, Second Movement, mm. 143–190.
   b. Debussy, *Feuilles mortes*, mm. 17–30.
   c. Hindemith, *Piano Sonata No. 2*, First Movement, mm. 63–112.

7–K.
SUMMARY OF CONTINUOUS
VARIATIONS

We speak of continuous variations when the theme is not a complete little piece in itself, but only a phrase, possibly two, and the successive variations appear with little or no perceptible break between them.

Continuous variations fall into two main types:

1. *Variations on a ground bass.* A melody in the lowest voice persistently recurs while the upper voices supply an ever-changing texture above it.

2. *Variations on ostinato harmonies.* The precise harmonic sequence persistently recurs throughout the variations, but neither the melody nor the bass of the original theme necessarily reappears during their course.

The principle of the ground bass is sometimes utilized to different ends.

1. *Ostinato figure.* The ground bass is a recurring bass motive rather than a complete melody. It does not control the formal structure of the composition, but acts as a bass line for certain sections within a composition in another form.

2. *Free ground bass.* The ground bass is a melody that recurs but not so exactly or persistently as the regular ground bass. Appearances of the ground bass might be separated by interludes, and the melody itself is subjected to various changes.

3. *Soprano ostinato.* The recurring melody is in the uppermost voice rather than the lowest.

8

THE TERNARY
FORMS

The discussion of ternary forms in Chapter 6 was chiefly concerned with methods of analysis. Our interest was centered upon dividing a composition into parts and discovering the general category, if any, into which it might fall. The time has now come for a second look at the ternary forms—some of the details, some unusual procedures, and, especially, the *composite ternary form*.

HISTORICAL NOTE ON TERNARY FORMS Compositions in ternary form existed as far back as the early Middle Ages. The textual arrangement of certain parts of the Mass, such as the Kyrie and Agnus Dei, conveniently accommodates a musical form based on the principle of statement, digression, restatement. The Kyrie of Gregorian Masses XII and XVI are among those ternary forms that can be traced back to the twelfth century and may well be of even earlier origin. The Agnus Dei of Mass XV is another. Nevertheless the ternary form did not occupy a conspicuous place in musical composition during the Medieval and Renaissance periods of music history. Only occasionally does one come across its use before the seventeenth century (for example, the chansons of Clément Janequin).

In the early part of the seventeenth century the ternary form began to make more frequent appearances, as in arias from the cantatas and operas of Luigi Rossi (1598–1653) and Monteverdi. The famous duet *Pur ti miro* from the latter's *Poppea* is a fully developed ternary form with repetition of the middle part (ABBA). During the course of the seventeenth century composers of opera, cantata, and oratorio began to rely more and more on the three-part plan for their arias. The third part often would not be written out but merely indicated by the words *da capo*, which directed the performers to repeat the first part, the soloist, to be sure, ornamenting it differently the second time.

The first half of the eighteenth century saw the rise of an instrumental genre analogous to the *da capo* aria and occurring in some of the dances of the late Baroque suite. A first dance could be followed by a second of the same type, after which the first would be performed again. An example is to be found in the two minuets of Bach's *French Suite No. 3*.

It was the instrumental dance, specifically the minuet (or scherzo) and trio (that is, the second minuet), that offered the most conspicuous use of the ternary idea during the late eighteenth and early nineteenth centuries. Nevertheless, ternary forms are encountered in other genres: *Dalla sua pace* from Mozart's *Don Giovanni* and the first movement of Haydn's *Quartet, Op. 76, No. 5*. In addition to the conventional minuet and trio, a spot sometimes chosen by the Classical composers for the ternary form was the slow movement of a sonata, trio, quartet, or symphony, as occurs in Haydn's *Symphony No. 92* ("Oxford"), Mozart's *Piano Sonata in D Major, K. 576*, and Beethoven's *Quartet, Op. 130*, the Cavatina.

Throughout the nineteenth century, composers continued to favor the ternary form for the slow movements of their large multimovement instrumental works. In addition, it is to be encountered again and again in songs and especially in short piano pieces. Many of the piano compositions of the Romantic composers, whether they were called nocturnes, preludes, romances, intermezzi, or some fanciful or descriptive title, exhibit one of the ternary forms. Nor is its use uncommon in this century. Prokofiev's *Piano Sonata No. 7*, Second Movement, Berg's *Lyric Suite* for string quartet, Third Movement, and Bartók's *Piano Concerto No. 3*, Second Movement, are but a few instances.

8–A.
CONNECTION OF PARTS ONE AND TWO

With the sole exception of the full sectional ternary, parts two and three of the ternary form are normally connected, for part two ends with a V_7 or some other chord which leads into the beginning of part three (see Ex. 6–8). In addition, many ternary forms include connective passages between parts one and two. There are four chief methods by which the composer can span the gap between these parts.

THE LINK **Example 8–1**

SCHUBERT: *Impromptu, Op. 90, No. 2*

The first three bars of Ex. 8–1 show the final cadence of part one. Measure 82 consists of a single major triad on G♭, III of the main tonality. This chord acts enharmonically as V of B minor, the key of part two. In this case a single chord, V in the new key, III in the original key, has joined part one with part two. This chord serves as a link between the end of the first part and the beginning of the next. In Ex. 8–2 the link consists of three tones that lead smoothly into the first note of the melody of part two.

Example 8–2

MOZART: *Sonata, K. 576*

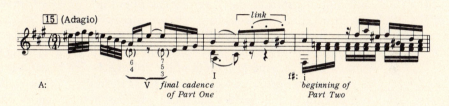

THE ELISION   **Example 8–3**

HAYDN: *Symphony No. 92 ("Oxford")*

In Ex. 8–3 parts one and two are connected by the device of the elided cadence (see Section 2–D). The device is used to bring about a continuity of movement between the two parts. Often, however, it does more, as in Ex. 8–3. The sudden beginning of part two in the opposite mode and in a contrasting character introduces an element of surprise.

Example 8–4

SCHUBERT: *Moments Musicaux, Op. 94, No. 4*

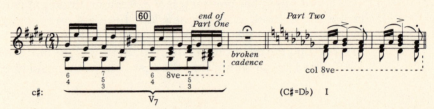

Rather than ending the first part with a complete conclusive cadence, Schubert in Ex. 8–4 proceeds as if he is going to do so, then suddenly breaks off before sounding the final tonic chord. A grand pause follows and then the middle part begins. The opening chord of part two resolves the chord that was sounding when the break occurred. A similar procedure is used by Chopin in his *Nocturne in F Major, Op. 15, No. 1.* In other situations the grand pause is sometimes filled in by a harping on a single tone, a brief flourish, or some other linking device. Such a link does not eliminate the broken cadence. The link as described above comes *after* the completion of the perfect cadence, whereas here it comes *instead* of its completion. A broken cadence differs from a half cadence in that the former does not have the rhythmic quality of a cadence at all. Rather than the feeling of comparative repose, the cadence is suddenly cut off in mid-motion.

Example 8–5

BRAHMS: *Ballade, Op. 118, No. 3*

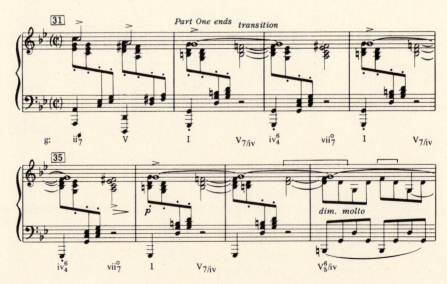

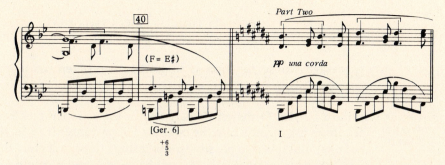

In Ex. 8–5, the final cadence of part one (mm. 31–32) is followed by a passage nine bars in length which connects it with part two (mm. 41 ff). Part one is in G minor, part two in B major, that is III by change of mode. Brahms concludes part one not on a G minor triad but on G major (the "Picardy third"). To this G major triad he adds the note f', turning it into V_7/iv, following it by iv and vii$^\circ_7$ (mm. 32–33). These two bars are repeated, after which mm. 36–40 prolong the seventh chord on G which has been treated as V_7/IV. With the entrance of the first B major triad of part two (m. 41) the listener realizes that the seventh chord on the note G has served as a musical pun, being the enharmonic equivalent of a chord of the augmented sixth (E♯–G–B–D) in the key of B.

The passage does more than merely effect an interesting and striking modulation from I to III. Instead of presenting us with an abrupt contrast as we go from part one to part two as Haydn had done (Ex. 8–3), Brahms gradually diminishes the energetic movement through mm. 32–37. In m. 38 he brings in a new flowing figure which anticipates the accompaniment of part two. Beyond this he introduces in mm. 38, 39, and 40 the motive (marked in brackets) from which the chief melody of part two is to be constructed. This type of passage is termed a transition or bridge.

The transition, like the link, serves to connect two parts of a composition. The connection by means of the link is achieved as expeditiously as possible, while the transition, taking longer, has time to prepare the listener for the new part.

EXERCISES

1. Contrast:
   a. Elision and broken cadence
   b. Link and transition (bridge)

2. In the following pieces, how are parts one and two connected?
   a. Schubert, *Moment Musical* (without Trio), mm. 15–17.
   b. Schumann, *Vogel als Prophet*, mm. 16–19.
   c. Beethoven, *Sonata, Op. 7*, Second Movement, mm. 23–25.
   d. Brahms, *Intermezzo, Op. 118, No. 2*, mm. 15–16.
   e. Brahms, *Intermezzo, Op. 119, No. 2*, mm. 33–36.

8–B.
CONNECTION OF PARTS TWO AND THREE

A passage whose function is to lead to a restatement is termed a *retransition*.

DOVETAILING OF PARTS TWO AND THREE

In most ternary forms either part two or the retransition closes on V_7 or vii°, resolving directly into the opening I of part three (that is, the return of part one). But it is also possible for part three to begin before the harmonic movement has reached the V_7 (or vii°) which ordinarily precedes it.

Example 8–6

SCHUMANN: *Romance, Op. 28, No. 2*

Part two of Schumann's *Romance* in F♯ major, for instance, reaches the vii°₇/V. But rather than moving on to V or V_7 before part three begins, the vii°₇/V moves to

$$\underset{V}{\overset{6-5}{\underset{4-3}{}}} \; (= \; I_4^6 - V)$$

as part three begins. The tonic chord that completes the harmonic movement is not sounded until the middle of the second bar after part three has begun. There is a conflict here between tonal structure and design, a conflict that results in a tight dovetailing of parts two and three.

Some dovetailing occurs by other means. Example 8–7 shows the opening phrase of part one (Ex. 8–7a), then skips to the last bar and a half of part two, continuing with the opening phrase of part three (= one) (Ex. 8–7b).

Example 8–7

SCHUMANN: *Frauenliebe und -Leben, No. 2*

Comparison of the two opening phrases shows the second (mm. 29 ff) to have an identical vocal melody but a different bass line. The original bass line moves upward in half steps from the note G to B♭, where it supports the V₇. In m. 28 the bass is on the note *d*, supporting the V₅⁶ chord. Contrary to the listener's expectations, this note *d* moves downwards to *d♭*, where it supports the first chord of part three, not as a I, but as a seventh chord on I in third inversion. It then proceeds downward by half steps to reach the V_7 (m. 31). The descending bass line, governing the harmonies which underlie the return of the melody of part one, serves to hide the seams between parts two and three.

ALTERNATE
HARMONIES FOR
CLOSE OF PART
TWO

As was mentioned above, the normal way of closing part two is by reaching the V_7 (or vii°). Sometimes, however, other chords are substituted. Such substitutions are almost obligatory when the opening theme of part three does not begin on I but on V. In such cases part two is likely to reach V/V or vii°/V. In Schumann's *Carnaval, Op. 9*, this situation occurs several times, the student being directed in particular to *No. 2* and *No. 3*. In the fourth piece, *Valse Noble,* the first part (in B♭ major) begins with a vii$^{o}_{7}$ in third inversion, moves to a V_7, thence to I_6, and so forth (Ex. 8–8a). Part two, expressing the submediant key (G minor) concludes with a V_7 in that key: the notes D–F♯–A–C. By reinterpreting the note F♯ as G♭ and a simple move of the soprano note *d"* to *e♭"*, Schumann arrives at the vii$^{o}_{7}$ which initiates the return of part one. Though an unusual procedure, the connection between the second and third parts could hardly be smoother (Ex. 8–8b).

Example 8–8

SCHUMANN: *Carnaval, No. 4*

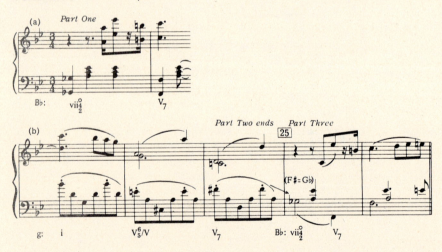

The preceding have all been illustrations of methods designed to bridge the gap between parts two and three so smoothly and subtly that the listener is hardly aware part three has begun until it is well under way. But the composer may desire to surprise the hearer by jumping abruptly into the beginning of part three. In that case, part two may cadence on a chord calculated to lead the listener's expectations in a direction other than that which the music is about to take.

Example 8–9

ROSSINI: *Stabat Mater*, Second Movement

Part two of the *Cujus animam* from Rossini's *Stabat Mater* expresses vi, the relative minor key. It comes to a semicadence on the dominant of that key (V/vi), while the voice descends stepwise unaccompanied. Melodically the voice part returns smoothly to the initial phrase (m. 4 of Ex. 8–9), but the entrance of the orchestra on I comes as a pleasant surprise. (See also the *alla danza tedesca* from Beethoven's *Quartet, Op. 130*, mm. 80–81.)

EXERCISES

3. Terms to define:
   Retransition
   Dovetailing of parts

4. In the pieces for Exercise 2 of this chapter, how are parts two and three connected?
   a. Schubert, *Moment Musical* (without Trio), mm. 39–53.
   b. Schumann, *Vogel als Prophet*, mm. 23–25.
   c. Beethoven, *Sonata, Op. 7*, Second Movement, mm. 37–51.
   d. Brahms, *Intermezzo, Op. 118, No. 2*, mm. 25–30.
   e. Brahms, *Intermezzo, Op. 119, No. 2*, mm. 67–72.

8–C.
THE PRELUDE AND POSTLUDE

Example 8–10

a. CHOPIN: *Mazurka, Op. 17, No. 4*
b. MENDELSSOHN: *Song without Words, Op. 30, No. 3*

Example 8–10 illustrates passages with which certain ternary forms by Chopin and Mendelssohn begin. In the first case (Ex. 8–10a) the pianist "strums" on a single chord, VI_6, decorated with nonharmonic tones. In the second (Ex. 8–10b) he plays a simple but complete harmonic movement, $I–V_7–I$. At the end of each piece the identical passage returns. In the latter case the passage does not bear any specific relationship to the composition it encloses. It seems to act as a frame for a piece rather than as an integral part of it. In the former case there is a definite relationship—the repeated chords in the left hand anticipate the chordal accompaniment of what is to come, and the tones b, c', d' in the left hand foreshadow the opening motive of the melodic line in m. 5. Still, it stands apart from the main body of the piece. We refer to such a passage as a prelude when it precedes a composition and a postlude when it follows, the two usually occurring together in a single work. The use of the prelude and postlude is virtually confined to short songs and lyric piano pieces of the Romantic composers (but see Beethoven's *Bagatelles, Op. 126, No. 6*).

Chopin's *Mazurka, Op. 17 No. 4*, an excerpt from which is quoted above, makes clear the distinction between a *postlude* and a *coda* (see Sec. 8–E), since its last twenty-four bars include both.

8–D.
THE INTRODUCTION

INTRODUCTION TO THE FIRST PHRASE Many ternary forms begin the first phrase with an introduction accomplished by one of the methods described in Section 4–A. Such an introduction is always very short, sometimes only a bar or less in length, and rarely more than four bars.

THE SINGLE PHRASE INTRODUCTION Some ternary forms are provided with short introductions which are not part of the first phrase but which exist as independent phrases. These are rarely more than a single phrase in length.

Example 8–11

GERSHWIN: *Prelude No. 3 in E flat Minor*

Copyright 1927 by New World Music Corporation. Used by permission.

As the ternary forms are not customarily provided with lengthy introductions, those of large proportions will be discussed in Chapter 12.

8–E.
THE CODA

In the course of the last two chapters we have had an introduction to the coda, a term referring to a section that is added to the end of a composition as a kind of appendage. At this point we shall take another look at the coda, considering it first from the point of view of tonal structure, then of design.

TONAL STRUCTURE OF THE CODA *Coda Prolonging the Final I by Chord Succession* The last five bars of Ex. 6–15 illustrated the coda in which the I, upon resolving the final V_7 in the perfect authentic cadence, is prolonged by a chord succession. (See also Ex. 5–5, last four measures.)

Coda Prolonging the Final I by Means of a Tonic Pedal Rather than a straightforward chord succession, many codas prolong the final I by means of a tonic pedal point. Normally, of course, the pedal point is in the lowest voice. Example 8–12 illustrates another possibility. This ternary form ends with a coda that prolongs the final I by means of a double pedal point (root and third of I) in the upper voices.

Example 8–12

PROKOFIEV: *Sonata No. 7, Op. 83*, Second Movement

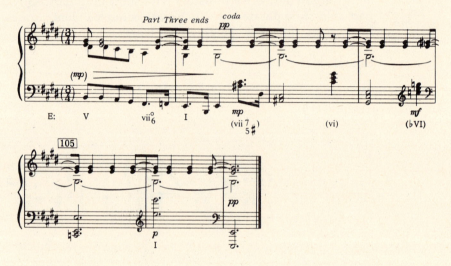

Coda Delaying the Final I by Means of Deceptive Cadence

Example 8–13

CHOPIN: *Nocturne, Op. 48, No. 1*

The ternary form of Ex. 8–13 behaves as if it will close with a conventional perfect authentic cadence (m. 71). But when the moment for the final I arrives, it is transformed into V$_2^4$/♭II (m. 72). Thereupon it progresses through ♭II$_6$ to V$_7$ and only then is the final i heard (m. 74). The deceptive cadence with which the coda begins delays by two bars the final resolution of V$_7$ to I.

In its first bar (m. 72) this coda emphasizes the chord of the "Neapolitan sixth." More often the tonal structure of the coda is devised to stress subdominant or submediant harmonies. The last four bars of Ex. 5–5, for instance, dwell on IV. The slow movement of Brahms' *Symphony No. 2* is a ternary form with a coda which begins with the deceptive cadence V$_7$–♭VI and which continues to emphasize this ♭VI throughout the coda. The prevalence of both IV and (♭)VI in many codas seems to be calculated by the composer as a means of establishing tonal equilibrium. Most compositions involve harmonic motion that begins on I, moves to III or V, or to III and then to V, then returns to I. The coda can reflect this move to III (up a third) by a move to VI (down a third) as in Brahms' *Nicht mehr zu dir zu gehen*. A move to V (up a fifth) is balanced by a move to IV (down a fifth), occurring in the aria *It is enough* from Mendelssohn's *Elijah*. On the other hand, the coda might reiterate a harmonic movement made earlier in the piece. In Berlioz' *Symphonie Fantastique* the middle part of the waltz appears suddenly in ♭VI. This striking harmonic turn is recalled for a few bars in the coda (mm. 36 ff from the end).

DESIGN OF THE CODA *Coda Extending the Final Phrase* The coda illustrated by the last four bars of Ex. 5–5 does no more than extend the final phrase by a continuation of the accompanimental figuration. There is no need to indicate such extensions of the final phrase by a separate letter in the symbolic representation of the design.

The Single Phrase Coda The coda of Ex. 6–15 consisted of a single phrase, made up almost entirely of new material. While the coda of new material is not rare, more commonly the composer makes use of material heard before. Often this is chosen from part one, but as frequently it is part two that provides the basis for the coda, as in Chopin's *Prelude No. 13*. The point of this procedure has to do with unity, for the effect is that of a kind of reconciliation of the mood of the second part with that of the first and third. From time to time the coda, even when only a single phrase in length, makes reference to both parts one and two. Example 8–14 presents the coda to the composition from which Ex. 8–4 was taken. It begins with a reference to part two, then concludes by a return to part one. The design of the piece is represented by the letters ABA–(BA).

Example 8–14

SCHUBERT: *Moments Musicaux, Op. 94, No. 4*

The Large Coda The coda to the Finale of Beethoven's "Eroica Symphony" is quite long and consists, as we have seen, of a number of sections. Codas to ternary forms, too, are sometimes long and divide themselves into sections. As with the shorter codas, the basis for the longer codas may be new or may come from one or more of the parts of the ternary form itself. Brahms concludes the second movement of his *Symphony No. 3* with a long coda in three sections. Section 1 (mm. 108–115) introduces a new melody derived from the cadence immediately preceding. Section 2 (mm. 115–121) recalls part two. Section 3 (mm. 122–134) is based on part one. The design of the entire movement would be symbolized by the letters ABA–(CBA).

The Codetta The standard explanation of the term *coda* is that it is an appended section at the end of a composition or movement, whereas when a part within the movement has such a "tailpiece" it is called a *codetta*. But a codetta may also occur at the end of a piece. The distinction between the two does not always lie in their respective positions in the piece, much less in their respective lengths, but in their functions. If the passage in question is acting as a conclusion to the entire piece or movement, it is a coda. If it is functioning merely as an appendage to the last part of the piece, it is a codetta. The value in attempting to distinguish between them is that such an attempt forces the analyst to scrutinize the quality and scope of the passage and thus to come to an understanding of its purpose in the work. The last five measures of Chopin's *Prelude No. 15 in D♭ Major* provides an example of a composition which ends with a codetta, for it serves merely to extend the last phrase of the piece by a modified repetition of the cadence. For all their brevity the last two measures of Chopin's *Prelude No. 13 in F♯ Major* have to be considered a coda. Since this passage recalls the middle part of the piece, it functions as an appendage to the whole.

8–F.
SUBDIVISION OF A PART: THE SECTION

Let us examine the *Andante cantabile* from Tchaikovsky's *Symphony No. 5*. The movement opens with an eight-measure phrase consisting of a series of slow chords. These serve both as a modulating transition from the previous movement and as a prelude. The familiar French horn melody leads directly into a passage marked *con moto* (mm. 24–32) in which the horn is joined by the oboe in a motivic interplay based on a new motive. The original horn melody is resumed, this time by the cellos, and leads into another tune (mm. 45–61) based on the motive of the *con moto* section previously heard. This comes to a perfect authentic cadence on I, the first strong conclusive cadence heard so far, marking the end of part one.

It is clear, then, that part one is itself divisible into several sections. After the introduction the horn melody with its accompaniment—that is, the *first theme*—makes up section 1 (mm. 8–24). The *con moto* passage with the motivic interplay is section 2 (mm. 24–32). The return of the first theme played by the cellos comprises section 3 (mm. 32–44). Section 4 (mm. 45–61) consists of the *second theme* which is based on the motive previously heard in section 2.

In representing in detail the design of a composition with subdivisions, it is necessary to differentiate the letters standing for a part from the letters standing for a section (a subdivision of a part). To do this we use capital letters for the parts and lower-case letters for the sections. Thus Tchaikovsky's *Andante cantabile*, part one, is indicated by the letter A and the sections into which it is subdivided by aba'b'.

An outline of the essential tonal structure of this movement is given as Ex. 8–15.

Example 8–15

TCHAIKOVSKY: *Symphony No. 5* (harmonic outline)

Outline
Summary
of
Tchaikovsky's
Symphony
No. 5,
Second
Movement

Bars	Division	Description	Basic Tonal Structure	Design Symbol
1–8	Prelude	Chords in low strings (quasi-transition from first movement)	$VI–IV–I–V_7–I$	– –
8–61	Part one	Two themes, alternating	$I–III–I$	A
8–24	Sec. 1	First theme (horn)	$I \rightarrow vii^{\varnothing}_{\frac{4}{3}}–III$	a
24–32	Sec. 2	Anticipation of second theme (horn and oboe)	III	b
32–44	Sec. 3	First theme modified (cellos)	$1 \rightarrow V^4_3$ [Fr. 6]	a'
45–61	Sec. 4	Second theme (violins)	$I \rightarrow V_7$ I	b'
61–66	Transition	Repetitions and sequence of final cadence of part one.	$I \rightarrow V_7/iii$	– – –
67–110	Part two	Third theme	$V_7/iii \rightarrow V_7/vii–V^4_2$	B
67–99	Sec. 1	Gradual increase of tension as third theme repeats in sequence and imitation.	$V_7/iii \rightarrow V_7/vii$	c
99–109	Sec. 2	Climax toward which sec. 1 was heading. Restatement of "motto" theme of the whole symphony, previously heard in first movement. Subsides to become the retransition.	V^4_2	d
110–170	Part three	Modified restatement of part one.	$I_6 \rightarrow V_7$ $(ii^{\varnothing}_{\frac{6}{5}})$ I	A'
110–127	Sec. 1	First theme (violins)	$I_6 \rightarrow V^4_3$	a
127–141	Sec. 2	First theme modified (winds)	$I_6 \rightarrow V^4_3$	a'
142–157	Sec. 3	Second theme (full)	$I \rightarrow V_7$	b'
158–170	Sec. 4	Modified "motto" theme as in part two, sec. 2, subsiding to become transition to coda	Passing–$ii^{\varnothing}_{\frac{6}{5}}$–I $^{\circ}7$	d'
170–184	Coda	Based on second theme	I (pedal)	b''

EXERCISES

5. Contrast coda with codetta.
6. Describe the tonal structure and design of the codas or codettas of the pieces for Exercise 2 of this chapter:
   a. Schubert, *Moment Musical* (without Trio), mm. 33–39.
   b. Schumann, *Vogel als Prophet*, mm. 16–18 and 40–42.
   c. Beethoven, *Sonata, Op. 7*, Second Movement, mm. 74–90.
   d. Brahms, *Intermezzo, Op. 118, No. 2*, mm. 38–48.
   e. Brahms, Intermezzo, *Op. 119, No. 2*, 99–104.
7. Making outline summaries, analyze the following in detail:
   a. Beethoven, *Quartet, Op. 135*, Third Movement (although this is the same movement listed in the exercises for Chapter 7 as a set of variations, it can also be understood as a ternary form).

b. Brahms, *Intermezzo, Op. 119, No. 2.*
c. Brahms, *Intermezzo, Op. 118, No. 6.*
d. Debussy, *Feuilles mortes.*

8–G.
INSTRUMENTAL COMPOSITE
TERNARY FORM: MINUET
(SCHERZO) AND TRIO

The minuet and trio, or scherzo and trio, familiar as one of the middle movements of most sonatas, trios, quartets, and symphonies of Haydn, Mozart, Beethoven, and Schubert, is a structural complex. The minuet or scherzo is a complete composition in itself (see Ex. 10–3). It usually exhibits a rounded binary form, but sometimes it is one of the ternaries. The Minuet from Mozart's *Serenade, K. 525* ("Eine kleine Nachtmusik"), for instance, is a sectional ternary on a miniature scale. In any case, in the music of the Classical composers it is almost always a two-reprise–‖ : A : ‖ ‖ : BA : ‖. The same observations hold true for the trio (see Ex. 6–3 and Ex. 6–6).

In performance, the minuet or scherzo is played, the trio follows, and then the minuet or scherzo is restated *da capo* without the repetitions. This practice lends to the two pieces an over-all aspect of a large full sectional ternary form:

A	B	A
‖ : a : ‖ ‖ : ba′ : ‖	‖ : a : ‖ ‖ : ba : ‖	aba′

Since this large form comprises two smaller forms, it is called a *composite*, or *compound*, ternary.

EXERCISE

8. Examine the composite ternaries in some or all of the following works: Bach, *Gavottes I* and *II, Minuets I* and *II*, Haydn, *Menuetto* and *Trio* from the "Clock Symphony," the minuet (scherzo) and trio from the Beethoven piano sonatas *Op. 2, No. 1, Op. 2, No. 3, Op. 28*, the second movement of the *Quartet, Op. 135*, and Chopin's *Mazurka No. 45*.

8–H.
INSTRUMENTAL DERIVATIONS
FROM COMPOSITE TERNARIES

THE REPEATED TRIO Beethoven lengthened the scherzos of his *Symphonies No. 4* and *No. 7* by the simple device of restating the trio after the scherzo proper had been played *da capo* and following this restatement with still another scherzo *da capo*, finishing with a short coda. The resulting design can be diagramed

A ‖ : BA : ‖. Such a representation is not misleading as is the diagram A–B–A–B–A, for in these symphonies, although the listener hears the scherzo three times and the trio twice, these are no more than repetitions within an over-all ternary form. We are not dealing with a genuine five-part form.

TWO TRIOS   In his *Clarinet Quintet, K. 581* Mozart employs two different trios which result in a composite five-part form: A–B–A–C–A. A number of Beethoven's successors used this procedure to arrive at lengthy movements. The most played example of the resulting composite five-part form, however, is not a minuet or scherzo at all, but the "Wedding March" from Mendelssohn's incidental music to *A Midsummer Night's Dream*. In this instance the first *da capo* of A is much abbreviated.

Many of the scherzos in the symphonies and chamber music of Schumann have two trios. Brahms also made use of the idea from time to time, as in his powerful *Scherzo, Op. 4*, for piano. In his *Symphony No. 2* the two trios of the *Allegretto grazioso*, though contrasting in character, are derived from the melody of the first part. The tune of the first trio is arrived at by applying a different meter and rhythm to the original melody, with only a few changes of the actual notes. The melody of the second trio, in a still different meter, grows out of motives occurring at the end of the original melody, or rather, from the motives as they appeared in the version of the first trio. Thus, while the first trio can be said to be a result of the original theme, the second trio is a result of the first trio.

Example 8–16

BRAHMS: *Symphony No. 2,* Third Movement

THE CHAIN OF WALTZES

The eminent Viennese waltz composers Johann Strauss, both father and son, Joseph Lanner, Emil Waldteufel, and others, generally followed a single procedure in their popular dances. They assembled a series of five contrasting waltzes preceded by an introduction in slow tempo that might anticipate motifs from the ensuing waltzes. Between the introduction and the first waltz came a few bars, called the "entry" (*Eingang*) which marked the waltz time. After the series of waltzes a lengthy coda was added based on the melodies of the various waltzes and ending brilliantly. The whole complex of the typical Viennese waltz, then, was introduction, entry, waltz A, waltz B, waltz C, waltz D, waltz E, finale (based on A and/or B, C, D, E). The introduction and coda are important in tying together an otherwise unrelated series of dances.

One of Chopin's waltzes for piano (*Op. 18*) is almost a chain of waltzes. It too consists of a series of five waltzes, but the fifth is like the first. The result is a composite five-part form, designed A–B–C–D–A, with coda.

Other possible groupings of the various parts of sectional forms can be easily discovered by a cursory perusal of march and ballet music or by an analysis of the potpourri overture to many a once-popular "grand opera" and to the operettas of Gilbert and Sullivan. From the formal point of view these pieces are always extremely simple to understand, for the parts are precise and clear cut. The listener has no trouble in identifying them and can, therefore, easily grasp the design whether or not the formal scheme is a usual one. Special mention, however, will be made of certain designs of an unusual kind which are occasionally found in the greatest music.

ISOLATED DERIVATIONS FROM THE COMPOSITE TERNARY

In considering the nature of his musical material, the composer may decide that none of the standard forms, if used in its usual way, will suit him. Since there can be no compulsion on the composer to use one of the established designs, it should not be surprising when variations from the fixed norm appear.

Thus, in his *Sonata, Op. 106* ("Hammerklavier"), Beethoven has a scherzo with two trios. But the second trio follows immediately after the first, omitting the first *da capo*. The result is represented as A–B–CA. Mozart had arrived at much the same design in the Finale of his *Sonata, K. 570*.

In his *Rhapsody in E♭ Major, Op. 119, No. 4*, Brahms arranges the parts in the order A B C B A, a pattern sometimes referred to as an *arch* (or *chiastic*) design. Chopin's *Waltz, Op. 34, No. 1*, is also designed as an arch: A B C D C B A–(BA).

The celebrated *alla turca* which closes Mozart's *Piano Sonata in A Major, K. 331*, is a composite ternary with a distinctive feature: between each large division and before the coda is heard a two-phrase period, of contrasting mode and character, which acts as a kind of refrain. Thus:

						Re-
	Re-		Re-			frain
A	frain	B	frain	A		Coda
‖ : a : ‖‖ : ba : ‖		‖ : a : ‖‖ : ba : ‖		‖ : a : ‖‖ : ba : ‖		

EXERCISE

9. Analyze:
   a. Chopin, *Mazurka No. 3* (consider mm. 1–8 a *Refrain*).
   b. Schubert, *Moment Musical in A flat major* (entire).
   c. Brahms, *Intermezzo, Op. 118, No. 2*.

8–I.
VOCAL COMPOSITE TERNARY
FORM: DA CAPO ARIA

The aria *Cara Sposa* from Handel's opera *Rinaldo*[1] illustrates a Baroque *da capo* aria. It begins with a largo movement in E minor in simple binary form. Part one of this movement extends to m. 46 where it closes with a perfect authentic cadence on III. Particularly striking is the use of the orchestra. It does not supply a subordinate accompaniment to the voice part so much as provide a musical texture of equal importance to the part allotted the soloist. There are two passages in the first part where the orchestra plays alone. First, the long opening phrase (mm. 1–12) is given to the orchestra, the soloist not entering until m. 12. Again, with the semicadence on V in m. 24, the orchestra plays alone (mm. 24–28). This second orchestral passage reproduces mm. 4–6 of the first orchestral passage. Because in the Baroque aria passages given to the orchestra alone are generally based on the opening passage, that is, on the return of material previously heard, we speak of them as *ritornellos*. This aria, then, begins with an orchestral ritornello (mm. 1–12), continues with voice and orchestra (mm. 12–24), introduces a second ritornello for orchestra (mm. 24–28), and continues with voice and orchestra to the conclusive cadence on III which closes part one (m. 46). Part two begins with voice and orchestra and continues to a conclusive cadence on i in m. 72. Another orchestral ritornello occurs at this point, reproducing all but the first three bars of the opening ritornello and bringing the largo movement to a close on i. To this point the aria is constructed as a composition complete in

[1] Reproduced in *Masterpieces of Music before 1750*, ed. by Parrish and Ohl. New York: Norton, 1951, No. 44.

itself—a simple binary form with the design AA' and the basic tonal structure:

$$V\text{–}I$$

$$i \rightarrow \text{of III} \rightarrow V\text{–}i$$

Rather than concluding here, the aria continues with an allegro movement of a completely contrasting character. It, too, is in two parts (mm. 82–86 and mm. 86–91), but unlike the largo it does not exhibit a complete harmonic movement. It is, instead, a progressive movement from III to VII (VII is also V/III) in part one and thence to a perfect authentic cadence on v at the conclusion of part two. At the end of the allegro the words *da capo* direct the performers to return to the beginning of the largo.

TONAL STRUCTURE OF THE BAROQUE DA CAPO ARIA It is apparent that this *da capo* aria is analogous to the minuet (scherzo) and trio in that it is a composite ternary form assembled from two binary forms placed together according to the principle of statement, digression, and restatement. Regarding tonal structure, the chief difference between them lies in the middle portion. In the instrumental composite ternary, the trio is a complete composition in itself showing harmonic independence—that is, it is a single complete harmonic movement. In the *da capo* aria, on the other hand, the middle portion is usually not a single complete harmonic movement, but rather progresses from one key to another. Handel's *Cara Sposa*, like many Baroque *da capo* arias in the minor mode, begins the middle portion in III and moves through another key (in this case VII) to a perfect authentic cadence on v. Bach does the same in the aria *Buss' und Reu'* from the *St. Matthew Passion*. A procedure frequently occurring in major-mode arias is to begin the middle portion on vi and progress to an authentic cadence on iii, the dominant of vi (*St. Matthew Passion, Ich will dir mein Herze schenken*). Often, then, the middle portion begins in the relative key, for III is the relative major of a minor key, vi the relative minor of a major key.

The following diagram sums up the previous observations. While it cannot be said that the *da capo* aria usually shows one of the following tonal structures, these are, at least, of fairly common occurrence.

A	B	A
Major: $I \rightarrow V\text{–}I$	$vi \rightarrow \dfrac{V\text{–}I}{\text{of iii}}$	$I \rightarrow V\text{–}I$
Minor: $i \rightarrow V\text{–}i$	$III \rightarrow \dfrac{V\text{–}I}{\text{of v}}$	$i \rightarrow V\text{–}i$

DESIGN *Contrast* In *Cara Sposa* the middle portion contrasts greatly with the outer portions, appropriately so since the text carries an entirely different emotion. The largo is an expression of grief, the allegro of defiance. However, should the words continue with approximately the same sentiment, as is often the case, the middle portion usually presents no striking contrast. In many cases, in fact, the second part shows strong motivic resemblances to the first (see *St. Matthew Passion, Ich will dir mein Herze schenken* and *Können Tränen*).

The Ritornello A distinctive feature of the late Baroque aria, common to both *da capo* and other arias, is the orchestral ritornello. The first portion of an aria invariably begins and ends with a ritornello. In addition, more or less brief snatches of the ritornello appear as interludes from time to time during the singing of this opening portion. Generally speaking, the middle portion makes little use of the ritornello idea.

From the thematic point of view these ritornellos are of two types. The more common type is that which is based on the vocalist's melody (see *HAM, No. 258*), either identical to it or a variation of it. The other type is that which is entirely different from the singer's part, but which is designed so that it can be heard simultaneously with it.

In illustration of the first type Ex. 8–17 shows the opening ritornello and the beginning of the soloist's part of a Baroque *da capo* aria. The first bar of the ritornello is an ornamentation of the first of the vocal melody.

Example 8–17

BACH: *St. Matthew Passion*, Part One

150

The second type is illustrated in Ex. 8–18, which shows the opening of the ritornello and of the voice part. While there is no thematic connection between the two, the ritornello is designed in such a way that it can, at least in its opening measures, be sounded simultaneously with the vocal melody.

Example 8–18

HANDEL: *Radamisto*, original version, Act III

The Abridged Restatement Composers sometimes substitute an abridged restatement of the first portion rather than allowing it to return *in toto*. Abridgements are made by omitting or compressing portions (see, for instance, *Arm, Arm Ye Brave* from Handel's *Judas Maccabaeus*).

COMPOSITE TERNARY IN OTHER VOCAL TYPES
While the *da capo* device is found mainly in connection with the Baroque solo aria, it is sometimes applied to other vocal media. For example, the charming duet for soprano and bass in Bach's *Cantata No. 140 (Wachet auf)* is in structure a typical *da capo* aria, as is the exquisite double chorus which concludes his *St. Matthew Passion*.

EXERCISE

10. Make a detailed analysis of Handel's "Father of Heaven" from *Judas Maccabaeus*.

8–J.
SUMMARY

The ternary forms of the great composers often show traits calling for special discussion. These traits have to do with the connection of parts. To increase the effect of continuity through the three parts of a ternary form composers have often connected parts one and two by any of the following devices:

1. *Link:* A short melodic fragment or a chord or two ties the end of part one, after the completion of its final cadence, to the beginning of part two.
2. *Elision:* The cadence of part one is elided so that part two begins as part one ends.
3. *Broken cadence:* The final cadence of part one is broken off before the resolution of its V_7, leaving a gap which arouses the listener's expectations of something to follow; the first chord of part two resolves the last chord of part one.
4. *Transition:* A modulating passage, at least a phrase in length, leads gradually from part one to part two.

Parts two and three do not always call for a special connecting device, since part two frequently ends on V_7 or a substituted chord, which in itself prepares the ear for the return of the first part. Sometimes, however, a retransition connects parts two and three. Occasionally parts two and three are harmonically "dovetailed," that is, part three begins with the final V of part two instead of waiting for its resolution to I.

Ternary forms are seldom provided with introductions longer than a single phrase, but both short and long codas are frequently found. In contrast to the nineteenth-century prelude and postlude, which act as a relatively independent frame for a composition, the introduction and coda are integral parts of it. Whether long or short, the coda either prolongs the final I which closes part three or, opening with a deceptive cadence, delays this final I. In doing so the coda often emphasizes IV or (♭)VI, occasionally ♭II or some other chord. Usually it takes its material from the ternary form itself though not uncommonly the coda introduces new material.

In large ternary forms each part frequently comprises a number of sections. A part may have its own short coda, termed in this case a codetta.

Statement, digression, restatement—the basic ternary principle—can be applied to other forms to create the composite ternary form. This is represented in vocal music mainly by the *da capo* aria and in instrumental music by the minuet and trio with its derivations. In both cases two binary forms are normally involved: the first is stated, then the second, followed by a restatement of the first.

9

THE RONDO

The word "rondo" is a generic name referring to those compositions that are distinguished by frequent recurrence of a *refrain*. The refrain is normally a self-contained, harmonically "closed" passage. It begins the rondo and reappears at least twice. The passages between appearances of the refrain are called *episodes* or *couplets*.

HISTORICAL NOTE ON THE BAROQUE AND CLASSICAL RONDO The rondo can be traced as far back as the medieval rondel, a poetic form used by the troubadours of Provence during the twelfth and thirteenth centuries. Consequently it has a long history prior to the era of tonal music. Its first appearance during the period under discussion here was in the music of the French composers of the seventeenth and early eighteenth centuries. (This early rondo will be distinguished from later ones by the retention for the former of the French spelling *rondeau*.)

The rondeau was sometimes used by Bach in his instrumental suites, where he adapted the form to a specific dance style. For instance, in the *Partita No. 3* for solo violin he includes a *Gavotte en Rondeau* with four couplets, and in the *English Suite No. 5* for harpsichord the first *Passepied* is a typical French rondeau with two couplets. The light, attractive nature of these dance melodies is particularly appropriate to the rondeau, which is, in essence, a piece for entertainment rather than one with deep emotional content. This cheerful, witty quality remained characteristic of many of the Classical rondos of Haydn, Mozart, and Beethoven, and hence came to be thought of as "rondo style." Actually, the Classical composers by no means limited their pieces in rondo form to this one style, and the so-called "rondo style" appears in compositions in other forms.

The refrain of the Classical rondo may have any character. Many, as we have just observed, are gay or humorous. Others are of the gently flowing *amabile* type (see Beethoven's *Piano Sonata, Op. 90*, Finale), wistful or melancholy (Mozart's *Rondo, K. 511*), shadowy and mysterious (Mozart's *Sonata, K. 310,* Finale), or passionate and dramatic (Beethoven's *Sonata Pathétique, Op. 13,* Finale). If, as sometimes happens, a rondo is not the finale but the slow movement to a sonata or symphony, the theme is likely to be a long-breathed melody expressive of peace and quietude (Beethoven's *Symphony No. 4, Adagio*). But whatever the mood, the rondo refrain will almost always have a definite, clearly melodious character. It is not fragmentary or made up of figuration, but instead is more in the nature of what is called a tune.[1]

The catalogues of works by Haydn, Mozart, Beethoven, and Schubert contain relatively few independent rondos. Their main use of the form was in connection with sonatas, chamber music, symphonies, and concertos. The rondo form, with its regular recurrence of the refrain set off by easily grasped episodes, is particularly appropriate to those lighthearted finales designed to leave the audience in a happy frame of mind. When, then, a rondo forms part of a large work, it is usually the last movement of that work.

9–A.
THE RONDEAU

Example 9–1

D'AQUIN: *Suite No. 3, La Joyeuse*

---

[1] This observation does not hold true for the refrain of the rondo which concludes Beethoven's *Piano Sonata, Op. 26.*

From *Suite No. 3* in E minor, edited by Y. Pessl (in a volume of dance suites for the harpsichord). Copyright Edward B. Marks Music Corporation. Used by permission.

The essentials of a complete French rondeau of the eighteenth century are given in Ex. 9–1. The refrain is a double period based on interruption of the harmonic movement ($i \rightarrow V \parallel i \rightarrow V_7 - i$) and completes a harmonic movement in E minor. Couplet 1 is a four-phrase period completing a harmonic movement on III (G major). A link leads back to the refrain. Couplet 2 is a five-phrase period based on a progressive harmonic movement from VII (D major) to V (B minor). The refrain is again restated. The refrain (A) and the two couplets (B and C) sounded in this order result in the design A-B-A-C-A: a small five-part form.

D'Aquin's rondeau illustrates the form used by many of the late seventeenth- and early eighteenth-century French composers. In the hands of François Couperin and Rameau, too, it was as simple. The refrain, a complete little piece in itself, was written out only once, the performers understanding that it was to be repeated between each couplet. There were no standard number of couplets, but there were always at least two, insuring a minimum of three appearances of the refrain.

Except for contrast of key the couplets rarely differ greatly in character from each other or from the refrain. The general sameness of character is often increased by actual thematic resemblances between refrain and couplet, as in Example 9–1.

EXERCISE

1. Analyze Couperin's *La Bandoline*.

9–B.
THE TYPICAL CLASSICAL RONDO

DESIGN   Among the various designs to be found in the rondos of the Classical composers, the one which appears more often than any other was derived from the French rondeau of three couplets by transposing couplet 1 to the tonic key and allowing it to serve as couplet 3.

Refrain	Episode 1	Refrain	Episode 2	Refrain	Episode 3	Refrain
A	B	A	C	A	B'	A
I	V	I		I	I	I

Such is the basic design of many rondos of the classical composers. Perhaps their partiality to it lies not so much in its apparent symmetry as in what Charles Rosen has called a "sensitivity to tonal relationships. . . . Material presented outside the tonic must have created, in the eighteenth century, a feeling of instability which demanded to be resolved."[2] The resolution of this instability was achieved by the restatement of the episode, however modified, in the tonic key.

In spite of the apparent similarity between the designs of a French rondeau and a Classical rondo there is much to distinguish them. Leaving aside the difference in musical styles between the Classical and the Baroque periods, the usual classical rondo gives the listener an entirely different impression from the old rondeau. The difference lies in the effect of continuity found in the Classical rondo. The rondeau, being extremely simple, made no use of transitions to connect the couplet with the refrain. The most that can be expected is a short link. The result is a chain of self-contained units following each other in sequence.

In the Classical rondo, on the other hand, although the refrain is harmonically complete in itself, often the episodes are not. Being "open" at one end, they lead smoothly back to the return of the theme. Usually the return is made by means of retransitions and these often become important sources of the rondo's charm. Through skilful use of the retransition the constantly returning theme is not met by the listener with boredom, but with a pleasant sense of recognition.

THE REFRAIN   The refrain of a Classical rondo is virtually always periodic in some way, not a single phrase, and so is harmonically closed. Other than that, there is no general description of its structure that will hold true enough of the time to be significant. Schubert's *Sonata in A Major, Op. posth.*, has a rondo refrain in binary form: two periods, the second one repeated.

---

[2] C. Rosen, *The Classical Style*. New York: Norton, 1971, pp. 72–3. A similar observation was made by E. T. Cone in *Musical Form and Musical Performance*. New York: Norton, 1968, p. 77.

The refrain of the last movement of Beethoven's *Sonata, Op. 14, No. 2*, is a short sectional ternary (A-BA).[3]

This period, returning as it does a number of times, is often treated to variation (see the variation rondo, Section 7–F). Some of the returns may be shortened either by actual omission or by the elimination of repetitions.

THE FIRST (AND THIRD) EPISODE

The chief task of the first episode is to express a contrasting key, usually V or III. This may be accomplished without definite melody by the use of scales, arpeggios, or figuration. Or the first episode may present a melody that contrasts with the tune of the refrain. On the other hand, it may be the refrain melody transposed into the new key.

Example 9–2

HAYDN: *Piano Sonata in C Major, No. 48*, Second Movement

The first episode is almost always in the same meter and tempo as the refrain.

If the rondo is in a major mode, the usual procedure is to let the first episode express V (as in Example 9–2). If the rondo is in a minor mode, the first episode is also apt to be in the dominant key, but it might very well express III (the relative major) instead. When the first episode returns near the end as the third episode, it is customarily transposed from the key in which it formerly appeared to I.

THE SECOND EPISODE

The second episode is often larger than any other single section and is a self-contained unit, such as a complete binary or ternary form. Frequently its change of key is marked by a new signature, and if a change of tempo or meter should occur within the rondo, it is likely to take place here. In all, it presents much more of a contrast to the chief quality of the rondo than do the other sections.

[3] Beethoven called this movement *Scherzo* because of its humorous style. Its form, however, is that of a rondo.

In a major-mode rondo the key expressed by the second episode is IV, vi, or the minor mode of I. In a minor-mode rondo the second episode is likely to be the major mode of I, or possibly iv or VI. But again there is no rule other than the fact that some change of key or mode will almost certainly take place.

THE TRANSITION AND RETRANSITIONS

In a few rondos the conclusive cadence of the refrain is followed immediately by the first episode with no transition at all, as in the old rondeau, though there may be a link to connect the two. Usually, however, there is provided between each refrain and its ensuing episode a modulatory transition such as was described in connection with the ternary form (see section 8–A). The transition may consist of no more than figuration of some kind or may continue with motives taken from the refrain melody. Sometimes the transition has a definite melody of its own.

The retransition connects an episode with a return of the refrain. As usually handled by the Classical composers, the retransition glides smoothly and almost imperceptibly into the melody of the refrain.

Example 9–3

MOZART: *Sonata, K. 333,* Third Movement

Example 9–3 illustrates the first part of a typical Classical rondo. The theme itself is a symmetrical period that is repeated with a few ornamentations (the repetition is not included in the illustration). The transition that follows presents at m. 16 a new, melodious idea, and at m. 21 a modulating figure in triplets that introduces the dominant key. The first episode can hardly be said to have a melody. It consists of a single motive, marked by overhanging brackets, repeated three times, the second and third times in a varied form. In m. 28 it becomes a running figure in sixteenth notes which continues throughout the next two bars. These come to an authentic perfect cadence on V at m. 36 connecting by elision with the retransition. Over chromatically rising thirds the note f'' is tapped out in a distinctive rhythm which appears in augmentation in the bass as a pedal point. A brief flourish in mm. 39–40 deflects this f'' into upper regions, but it soon returns and gracefully becomes the first note of the refrain melody.

There is a special transitional device, the false return, which Beethoven seems to have particularly enjoyed using. After an episode, usually the second, the retransition is designed to lead not back to I but to another key, often IV, in which the refrain melody seems to return. But after a few bars the real refrain begins in I and the listener finds that what he had thought was the refrain was only an anticipation of its initial phrase. At times the device has the effect of a joke on the listener. As used in Example 9–4, however, it is not in the least amusing but results in a peculiar poignancy. It is as if the second violin longs to play the "sweetly melancholy" theme. It manages two bars of the melody but the first violin takes over. Trying again, the second violin succeeds this time in playing four bars, only to be forced to give in to the first violin, who, after all, knows the right key.

Example 9–4

BEETHOVEN: *Quartet, Op. 132*

In the Classical rondo scheme episode 3, like the refrains which precede and follow it, is in the tonic key. Since the normal purpose of the transition is to modulate from the key of one section or part to the key of the next, one might well question the necessity of a transition between the last episode and its surrounding refrains. In some cases the composer does simply omit the transition. Usually, however, the transition is utilized as a means of providing temporary relief from tonic harmonies. The transition in this case is constructed to set up chords other than I as secondary tonics. Usually it strays quickly into rather remote regions, such as ♭VI or ♭III, or moves restlessly from secondary tonic to secondary tonic.

In the E major rondo which concludes Beethoven's *Sonata, Op. 90*, the retransition between the final appearances of the episode and refrain begins on I, passes to ♭VI and thence through ♭vii to II. The supertonic in turn progresses to V, which is elaborately prolonged to cover nine bars, at length slipping almost imperceptibly into the refrain (Example 9–5a). Example 9–5b, showing the essential voice leading of the outer voices, reveals how they move stepwise in contrary motion from the I to the V$^6_3$.

Example 9–5

BEETHOVEN: *Sonata, Op. 90*, Second Movement (harmonic outline of retransition, mm. 201–231)

b.

E: I ———————————→ V⁶₅ I

The whole retransition covers a space of thirty bars. This provides the relief of harmonies distant from I and a degree of emotional contrast as well. Both episode and refrain have here a quiet, gently flowing character. The retransition builds to a climax, quickly subsides to a pianissimo passage of a mysterious quality, then, with a great up and down swell on II and V⁶₅ glides into the refrain. After the retransition's tortuous path the reappearance of the refrain come as a soothing return to a familiar landscape.

BASIC TONAL STRUCTURE In all but a few Classical rondos, each appearance of the refrain is in the tonic key. The first episode expresses III or V, the former usually but not always being reserved for minor-mode rondos, the latter for pieces in either major or minor modes. The second episode not infrequently remains in the tonic key with a change to the opposite mode. Otherwise it might express iii, IV, or vi. The third episode transposes the first episode to I. The tonal structure of the usual Classical rondo can be expressed succinctly as:

	A	B	A	C	A	B′	A
Major mode:	I	V	I	i	I	I	I
				(or iii, IV, vi)			
Minor mode:	i	III (v)	i	I (or iv, VI)	i	i	i

FORM A glance at the schematic representation of the rondo design A-BA-C-A-BA shows that the seven sections group themselves quite naturally into three parts:

		Part Three	
Part One	*Part Two*	*(Equals Part One)*	*(Plus Coda)*
A–B A	C	A–B′ A	
I V I	opposite	I	
(III)	mode or related key		

In this light one perceives an over-all composite sectional ternary structure, part three being a partly transposed version of part one, both surrounding a central part. The individualized treatment of the second episode (that is, part two) often bears out this ternary conception of the rondo.

EXERCISE

2.   Analyze the Third Movement of Beethoven's *Sonata, Op. 13.*

9–C.

OTHER DESIGNS IN THE CLASSICAL RONDO

ISOLATED DESIGNS Though the rondo just discussed is found more often than any other one type in the music of Haydn, Mozart, Beethoven, and Schubert, it is not at all unusual to find different designs, some involving a great number of episodes, others involving fewer episodes. Sometimes two episodes are placed adjacently, omitting the normal return of the refrain between them. Below are listed some of the various designs to be found isolated among the works of the classical composers.

A B A C A D A B' A	Mozart: *Sonata, K. 281*, Finale
A B A C A B'—(Transition)	Mozart: *Sonata, K. 310*, Finale
A B C A D A—(A)	Haydn: *Trio in G Major*, Finale ("Rondo all' Ongarese")
A B A C A D A—(BCDA)	Beethoven: *Violin Sonata No. 4, Op. 23*, Finale
A B A C D A E A B'—(A)	Mozart: *Rondo, K. 494*
A B A B' A—(Transition and New)	Mozart: *Sonata, K. 457*, Finale

THE SMALL RONDO FORM There is a particular rondo structure which appears often enough to warrant special mention. It consists in abbreviating the normal rondo structure by omitting the return of the first episode. The result is the design A B A C A, referred to as a small rondo.[4]

Immediately the perplexing question arises: How can a small rondo be distinguished from the five-part form, which is also an A B A C A design, or from the minuet or scherzo with two trios? The distinction lies in the continuity of the rondo. The five-part form, including the rondeau with two couplets, and the scherzo with two trios are built up mostly by placing self-contained sections or parts alongside each other with frequent com-

---

[4] Some theorists call this the "second rondo," the "first rondo" being our ternary form (ABA), and the "third rondo" being the typical Classical one (ABACAB'A).

plete cadences and a minimum of transitionary passages. While there may be a retransition from B back to A, B being harmonically closed, this retransition will begin after a definite and conclusive cadence. In the rondo, on the other hand, the espisodes are usually "open," or at least lead into the retransition with no perceptible break. Thus, while the fundamental designs are identical, the total effect of the two forms is different.

The appellation "small rondo form" seems to imply that its use will result in a short rondo. This is not necessarily the case, however. The term is used merely to indicate an abbreviation of the usual design. Actually one of Mozart's longest keyboard rondos exhibits this form, the *Rondo in A Minor K. 511*. Its great size is due to the fact that each section is in itself quite long. The refrain consists of thirty bars of 6/8 time in an andante tempo, and the first episode with its retransition contains fifty bars. Each of these sections is itself a ternary form, with statement, digression, and restatement.

The small rondo form only occasionally appears as a fast final movement of a sonata. But if a slow movement is cast in a rondo form, it is usually a small rondo, examples being the slow movements of Mozart's *Piano Sonata, K. 457,* and Beethoven's *Sonata Pathétique, Op. 13,* and *Quartet, Op. 74.*

Particularly interesting is Mozart's application of the small rondo form to vocal music. On a small scale his song *An Chloe* is a little "rondino" with a delightful variation of the refrain on its third appearance. On a larger scale Donna Elvira's aria *Mi tradì quell'alma ingrate* from *Don Giovanni* is a small rondo form in which a single motive appears in both voice part and accompaniment during the refrain and both episodes. When the refrain and all episodes are based on the same theme, we speak of a "monothematic rondo." The *Agnus Dei* from the *Mass in C Major, K. 317* ("Coronation"), is also a small rondo.

THE SONATA RONDO   Frequently the second episode of a Classical rondo does not present new material but is devoted instead to a development of the ideas heard in the refrain or episode 1 or, in some cases, a transition. In this case episode 2 takes on the aspect of the development section of sonata form, to be discussed in Chapter 11. For that reason our discussion of the sonata rondo must be postponed until then, although the basic design of this hybrid form is simple enough:

Refrain	Episode 1	Refrain	Episode 2	Refrain	Episode 3	Refrain
A	B	A	Development (of A, B, or transition)	A	B′	A
						plus Coda

THE FINAL REFRAIN AND CODA   Sometimes the final refrain is not stated in its entirety. Rather, its beginning is heard and then it merges with the coda. One can hold that in these situations there is no final refrain but that the coda begins with the opening passage of the refrain. Which point of view best expresses a particular situation resolves itself around the question of the length of the partial restatement of the refrain. For example, in the rondo that closes Mozart's *Piano Concerto in D Minor, K. 466*, the final statement of the refrain (mm. 346–352) is abruptly cut off after only six bars, at which point the coda begins. A plausible argument for considering those six bars not as a return of the refrain but as the actual beginning of the coda could easily be made. In the *Concerto in C Major, K. 415*, Mozart has shortened the refrain by omitting its repetition by the orchestra, but has not cut out any essential part of it. Although the coda connects with the refrain's ending without a perceptible break, it would not seem that this case justifies considering the final appearance of the refrain as no more than the beginning of the coda. On the contrary it is a genuine reappearance which then merges with the coda.

EXERCISE

3. Analyze the Finale of Haydn's *Symphony No. 101* ("Clock").

9–D.
CLASSICAL RONDOS LACKING CONTINUITY

We have emphasized that the difference between the Classical rondo and a similarly designed derivation from the ternary form is that the former exhibits a general continuity of movement while the latter does not. Having absorbed this distinction, we discover that some Classical rondos—often so labeled by their composers—do not display the continuity described as distinctive of the Classical rondo, but are loaded with full stops. They seem to be in this respect more like the old French rondeau than a composition of the Classical era.

To explain this seeming discrepancy one must remember that our description of the typical Classical rondo is based not on eighteenth-century books of musical theory, but on deductions drawn from observation of what Haydn and Mozart actually did. These are the men who, along with certain lesser figures, created the Classical rondo. Therefore it stands to reason that when they first began to compose rondos, their starting point was not *our* idea of the Classical rondo but something more like the French rondeau. (See, for instance, the rondo Finales to *Sonatas, K. 26* and *K. 30*, by the nine-year-old Mozart.) When Beethoven and Schubert began to compose, their idea of the rondo was based on those of Haydn, Mozart, and their contemporaries. It is for this reason that their rondos generally conform to our idea of the typical Classical rondo, whereas Haydn's and Mozart's sometimes do not.[5]

HISTORICAL NOTE ON THE RONDO AFTER THE CLASSICAL PERIOD The chief appearance of the rondo form during the Romantic era was as a concerto finale (see Section 13–C). Otherwise, the majority of Romantic composers had little use for the form. Among the works of Chopin and Weber are a few piano rondos in a virtuoso style. Mendelssohn wrote a brilliant *Rondo Capriccio* for piano and orchestra. But Wagner and the Italians were writing only opera, and the arch-Romanticists Berlioz and Liszt, turning their attention to program music and new forms and genres, had little use for the worn-out rondo.

In the piano music of Schumann there are a number of rondolike structures. The *Novellett in E Major, Op. 21, No. 7,* for instance, is an eight-part form with the design A–B–CA–D–A–CA. The fourth piece, *Grillen* (that is, *Caprices*), of the *Phantasiestücke, Op. 12,* is in design and tonal structure a typical Classical rondo. Yet these pieces cannot be considered real rondos, nor does Schumann call them so. The Classical composers had taken what was originally a form made up of a number of separate sections—with the seams still showing—and worked it into a continuous and coherent whole. Schumann's structures consist, like the old rondeau, of a series of little pieces in a row, but unlike the rondeau his pieces stand in strong contrast to each other with little relationship among them. They are delightful music but are not real rondos, despite the rondo principle underlying their structure.

The only Romantic composer who showed a decided interest in the rondo was Brahms. Most of his works in rondo form are of the sonata-rondo type (see Section 9–C). A notable example of a simple rondo by Brahms is the great *Rondo alla Zingarese,* which forms the Finale to the *Quartet for Piano and Strings, Op. 25,* and uses four distinct episodes, in addition to a cadenzalike section before the final appearance of the refrain. The result is a work of twelve sections, which seem to group themselves according to mode into three parts.

	Part One	*Part Two*	*Part Three*
	(Minor)	(Major)	(Minor)
Tonal Structure	i → v i III i	I vi I I	i → V (V) i
Design	AB A C A	D E C D	B Cadenza A (E C D)

Outline of Brahms' Piano Quartet, Op. 25, Fourth Movement

At the very end of the nineteenth century Richard Strauss wrote a symphonic poem, *Till Eulenspiegel's Merry Pranks,* which claims in its title

[5] But see Beethoven, *Quartet, Op. 18, No. 4,* Finale, for an exception.

to be a rondeau "after the old-fashioned roguish manner." "Thus," writes Leichtentritt, "the listener is warned to accept the rondo as one of Till's 'merry pranks.' "[6] Indeed, if this is a rondo at all, it is one only in the sense that two motives, representing the hero, make frequent reappearances throughout the work. Another interesting rondo written about the same time is the great Finale to Mahler's *Symphony No. 5.*

Certain composers of the first half of the twentieth century have continued to compose rondos which, for all their change in musical style, do not show any outstanding alteration of design from those of the Classical era. One such piece is the finale of Prokoviev's *Piano Sonata No. 4 in C Minor, Op. 29.* In tonal structure, to be sure, novelties are to be found. Hindemith closes his *Sonata No. 1 for Organ* with a small rondo form in E♭. While the second episode expresses a key conventional enough in the late eighteenth and early nineteenth centuries (♭VI), the first episode is in the key of A, a tritone distant from E♭.

A number of works by members of the "second Viennese school" show a design based on the rondo principle, such as the Second Movement of Webern's *Quartet for Clarinet, Tenor Saxophone, Violin, and Piano, Op. 22*—the structure of which he compared to the last movement of Beethoven's *Piano Sonata Op. 14, No. 2*—and the Finale of Schoenberg's *Quartet No. 3.* Alban Berg seems to have been partial to the rondo, having used it twice in *Wozzeck* (the last scenes of Acts I and II), in the finale of the *Chamber Concerto,* the second movement of the *Lyric Suite,* and in the first movement of the *Lulu Symphony.*

9–E.
SUMMARY

The principle of the rondo lies in the statement of a passage of music, the refrain, and its return at intervals after contrasting episodes or couplets. It is thus allied to the ternary forms whose chief characteristic is also statement, digression, and restatement. In the rondo, however, more than one restatement is always present.

The rondeau of the seventeenth and early eighteenth centuries was an aggregation of a number of miniature pieces with little contrast among them other than that of key. They were assembled as refrain, couplet 1, refrain, couplet 2, refrain, and so on, either without connective passages between them or with no more than a simple link. Some of the rondos of Haydn and Mozart are similar to these, but the typical Classical rondo was given a much more continuous aspect by the judicious use of transitions, especially retransitions leading into the return of the refrain. While many different designs are to be found in the rondos of the Classical composers, the typical design is arranged as a composite ternary form.

---

[6] Hugo Leichtentritt, *Musical Form.* Cambridge, Mass.: Harvard University Press, 1951, p. 120.

10

THE BINARY FORMS

HISTORICAL NOTE ON THE BINARY FORMS AND THE SUITE During the late seventeenth and early eighteenth centuries instrumental music depended on the binary form to a greater extent than on any other. The vast majority of stylized dance pieces, of which Baroque sonatas and suites are full, as well as many slow movements of concertos and other large works, exhibit binary forms.

The binary form is characteristic of the individual pieces making up French and German lute and keyboard suites during the second half of the seventeenth century (for example, Chambonnières and Froberger; see No. 35 in *Masterpieces of Music Before 1750*, New York: Norton, 1951). A Baroque suite consists of a number of dances, all in the same key. While no standard number or type of dances were used consistently, many suites include an *allemande, courante* (or *corrente*), *sarabande*, and *gigue*.

Dance Type	Meter	Tempo and Character
Allemande	Duple	Moderate; sombre, stately
Courante	Triple	Moderate fast; *corrente* faster
Sarabande	Triple	Slow; stately
Gigue (*Giga*)	Compound duple (6/8 or 12/8)	Fast and vivacious

Most suites comprise at least four pieces, some as many as twenty or more. Additional dances often appearing, especially in the eighteenth century, are:

Dance Type	Meter	Tempo and Character
Bourrée	Duple	Lively
Gavotte	Duple (¢ or 4/4, each phrase starting on third quarter)	Moderately fast
Minuet	Triple	Moderate; stately
Passepied	Triple	Lively

Bach's *French* and *English Suites* all include the *allemande, courante, sarabande,* and *gigue* in that order as well as a few other dances. These are inserted between the *sarabande* and *gigue* or occasionally between the *courante* and *sarabande.* Some of the dances are provided with doubles. In addition, each of the *English Suites* opens with a prelude.

In Germany the suite was also called a *partita,* in France an *ordre,* and in England a *lesson.*

The two-part form was by no means limited to music in dance style. Some of the preludes of Bach's *Well-Tempered Clavier* are constructed along these lines, as are many sonata movements (for example, each of the three movements of the *Organ Sonata No. 1*) and cantata sinfonias (for example *Ich steh' mit einem Fuss im Grabe, No. 156*). Much of the vocal music of the Baroque era is also in binary form.

Bach and Handel made occasional use of the balanced and rounded binary forms but relied mainly on the simple binary. Domenico Scarlatti, on the other hand, consistently wrote balanced binaries. In the late eighteenth century it was the rounded binary that came into normal use, particularly in the instrumental minuet and scherzo, though the other types were not totally absent. Throughout the nineteenth century the binary form—especially the rounded type—is frequently found. Usually, however, it was used either on a small scale, as we have already seen in certain of Schubert's songs and Chopin's preludes, or as one division of a composite ternary form. A sole exception is the opera aria, which, during the latter half of the eighteenth century, had dropped the undramatic *da capo* idea. Instead many arias and some ensemble numbers were constructed as large composite binary forms: a slow part followed by a fast one (for example, *Batti, batti* from Mozart's *Don Giovanni*). This scheme, ideally suited to the depiction of a dramatic change in emotion or situation, continued through the first half of the nineteenth century as a standard form for the opera aria. The slow part was often called *cavatina,* the fast part *cabaletta,* each frequently being introduced by a recitative. (See Bellini, *Come per me sereno* from *La Sonnambula.*) One of the last and most popular examples of the *cavatina-cabaletta* construction is *Ah, fors'è lui* and *Sempre libera* from Act I of Verdi's *La Traviata.* In this century, however, it has been revived by Stravinsky for the closing scene of the first act in his opera, *The Rake's Progress.*

10–A.
SUBDIVISION OF BINARY FORMS

Let us examine two binary forms, a simple binary by Bach and a rounded binary by Haydn.

Example 10–1

BACH: *French Suite No. 3*, Minuet

Example 10–1 illustrates a late Baroque keyboard minuet in simple binary form. Dominating is a melody of the *perpetuum mobile* type constructed from the motives, a, a′, and b. Part one is a two-phrase period comprising a progressive movement from i to III. Beginning where part one leaves off, part two progresses from III to a perfect authentic cadence on v (m. 24). Measures 25–26 emphasize iv and, by means of a sequential repetition, emphasize V again (mm. 27–28). In m. 29 this V becomes a seventh chord (V$_5^6$) leading back to I.

Aside from the cadence in mm. 15–16 which divides part one from part two and that which closes the minuet, the design shows one perfect authentic cadence. This occurs at mm. 23–24. Although the strength of this cadence would seem to be as great as that on III which brings part one to a close, the cadence is weakened to the point of being nondivisive by two factors. First, motive a, which acts as a bridge in the left hand, provides continued motion in eighth notes. Compared with the definite conclusive quality of the three-quarter notes played by the left hand in m. 16, the steady eighth-note motion tends to weaken the divisive effect of this cadence. The second factor is that *e* is introduced on the third beat of the bar as a passing tone leading into the beginning of the next phrase, and this passing tone propels the listener on. Other design factors are not divisive. Unity of tempo, texture, and rhythm prevails, and the melodic motives of part one are, with the exception of motive c and its derivatives, the same as those of part two.

The attentive listener will sense that the character of the music from m. 17 to m. 31, while not contrasting, is subtly different from that which precedes and follows it. The effect results from the greater degree of tension manifested in this section. Undoubtedly the difference is partially due to the introduction of the new, rhythmically interesting motives c and c". More significant, however, is the effect of the secondary tonics which occur here on both iv (mm. 25–26) and v (mm. 22–23; 27–28). By emphasizing first one chord, then another, the harmony brings about a sensation of energetic movement. Combined with the steady rise of the melody (mm. 25–30) just before the relaxing return of the tonic (m. 31), these secondary tonics imbue the section with great vitality. Due to the distance from the tonic that the harmony travels in bringing in secondary tonics, the sections opening part two are called the departure or digression and the section in which the main key reappears is called the return. Example 10–2 is a harmonic outline of the piece.

Example 10–2

BACH: *French Suite No. 3*, Minuet (harmonic outline)

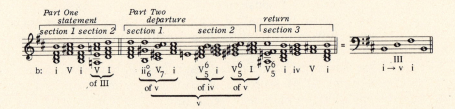

Example 10–3

HAYDN: *Quartet, Op. 76, No. 5*, Third Movement

Example 10–3 is one of Haydn's minuets in rounded binary form. Part one is a phrase with a progressive harmonic movement from I to V. It will be remembered that when part one closes on V in the rounded binary, part two begins by prolonging this V until the restatement begins (see Section 6–D). Example 10–3 accomplishes this prolongation by an interesting use of a succession within a succession. The digression leaves the cadential V by treating ii as a secondary tonic (mm. 9–10), these bars repeating sequentially on I. This I is immediately treated as the dominant of IV (mm. 11–12). Measures 13–15 outline the notes of the supertonic triad, preceding each with a lower appoggiatura, leading into the return of V (see Ex. 10–4).

Example 10–4

HAYDN: *Quartet, Op. 76, No. 5*, Minuet (harmonic outline of departure)

Two features of part one should be particularly noted: (1) the three-note motive in m. 4, marked with an overhanging bracket, and (2) the *sforzando* on the third beat of m. 6. Haydn has provided himself with a three-note motive and a misplaced accent—two bits of material which he exploits fully. He begins his digression by combining the two, with the result that mm. 9–11 are rhythmically askew: four bars of 2/4 meter are injected into three bars of 3/4. A unison cascade on the first two notes of the motive follows, during which one loses track of the 3/4 meter altogether. This passage leads into the restatement. Thus the entire digression is constructed by *motivic development* from the two fragments of material chosen from part one.

The digression, with its rhythmic surprises, is both exciting and humorous. The modified bars of the restatement (mm. 23–24) provide a further surprise, for they are played a delicate *piano* rather than *forte* with a *sforzando* as they had first appeared. And now, as if angry at having been excluded from the graceful ending of the restatement, the cello bursts in with the three-note motive and the misplaced accents, the other instruments immediately joining the fray. Thus while part one is balanced by the first phrase of the expanded restatement, the digression is balanced by the second. The complete design of Ex. 10–3 is, therefore, an unusual AB‖A′B′.

Certain features occurring in one or both of the Bach and Haydn examples just examined should be noted.

1. Part one is shorter than part two.

2. Part one can be a single phrase or it can be a period divisible into sections. Part two is divisible into sections.

3. Part two is based wholly or partially on material first heard in part one.

4. (a) When part one ends on III, part two begins with a progressive movement connecting this III with the V that ushers in the return to the tonic key (see Ex. 10–5a). (b) When part one ends on V, part two begins with a prolongation of this V until it ushers in the return to the tonic key (see Ex. 10–5b). In Ex. 6–2 and 6–3 this prolongation was accomplished for the most part by a simple extension of the V with a dominant pedal point in the lowest voice. But we have now observed that the prolongation may take the form of a chord succession beginning and ending with V.

Example 10–5

Typical basic tonal structure of a Classical continuous rounded binary

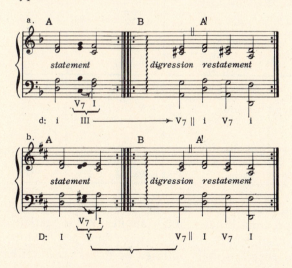

5. The initial section of part two, in its task of progressing to or prolonging V, is given to bringing about a feeling of energy with an increase of tension. This is done partly by harmonic restlessness due to the estab-

lishment of a series of secondary tonics, and partly through increased rhythmic and textural complexity. The increase in tension may continue through more than just the initial section of part two, as happens in the example from Bach. The sections opening part two, given over to such increase in tension, can be referred to collectively as the departure or the digression.

Examination of many binary forms of the great composers of the tonal era reveals that the observations deduced from the two previous examples may be considered typical for the binary froms as a whole. Nevertheless, it will be advantageous to consider the binary form as used by Domenico Scarlatti for one of his harpsichord sonatas. We shall examine the *Sonata in A Minor*, No. 175 in Kirkpatrick's catalogue, by means of a summary outline.[1]

Outline Summary of Scarlatti's Sonata in A Minor, K. 175

Bars	Division	Basic Tonal Structure	Design Symbol
1–51(52)	Part One	$i \rightarrow$ V–I (of V)	A
1–16	Section 1: opening section	$i \rightarrow$ V	a
16–32	Section 2: modulating section	$i \rightarrow$ V$^6_5$–i (of iv) V–i–V (of v)	b
32–41	Section 3: closing section	I $\rightarrow$ IV–V–I (of V)	c
41–51(52)	Section 4: codetta	I–IV–V–I (of V)	a'
52–103	Part Two	$ii \rightarrow$ V–I ♯	A'
52–66	Section 1: departure	ii° V–I (of ii) –V/V	d
66–84	Section 2: departure	V/V $\rightarrow$ IV–V	b'
84–96	Section 3: closing section	I $\rightarrow$ IV–V–I	c'
96–103	Section 4: codetta	I–IV–V–I	a''

This outline reveals a much longer and more complex structure than either of our previous binary-form examples. While Scarlatti's sonatas are normally balanced binaries, they do not follow a stereotyped pattern in details. The particular sonata outlined here, then, cannot be considered typical. Rather, it illustrates one way of subdividing the parts of a bal-

[1] This sonata is reproduced in *HAM*, No. 274, and in Scarlatti, *Sixty Sonatas*, ed. by Ralph Kirkpatrick. New York: Schirmer, Vol. 1, No. XXI. Only the latter corresponds fully to Scarlatti's intentions.

anced binary form. In other sonatas the transposed restatement of part two might involve more or fewer sections. The departure might be reduced drastically, or more than one codetta might appear. Scarlatti's balanced binary form served him as a broad framework within which he constructed a great variety of designs.

Particular notice should be taken of the unusual tonal structure. Since the piece is in the minor mode, one would expect that the related key area in part one would be the dominant minor. Instead, the major mode is substituted. For this reason, the corresponding passages in part two are in the tonic major.[2]

10–B.
CONNECTION OF PARTS ONE AND TWO

Example 10–6

SCHUBERT: *Twelve Ländler, No. 1*

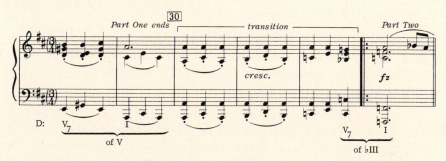

Just as parts one and two of the ternary forms are often connected for greater continuity, so are parts one and two of the binary forms. In Ex. 10–6 part one ends with the perfect authentic cadence (mm. 28–29) and is followed by a three-bar transition (mm. 30–32) leading into part two. (See also Bach, *WTC, Prelude No. 10*, mm. 21–22.)

More commonly the link is used as a connective device (Bach, *WTC, Prelude No. 4*, m. 14). The use of elision or broken cadence is extremely rare, an exceptional case being the elision in m. 6 of *WTC, Prelude No. 23*.

10–C.
CODETTA AND CODA

The outline summary of Scarlatti's *Sonata, K. 175* (section 10–A), shows that section 4 of each part is a codetta. The longer simple and rounded

---

[2] For a detailed examination of form in Scarlatti's sonatas see Ralph Kirkpatrick, *Domenico Scarlatti*. Princeton, N. J.: Princeton University Press, 1953, Chap. XI.

binaries also often include codettas, as in the Minuet of Haydn's *Symphony No. 101* ("Clock"), mm. 20–28; mm. 72–80 (in Burkhart's *Anthology*).

Frequently the binary form concludes with a more or less lengthy coda. When the two parts are repeated, the coda usually begins after the repetition of the second part. Occasionally, however, it is included in the repetition (*WTC, Prelude No. 24,* last five-and-one-half bars).

EXERCISE

1. Analyze the following music. Subdivide those parts that are susceptible to subdivision and label each section appropriately. Construct a harmonic outline.
   a. Scarlatti, *Sonata, K. 380.*
   b. Mendelssohn, *Song Without Words, Op. 62, No. 1.*
   c. Brahms, *Intermezzo, Op. 76, No. 4.*
   d. Wolf, *In der Frühe.*

10–D.
THE COMPOSITE BINARY FORM: OPERATIC ARIA

Let us examine the soprano aria *Tacea la notte placida* from Verdi's *Il Trovatore.* After a five-bar introduction Leonora begins an andante, 6/8 meter, in Ab minor, quiet and restrained. With the words *"dolci s'udiro e flebili"* the mode changes to major, the mood becomes expansive. These two passages, contrasting in nature, comprise a small simple continuous binary form. The following stanza constitutes a repetition, slightly varied, of the first, and leads into a climactic coda ending with a perfect authentic cadence in Ab major. A passage in a kind of recitative style ensues, a duet between Leonora and her companion Inez. The meter now changes to 4/4, the tempo to allegro giusto and, after a lengthy orchestral introduction, Leonora sings a brilliant coloratura aria, a sectional rounded binary in the same key. After a brief interjection by Inez the aria is repeated, concluding with a fifteen-bar coda in which the two voices are joined.

Tacea la notte placida contains two independent and contrasting forms, placed adjacently to comprise a composite binary form. The first half in slower tempo is called the *cavatina,* the half in quick tempo is the *cabaletta.*

It will be remembered that the composite ternary form of the *da capo* aria and the minuet (scherzo) and trio is the result of a combination of two independent forms according to the principle of statement, digression, restatement. Like *Tacea la notte placida,* many opera arias of the late eighteenth and early nineteenth centuries show an analogous composite binary form. The two halves are always of a contrasting character. Usually they are placed as in Verdi's aria, the cavatina before the cabaletta, and it is only when they are so arranged that these terms are used. Sometimes, however, depending on the text, the slower half follows, as happens in Leporello's celebrated *Madamina* in Mozart's *Don Giovanni*.

EXERCISE

2. Analyze one or more (not in Burkhart's *Anthology*):
    a. Mozart, *Don Giovanni, No. 4* ("Madamina—Nella bionda")
    b. Mozart, *Don Giovanni, No. 7* ("Là ci darem la mano—Andiam, andiam")
    c. Mozart, *Don Giovanni, No. 12* ("Batti, batti—Pace, pace, o vita")
    d. Mozart, *Magic Flute, No. 4* ("O zittre nicht—Du, du, du")
    e. Beethoven, *Fidelio, No. 9* ("Abscheulicher!—Ich folg' dem innern Triebe")
    f. Bellini, *La Sonnambula, No. 4* ("Come per me sereno—Sovra il sen la man")
    g. Verdi, *La Traviata, No. 6* ("Ah, fors'è lui—Sempre libera")
    h. Stravinsky, *The Rake's Progress, Act I, Sc. 3* ("Quietly night—I go, I go to him")

10–E.
SUMMARY

As in the ternary forms, the parts of a binary form are often susceptible to subdivision—part one frequently, part two almost always. Ordinarily the initial section of part two, referred to as the departure or digression, is particularly interesting. This is the section which, in prolonging the V which concluded part one or progressing from the final III of part one to the V, moves restlessly from secondary tonic to secondary tonic, resulting in an effect of tension or vitality. Upon the return of the tonic key, or shortly thereafter, this tension is released.

As in ternary forms, the parts of a binary form may be connected by a link or transition. Each part may close with a codetta, and a coda often concludes the whole.

Many opera arias consist of a combination of two independent forms of a contrasting character. The result is termed the composite binary form.

11

THE SONATA
FORM

HISTORICAL NOTE ON SONATA AND SONATA FORM For the past two hundred years the term "sonata" has usually been reserved for works performed by one or two players only. Sonatas for three performers are called trios, those for four quartets, those for orchestra symphonies. Although the number of performers vary, such works have so many important formal characteristics in common that we can refer to them all as sonatas.

The history of the sonata is complicated by the fact that the history of the term does not coincide with the history of the genre itself. During the sixteenth century and before, the *word* "sonata," meaning a piece to be "sounded" on instruments, could denote any type of instrumental composition. As a *genre* the sonata was a piece in several contrasting sections for one or more instruments which, by the early seventeenth century, could be designated by a variety of terms. *Ricercare, canzona, sinfonia, capriccio,* along with *sonata,* appeared as titles of such pieces, to all appearances sometimes indiscriminately. About the middle of the sixteenth century the style and technique of the French chanson, a polyphonic composition based on imitative counterpoint and comprising a number of distinct sections, was transferred to the keyboard (*HAM* Nos. 91 and 118) and thence to the instrumental ensemble to become the *canzon da* [or *per*] *sonar(e)* (*HAM* Nos. 136 and 175). In the early part of the seventeenth century Italian composers such as Fontana, Landi, and Merula were writing sonatas with fewer sections, each of these enlarged—that is sonatas in several movements (*HAM* Nos. 198, 208, and 210).

Due to the enormous number and types of compositions being written in various countries by many composers, the sonata's history in the seventeenth century is extremely complex. Here it will suffice to point out that by around 1660 two chief classes of sonatas had emerged. Both of these were commonly written for two instruments, such as violins, with

178

basso continuo (ordinarily performed by a violoncello or viola da gamba along with organ, harpsichord, or some other instrument capable of producing harmonies). The distinction between them has to do with style and often with the number of movements. One type consisted mostly of pieces in dance rhythms—essentially it was a suite of dances—and was called *sonata da camera* (chamber sonata). The other was normally made up of pieces in a more sober style, the fast movements often in an imitative texture, and since this type was frequently played in church, it came to be known as the *sonata da chiesa*. These types were fairly well standardized by Corelli, the *sonata da chiesa* consisting of four movements (slow-fast-slow-fast). Composers of the next generation, such as dall'Abaco, Geminiani, and Telemann, as well as Handel and Bach, continued and developed the *sonata da chiesa* type, often transferring it to other performing media, such as a solo instrument (usually flute or violin) with continuo. The *sonata da camera* most often consisted of a prelude followed by two or more dances, around three to six movements in all. Such compositions bear a close relationship to the keyboard suite which had been cultivated all over Europe during the late sixteenth and seventeeth centuries. During the eighteenth century sets of dance pieces came to be called suites or partitas rather than *sonate da camera*. Late eighteenth-century composers, including Haydn and Mozart, usually called them *serenades, cassations, notturni* or *divertimenti*, and wrote them as music for social functions. As such they were of an appropriate quality—light-hearted, entertaining, diverting, or merely pretty. With some notable exceptions (e.g., Mozart, *K. 563*), such works are not characterized by profundity or intellectual content. Austrian and South German composers generally included at least six movements (two minuets and two slow movements in addition to the outer fast movements). Beethoven's *Septet, Op. 20,* is properly included in the suite category, along with his two *Serenades, Op. 8* and *Op. 25.* Schubert's *Octet,* modelled after Beethoven's *Septet,* is another example.

As for the sonata proper, two generally observed standard movement schemes had emerged by the end of the first half of the eighteenth century: the four-movement and three-movement schemes. The three-movement scheme (fast-slow-fast) has been common since the beginning of the eighteenth century when it was used not only in chamber music but as the standard scheme of the Italian opera overture, the *sinfonia.* In the later eighteenth century and the nineteenth this three-movement scheme was for the most part restricted to works for one or two performers, for instance, sonatas for piano and sonatas for violin or some other solo instrument and piano. The four-movement scheme has been associated since the time of Beethoven with sonatas requiring any number of performers from one (Beethoven's *Op. 2* piano sonatas) to several hundred (Beethoven's *Symphony No. 9*).

When a sonata has four movements, either of two schemes is likely to be found. The slow-fast-slow-fast pattern was typical of the Baroque *sonata da chiesa*, but has only rarely occurred since then (Haydn, *Symphony No. 34 in D Minor*; Brahms, *Horn Trio, Op. 40*; Franck, *Violin Sonata*). The four-movement scheme of the Classical composers was first established in some symphonies by Johann Stamitz and other composers working in Mann-heim around 1750, who may have been influenced in this regard by a 1740 symphony of the Austrian G. M. Monn. This movement scheme comprises two fast movements surrounding two middle movements. One of these middle movements is generally slow, the other a minuet. By speeding up the minuet, Beethoven in effect created the *scherzo* and, from his time on, the minuet normally gave up its place to the scherzo.

From time to time sonatas with schemes of more or fewer than the standard three or four movements are to be found. One-movement sonatas are represented by the eighteenth century Italian keyboard com-posers, especially Domenico Scarlatti. It is now known, however, that Scarlatti ordinarily grouped his sonatas in pairs so that the majority of them should more properly be thought of as forming sonatas in two movements. The sonata consisting of a single movement was revived in the nineteenth century by Liszt (*Piano Sonata in B Minor*) and is not infrequent in the twentieth century (Sibelius, *Symphony No. 7*; Berg, *Piano Sonata*; Schoenberg, *String Trio*). It should be noted that often a sonata which is ostensibly in one movement actually contains several movements played without pauses (Barber, *Symphony in One Movement*; Schoenberg, *Chamber Symphony No. 1*). Two-movement sonatas were written by the Classical composers (e.g., Mozart's violin sonatas K. 301, 302, 304 and 305 and Beethoven's piano sonatas Opp. 49, 54, 78, 90, 111), but after Beeth-oven they are not found among the great music of the nineteenth century unless Schubert's *Symphony No. 8* ("Unfinished") is included in this group. The two-movement sonata is not uncommon in the twentieth century (Schoenberg, *Chamber Symphony No. 2*; Prokoviev, *Symphony No. 2*; Webern, *Symphony Op. 21*; Berg, *String Quartet, Op. 3*).

The sonata sometimes includes five and occasionally more movements. The greater number comes about by the addition of a special characteristic movement to the standard four. Beethoven's *Symphony No. 6* ("Pastoral") adds the storm scene, Berlioz' *Symphonie Fantastique* the "March to the Scaffold," Schubert's *Piano Quintet in A Major* a set of variations on his song "The Trout." Beethoven's late quartets, considered in chronological order, show a progression in the number of movements: the E♭ Major, *Op. 127*, has the standard four; the A Minor, *Op. 132*, adds a short march to make five; the B♭ Major, *Op. 130*, includes two dance movements and two slow movements to make six, but because of the style of the music this work can by no means be considered a serenade or divertimento; and the C♯ Minor, *Op. 131*, precedes the standard four movements with a slow fugue and places a short transitional movement before the slow movement and a brief slow movement before the finale. The result is a seven-movement work played without pause.

Sometimes a theme appears in more than one movement of a work. For example, in Brahms' *Violin Sonata No. 1*, the second episode of the concluding rondo makes use of the theme which opened the slow movement. Such treatment is termed "cyclic." The cyclic principle was common early in the history of the sonata (e.g., the *sonata da chiesa* of Vitali, No. 241 in Schering's *Geschichte der Musik in Beispielen*), but the principle waned and was not revived and further developed until the time of Beethoven and the Romantic composers. Berlioz' first two symphonies (*Fantastique* and *Harold in Italy*) make use of a certain theme (the *"idée fixe"*) which appears in every movement. Brahms sometimes restates the opening theme of the first movement during the finale (*Symphony No. 3, String Quartet No. 3, Clarinet Quintet*). The Finale of Bruckner's *Symphony No. 8* includes a simultaneous statement of the principal themes of the three preceding movements. During the last half of the nineteenth century French composers (Franck, Saint-Saëns, d'Indy, and others) particularly emphasized cyclic treatment in their sonatas.

The term "cyclic" refers to compositions in which entire themes are openly and obviously transferred to movements other than that in which they were first heard. Many sonatas which cannot reasonably be termed "cyclic" have subtle relationships between themes of different movements (e.g., Mozart, *Clarinet Quintet, K. 581*, first movement, second theme and second movement, first theme; Beethoven, *Sonata Pathétique, Op. 13*, first movement, second theme and last movement, first theme).

Any discussion of the formal aspect of the sonata must make clear the distinction between the movement scheme and the sonata form. The term *movement scheme* refers to the number and tempo or type of the individual movements comprising the whole sonata. The *sonata form* is a standard form exhibited by certain single movements. Not every movement in a sonata is a sonata form. Some are binary forms, others are ternaries, rondos, and so on. Sonata form is a form which throughout history has played such a large role in the various sonata movements that the name has been attached to it.

The particular form known today as sonata form (often inaptly called "sonata-allegro form" or "first-movement form") has, from the second quarter of the eighteenth century, been associated with the Italian opera sinfonia, as well as with the sonata. The vast majority of movements in the sonatas and opera sinfonie of the late seventeenth and early eighteenth centuries were continuous binaries—simple, balanced, and sometimes rounded. Around 1720 a few sonata movements of certain composers, though still in continuous binary form, began to take on all the essential characteristics of what was later to become standardized as sonata form.

Examples of such movements are the finales of Veracini's *Violin Sonatas No. 1* and *No. 6* (1721), the first movement of Francesco Conti's Overture to *Pallade Trionfante* (1721), and the second movement of the *Violin Sonata in B♭* (1717) by G. B. Somis, as well as the fourth movement of his *Violin Sonata in D Minor* (ca. 1725) published in Einstein's *A Short History of Music* (2nd ed., New York, 1938). During the 1730's this rudimentary sonata form became more and more frequent and was the preferred form for the first movements of the opera *sinfonie* of the Neapolitan composers G. B. Pergolesi and Leonardo Leo. By 1742, it had found its way to Berlin in the "Prussian" sonatas of C. P. E. Bach. In the latter half of the eighteenth century and the first quarter of the nineteenth century sonata form was so prevalent throughout Europe that it constituted the most important single form, extending its influence beyond the sonata as far as the realm of opera (for example, Mozart's *Don Giovanni*, Nos. 3 and 15). But this is not to say that sonata form was a fixed, unchangeable blueprint according to which composers constructed their works. On the contrary, the form remained stable only in its broadest outlines. Each of the great Classical composers treated it according to his own creative impulses and in constantly fresh ways. Only after Beethoven did the sonata form tend at times to petrify into a stereotype, as it seems to have in the first movement of Grieg's *Piano Concerto in A Minor*.

Throughout the Classical and Romantic periods it is the first movements of sonatas, chamber music, and symphonies that are usually, but by no means always, sonata forms. Any of the other movements may or may not be in this form. Slow movements and finales are very often in this form; exceptionally a minuet or scherzo, discounting the trio, may be (Mozart, *Quartet, K. 387*; Beethoven, *Symphony No. 9*; Schubert, *Symphony No. 9*). The Classical overture is ordinarily either a sonata form or its relative the sonatina, which we will discuss in Chapter 12.

The sonata form has found a place in certain music of the first half of the twentieth century (Hindemith, Prokoviev, Bartók). Schoenberg managed to follow its design even in twelve-tone works (*Quartets No. 3* and *No. 4*), but composers after 1950 have rarely found it useful.

11–A.
THE GENERAL ASPECT OF SONATA FORM

The sonata form originated as a type of continuous binary form, the two parts of which, like those of the rounded and balanced binary, are subdivided in a particular way. Example 11–1, the first movement of a Neapolitan opera overture dating from the year 1739, illustrates the sectional pattern of the first part of a typical sonata form.

Example 11–1

LEO: *Amor vuol sofferenza, Sinfonia*

Part one extends to m. 23 and is made up of four sections. The *primary key section*, because of its opening position, is usually called the first or principal theme (abbreviated *PT*). In this case it is a single phrase in length (mm. 1–6). The imperfect cadence with which it ends continues the sixteenth note motion to give the effect of merging with the next section (mm. 6–14). This section, making use of a motive from the primary key section, modulates to the dominant key and cadences there. It is, then, a *transition* or bridge.

The *related key section* (mm. 14–21) expresses the dominant key throughout, the first four-and-one-half bars in the minor mode, the remainder major. The second or subordinate theme (*ST*), as this section is usually called, offers, in this case, an extreme initial contrast to the first theme motivically, rhythmically, and in its quasi-contrapuntal two-voice texture. Though contrast in character between first and second themes occurs with great frequency, it is not a *sine qua non* of the sonata form. On the contrary, often, in what are called monothematic sonata forms, the two themes are similar if not virtually identical, and elements of a melody may be used in both principal and subordinate themes. What is essential to this form is the change of key.

The *closing section* (mm. 21–23) is so named because it concludes part one. Its chief purpose is to reconfirm the new key, often, as in this case, with reiterated tonic and dominant harmonies, along with a tonic pedal point. Some closing sections have melodic lines which contrast with the first and second themes. Some closing themes—and this is true for some first and second themes as well—exhibit no clearly melodic aspect whatsoever, consisting instead of arpeggios, scales, or some other figuration appropriate to the performing medium [see the Finale of Beethoven's *Sonata, Op. 27, No. 2* ("Moonlight")].

The chief musical material of the piece is set forth or "exposed" in the four sections of part one. The first part of a sonata form is therefore called the exposition. The four sections of the exposition (primary key section, transition, related key section, and closing section) appear in the majority of cases as they do in Ex. 11–1, though in later works usually much expanded. It is not rare, however, for there to be more or fewer sections, as will be demonstrated in future examples.

The second part of the typical sonata form opens like that of any other continuous binary form with a departure (digression) prolonging the concluding V of the exposition or, in cases where part one ends on III, progressing to V. As in the rounded binary, this V brings about interruption of the harmonic movement, followed by a return to the beginning and a complete harmonic movement on I. The return, as we have seen in connection with the simple and rounded binaries, is crucial, for it is here that the harmonic movement is completed. We have noted that in the balanced binary the final passages of part one return transposed to the tonic key as the final passages of part two. The typical sonata form, as it appeared in the eighteenth century, is a combination of rounded and balanced binary. It begins the return with a restatement of the opening of part one, as in the rounded binary, and it closes with a restatement of the final sections (second and closing themes) of part one transposed to the tonic, as in the balanced binary.

The terms universally employed today for the departure and return are, when used in connection with the sonata form, development and recapitulation, respectively. The term "development" indicates that the section is often devoted to motivic development based on themes heard in the exposition. The term "recapitulation" implies a return of a number of themes rather than a single one. (As we shall see in Sections 11–F and 11–G, these terms can be misleading. They are descriptive of events which often do take place, but they do not indicate the essential *function* of the second part of the sonata form. Moreover, their use can carry the implication that motivic development and/or thematic restatement somehow "ought" to take place in these sections. But this is by no means the case.)

The following outline of the sonata form shows its relationship to the rounded binary and the balanced binary:

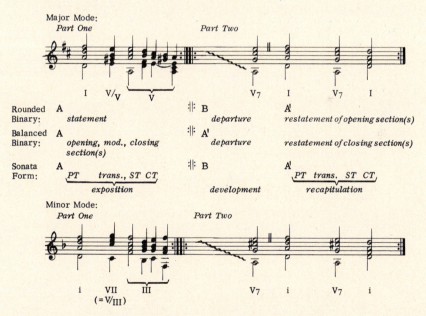

Since the sonata form grew almost imperceptibly out of the various types of continuous binaries, the practice of repeating each part was at first regularly followed. But in many of their later works, Haydn and Mozart dropped the repetition of part two, and Beethoven and Schubert did the same. In only a few works of the latter composers (Beethoven's

Sonatas, Op. 78 and *Op. 79*, and Schubert's *Sonata in A Major, Op. 120*, for instance) are the development and recapitulation sections also repeated. In the Finale of the *Sonata, Op. 57* ("Appassionata"), Beethoven repeats the development and recapitulation sections, but not the exposition. In most cases the exposition was repeated by all Classical composers and often by the Romantics as well. When sonata form is used for an overture, neither part is customarily repeated.

Having outlined the main features of sonata form, we shall consider it in greater detail in the next sections.

11–B.
PRIMARY KEY SECTION (FIRST THEME OR GROUP)

Example 11–2 is the first theme group from the exposition of the opening movement in Brahms' *Symphony No. 1 in C Minor*.

Example 11–2

BRAHMS: *Symphony No. 1 in C Minor*, First Movement

The first phrase acts as an introduction. Phrase 2 presents the theme's first real melody, A, which ends with a half cadence on V (m. 46). Motivically similar, phrase 3 makes this V a secondary tonic by means of the perfect, though inconclusive, cadence $V^7/V–V$ (mm. 50–51). Phrase 4 presents a different melody, B (its opening motive derived from mm. 45–46 of A). It closes with a half cadence on V (mm. 56–57). Phrase 5, similar to 4 though extended, closes the harmonic movement with a perfect authentic cadence on i (mm. 69–70). The four phrases of mm. 42–70 have formed a contrasting double period. Phrase 6 takes up the melody A again, semicadencing in mm. 77–78. Phrase 7 is similar and closes the second complete harmonic movement with a perfect authentic cadence on i. Phrases 6 and 7, then, are recognizable as a symmetrical parallel period. The seven phrases which comprise the first theme thus form themselves into two groups preceded by an introduction, and are characterized by a design involving statement, digression, and modified restatement. It will be observed that the double period (mm. 42–70) encompasses both the statement and digression, while the second period presents the modified restatement.

The "symmetry" of the double period lies in the balancing of the two-phrase antecedent by the two-phrase consequent. Each phrase, however, is longer than the preceding one (four bars, five-and-one-half bars, six bars, thirteen bars). Similarly, in the next period the eight-bar antecedent is followed by an eleven-bar consequent. The enormous drive of this powerful theme is partly due to the growth in the length of its phrases.

The exposition of a sonata form comprises the first part; the principal theme comprises the first section of that part. A subdivision of the principal theme is referred to as a subsection. The introduction and two groups of Brahms' first theme, then, become three subsections of that theme. The entire first theme group can be outlined as shown below.

Bars	Phrase	Division	Tonal Structure	Design
38–42	Phrase 1	Subsection 1: introduction	$I \rightarrow V_7–I$	—
42–70	Phrases 2–5	Subsection 2: double period	$I \rightarrow V_7–I$	AB
70–89	Phrases 6, 7	Subsection 3: period	$I \rightarrow V_7–I$	A'

It will be observed that Ex. 11–2, though comprising only the first theme group of a sonata-form exposition and therefore not a part in itself, nonetheless concludes with a perfect authentic cadence. The strength of this cadence has been emphasized and it has been presented as capable of dividing a composition into parts. But it is not rare for longer works, in which the parts are further divided into sections and subsections, to use the perfect authentic cadence as a means of marking the end of a section or subsection as well as the end of a part. In our example and in similar cases the rhythmic motion of the accompaniment helps to drive through the cadence. Moreover, compared to those at the end of the exposition, the cadence is not of divisive strength. (The first movement of Schubert's "Unfinished Symphony" is similar in this respect to the first movement of Brahms' *Symphony No. 1*.)

Although the tonal structure of Ex. 11–2 divides the first theme into two unequal subsections plus introduction, the melodic arrangement imposes on the section a ternary design: AB–A'. It is doubtful whether music literature has another principal theme constructed quite like this one. Examination of the first theme of Ex. 11–3 will show it to be very different. There the single melody is presented without introduction and as a symmetrical period. This period is then repeated in a varied version and followed by a codetta. Actually, sonata form first themes have been constructed in innumerable ways. In Mozart's little *Sonata in C Major, K. 545*, the first theme consists of a single four-bar phrase, while in his *Symphony No. 38* ("Prague") it is a section of thirty-five bars in two distinct subsections, each of which can be further subdivided, the whole containing no less than seven different melodic ideas.

In a lengthy movement the primary key section may be a theme group containing within itself several subsections and a number of ideas. It is usually not difficult to determine how far the first theme or theme group extends, for the whole section will express the tonic key. There may be temporary secondary tonics, but as long as a return to the original tonic is effected, the various subsections are considered part of the first theme group.

EXERCISE

1. Each of the following passages is the primary key section of a sonata-form movement. Identify and compare their formal characteristics.
    a. Mozart, *Sonata, K. 333*, Second Movement, mm. 1–8
    b. Beethoven, *Sonata, Op. 2, No. 1*, First Movement, mm. 1–8
    c. Hindemith, *Piano Sonata No. 2*, First Movement, mm. 1–26

11–C.
THE TRANSITION

Example 11–3 illustrates the first theme and transition from the exposition of the first movement of one of Haydn's piano sonatas.

Example 11–3

HAYDN: *Sonata in C Major, No. 35,* First Movement

The first theme (mm. 1–16) consists of the statement and varied repetition of an eight-bar symmetrical period, closing with a perfect authentic cadence on I. This I is sustained as a codetta and leads directly into the transition, which begins with no break in the flow of the music. The transition theme is clearly related to the first theme in that it is built entirely out of the latter's chief motives.

MODULATORY ASPECT OF THE TRANSITION

From m. 20 to m. 23 the main tonality of C is expressed. With the last beat of m. 23, the note $f''\sharp$ is introduced and maintained from then on. No other chromatic alteration is made until m. 31, when the note $c'\sharp$ appears in the bass, passing between a c' and a d'. The harmonies of mm. 23–35 express the key of G major, the dominant aspect of the main tonality of C. When the note $f''\sharp$ is first introduced in m. 23, the listener does not know whether it presages a real change of key or whether it acts as a mere secondary dominant of V. But as it continues to appear through a number of bars, the listener's bearings begin to change, and the original tonality recedes. With the note $c'\sharp$ in m. 31 the D major chord (V in the key of G) that begins m. 32 is made a secondary tonic. When a dominant chord in the new key is preceded by its own (secondary) dominant, the home key is no longer on a prominent level of the hearer's consciousness, and the modulation is complete.

On the basis of first one and then another chromatic alteration, we can divide the modulatory aspect of the transition into three phases.

1. Phase 1 is that part before the modulation begins to set in (mm. 20–23).
2. Phase 2 contains the deflection away from the tonic key by the introduction of the leading tone, in this case the note $f''\sharp$ of the new key (mm. 23–31).
3. Phase 3 begins with the leading tone to V in the new key, as in V/V or vii°/V. In our example phase 3 begins with the appearance of the note $c'\sharp$ and continues to the end of the transition and the beginning of the second theme (mm. 31–35).

Locating the beginning of each phase can be simplified by looking for the chromatic alteration which appears at the point where the new phase begins. If the modulation is to be from I to V, the point at which the second phase begins will be marked by a raising of the fourth degree of the scale, and the third phase will be marked by a raising of the first degree. In other words, in a piece in F major the beginning of phase 2 will contain a B♮ somewhere in the texture, the third phase will contain an F♯. In order not to be misled one must make sure that these chromatic alterations actually reflect an essential modulatory change and are not merely passing secondary dominants or chromatic ornamentation of some kind (such as the b'-flats in mm. 16 and 18 of Ex. 11–3).

Since the modulation is often not to V but to III or even VI, the preceding observations about chromatic alteration will not always apply. If the following facts are kept in mind, the student should have no trouble in recognizing the various phases of modulation in a transition:

1. The beginning of phase 2 is marked by the appearance of the leading tone of the new key; this leading tone usually appears as an element of V in the new key, sometimes of vii°.
2. The beginning of phase 3 is marked by the leading tone to V (i.e., ♯4) of the new key. This note is an element of the V/V or vii$^{\circ}_{7}$/V of the new key.

Note: In the minor mode phase 2 of a modulation from I to III does not
      necessitate a chromatic alteration, because in the natural minor VII
      is also V/III.

Most transitions of the Classic and Romantic composers make use of this
three-phase model of modulation, but modifications of it occur from time
to time. In the first movement of Beethoven's *Sonata in C major, Op. 53*
("Waldstein"), the leading tone to V of the new key (appropriate to phase
3) is introduced in m. 22, whereas the leading tone of the new key
(appropriate to phase 2) is not heard until m. 23. This reversal is somewhat
mitigated in that the leading tone to V in this case is an element not of V or
vii°, but of the Italian 6th. The true phase 3 begins in m. 27.

Sometimes secondary tonics other than those strictly needed for phases
2 and 3 are introduced (see Ex. 11–4).

Example 11–4

BRAHMS: *Quartet in A minor, Op. 51 No. 2,* First Movement (reduction)

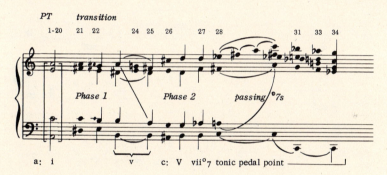

In the example above, phase 2 of the modulation begins in m. 26 and
phase 3 in m. 40. Before phase 2 there has been a brief secondary tonic on
v, and between phases 2 and 3 Brahms stresses the flat submediant of the
new key by treating it as a secondary tonic for three bars. Although the
new key is to be C major, the modulation during the transition is to C

191

minor. Thus mm. 35–38, in A♭ major, stress the submediant aspect of C minor. The result is more appropriate to the style of this quartet than a direct modulation from A minor to C major ever could be.

DEPENDENT AND INDEPENDENT TRANSITIONS

To return to Ex. 11–3, the transition begins in m. 20, its first notes forming an elided cadence with the codetta of the first theme. Though motivically related to that theme, it has its own melodic line and rhythmic aspect. It therefore has a clear beginning and is to be spoken of as an independent transition.

Example 11–5

MOZART: *Sonata, K. 333,* First Movement

The transition of Ex. 11–5 is different in that its beginning is not clearly set off in the listener's mind. One hears the beginning of the first theme transposed to the lower octave and might well assume that this is to be a varied repetition of the exposition's initial section. Instead, the presumed first theme is soon deflected in its course and takes on the aspect of a transition. The process of deflection is known as *dissolution* for it involves the gradual disappearance of the first theme. Such a transition is considered dependent in that its transitory aspect emerges only gradually from what the listener supposes to be a restatement of the first theme.

Both dependent and independent transitions are frequently to be found in the music of the Classical and Romantic composers.

THE FUNCTION OF THE TRANSITION

Modulation is only one of the functions that a transition can perform. Consideration of other aspects will reveal a variety of uses to which it can be put. In Ex. 11–3 mm. 20–26 of the transition are based on motive b from the first theme, while mm. 27–31 are devoted to motive a'. The transition here provides motivic development quite apart from the actual development section which will appear later. In addition, the progressive harmony combines with the melodic ascent throughout mm. 20–32 to produce a certain amount of tension. This transition thus achieves at least three things: (1) modulation to the new key; (2) development of motives of the first theme; and (3) contrast in degree of tension, an aspect of the music's shape.

Being a dependent transition, Ex. 11–5 recalls the initial notes of the first theme. Aside from this there are certain motivic references to the first theme, but these do not assert themselves as a characteristic of the transition. Rather, this is an example of a transition that introduces new material. This new material is not suddenly brought in without motivation but grows almost imperceptibly out of what has gone before. The passage from m. 15 (beat three) to m. 16 (beat three) is a variant of the motive immediately preceding and is transformed in turn into mm. 17–19. M. 20 is a variant of m. 18. The top line of m. 21 is a restatement of m. 19, while the lower figures are derived from m. 20 (the b-natural to c in sixteenth notes on the latter half of each beat).

The transition that connects the first and second themes of Brahms' *Symphony No. 1* is an independent transition, a phrase group of four phrases, consisting partly of new and partly of previously heard material. The illustration in Ex. 11–6 begins at the point where Ex. 11–2 left off.

Example 11–6

BRAHMS: *Symphony No. 1*

There are two features of this transition which should be especially noted. The first is that, although it is to lead to the major mode of III (that is, E♭), the transition emphasizes the minor mode of that key. Emphasis in the transition on the opposite mode is a useful device, for the listener does not tire of the new key's harmonies before the second theme begins. The Classical composers also used this practice to good advantage.

The second feature to be noted is the length of this transition. From the modulatory standpoint it need not have been so long, since it attains its objective, the establishment of the key of E♭ by means of vii/V of that key in its seventh bar (m. 96). Yet it continues for twenty-four more bars. There are two reasons for the length of this transition. The first is a matter of proportion. The first theme (Ex. 11–2) is quite long in itself, as are the second and closing themes (see Ex. 11–6), and it is reasonable that the size of the transition that connects them be in keeping with their length. Perhaps more important in this case, however, is the other reason. The first theme is of a violent and stormy nature, the second theme is quiet and restrained. Brahms has calculated that it will take some time to effect this emotional change, for the listener must be psychologically prepared if the mood of the second theme is to be convincing. A hearing of the exposition of this remarkable movement will demonstrate the gradual change from one quality to another which takes place during the transition.

On the basis of our examination of Ex. 11–6 we can deduce that an additional function of a transition may be to prepare the listener for the section that is to follow. Sometimes the transition goes further and actually anticipates the ensuing section by introducing a characteristic rhythm or motive (see Ex. 8–5). In these cases the transition can be compared to the fade-out/fade-in of film technique.

To summarize, there are six common functions that a transition may perform.

1. Modulation to the new key
2. Development of a motive or motives from the first theme
3. Introduction of a mood which contrasts with that of both first and second themes
4. Introduction of new material which contrasts thematically with both first and second themes
5. Preparation of the listener for the second theme by gradual change from one mood to another
6. Preparation of the listener for the second theme by anticipation of its characteristic rhythm or melodic motive

It is obvious that no single transition can perform all these functions, since some are mutually exclusive (Nos. 3 and 5, for instance, or 4 and 6). Most transitions are concerned with several of them. No one function is an indispensable feature of any transition, not even the first, as the following paragraphs will demonstrate.

THE PARTIALLY MODULATING TRANSITION The three phases of modulation are to be found in the majority of transitions. The third phase, introducing V of the new key as a secondary tonic, undermines the listener's sense of the original key as "home." These transitions can, then, be thought of as complete from the modulatory standpoint. Some, however, do not bring in phase 3. Instead, the secondary section enters in the new key after phase 2 has run its course. In other words, the transition prepares for the second theme by introducing the new key with its regular V, not a secondary tonic on V. Since the listener's feeling for the original key has not disappeared upon the entrance of the second theme, this type of transition will be called partially modulating. A number of piano sonatas by Mozart contain partially modulating transitions (*K. 279*, First Movement; *K. 281*, Second Movement; *K. 309*, First Movement), and such transitions occur from time to time in the works of most other composers as well. (For a partially modulating transition in a rondo see Ex. 9–3.)

THE NON–
MODULATING
TRANSITION

Example 11–7

HAYDN: *Sonata in D Major, No. 37,* First Movement

Example 11–7 illustrates a type of transition not infrequently found among eighteenth-century composers. In this type no modulation takes place at all. Instead, the transition ends with a semicadence on V and the second theme follows immediately in the new key.

The nonmodulating transition seems to be found only in major mode sonata forms whose second theme is in the dominant key. (See Mozart's piano sonatas, *K. 284* and *311*, first movements.)

TRANSITION
WITH DECEPTIVE
MODULATION

In his *Trio, Op. 99,* for piano, violin, and cello, Schubert makes use of an interesting and effective modulatory device. The first movement, in Bᵇ major, presents the first theme in I followed by a transition leading to III. Leaving B♭ major in m. 35, the transition moves with apparent sureness of purpose to the key of D major. The listener, expecting the second theme in this key, is surprised to hear it enter instead in F major, the dominant. It is, of course, not possible to describe the particular effect of such deceptive modulations. They must be heard to be appreciated. Although the deceptive modulation can be found in the music of most Classical and Romantic composers, no one seems to have been quite so fond of it as Schubert.

Not all apparently deceptive modulations actually are so. For instance, in the Finale of Beethoven's *Symphony No. 8 in F major,* the transition (mm. 28–47) includes a partial modulation to the dominant key, C major, whereas the second theme begins in ♭III, A-flat major (m. 48). But it soon moves to C major (m. 60). What has happened here is not, in the larger sense, a deceptive modulation at all, but a deceptive beginning for the second theme. In other words, the related key section is in the usual dominant key (to which the transition had modulated) but its first phrase uses ♭VI of that key as a secondary tonic.

OMISSION OF
THE TRANSITION

Another device occurring several times in the music of Schubert, but rarely used by other composers, is the appearance of the second theme immediately after the first theme without an intervening transition. In this case, Schubert bridges over the gap by means of a short link, no more than a chord or two, or several unaccompanied tones. Well-known examples are to be found in the first movements of the "Unfinished Symphony" (mm. 38–41) and the *Symphony No. 9 in C Major* (mm. 132–133). The second movement of Mozart's piano *Sonata, K. 280,* provides neither transition nor link.

EXERCISE

2. The following passages are the transitions from the expositions of the sonata forms dealt with in Exercise 1:
   a. Mozart: mm. 8–13
   b. Beethoven: mm. 8–20
   c. Hindemith: mm. 26–40
   (1) Considering these transitions in the above order, locate the beginning of phase 2 and of phase 3, if present, of the modulations: first, look ahead to discover the key of the second theme; then locate the first appearance of V of the new key; finally, locate the first appearance of V/V, if any, of the new key.
   (2) Which are "dependent" and which "independent" transitions?
   (3) Describe the functions performed by each.

11–D.
RELATED KEY SECTION (SECOND
THEME OR GROUP)

RELATIONSHIP
OF FIRST AND
SECOND THEMES

Like the first theme, the second theme consists, in shorter movements, of a single section; in long movements it will probably comprise a group of subsections. Often the second theme is of a character contrasting with the first theme; sometimes it is not. In so-called monothematic first movements, common in the works of the Classical composers, the second theme is closely related to the first theme, although here there is generally some element of contrast, perhaps in texture or harmonic rhythm. In longer works where the second theme forms a group of subsections, at least one or two of these will probably contrast with the first. But there is no standard practice in this regard. The sole feature that invariably distinguishes the second theme from the first is the change of key.

Except in the late Romantic period the tempo and meter of the first theme are shared by the second. (It is, in fact, unusual for these to change anywhere in the movement until the coda is reached—the very meaning of "movement" is close to "tempo.") Toward the end of the nineteenth century composers often used tempo and meter changes to help imbue the second theme with an entirely new character. In Tchaikovsky's symphonies and overtures such far-reaching contrasts are the rule.

KEY OF SECOND THEME
Previous to Beethoven the second theme very rarely expressed a key other than III or v for sonatas in the minor mode, or V for sonatas in major mode. In the *Sonata, Op. 31, No. 1*, and in the *Sonata, Op. 53* ("Waldstein"), the second and closing themes of the first movements express III although both these sonatas are in the major mode.

In his later works Beethoven frequently substituted VI as the key of the secondary and closing themes (for instance, the first movements of *Symphony No. 9, Quartets Op. 95, Op. 130, Op. 132*, and *Piano Sonata, Op. 106*). Schubert did the same in the first movement of his "Unfinished Symphony."

By the use of mode mixture the keys of III or VI often occur in a higher or lower position than might be expected. For instance, the Finale of Beethoven's *Symphony No. 8* in F major uses the key of A♭ major for the beginning of the second theme: III of F minor rather than F major. In Mahler's *Symphony No. 2* in C minor the second theme is in E major: III of the major, rather than the minor, mode of C. The use of mode mixture in the selection of related keys is very common.

Occasionally the second theme does not express a single key but progresses from one to another. In the first movements of Schubert's *Quintet in C Major* and the *Quartet in D Minor* ("Death and the Maiden") the second theme begins with III, then moves to V. In the first movement of Beethoven's *Symphony No. 8* the progression is from VI to V.

The second theme often comes to a close with an authentic cadence. At other times the final phrase of the second theme leads by means of the elided cadence into the first phrase of the closing theme. From time to time, of course, exceptions occur. Example 11–8 is a case where the second theme comes to a semicadence (V_7), after which the closing section commences on I.

Example 11–8

BRUCKNER: *Symphony No. 7*

EXERCISE

3. The following passages are the second themes or theme groups from the expositions of the sonata forms dealt with in Exercises 1 and 2:
   a. Mozart: mm. 14–21
   b. Beethoven: mm. 20–41
   c. Hindemith: mm. 41–63
   (1) Considering these second themes in the order above, identify the type of larger unit displayed (period, phrase chain, phrase group), if any.
   (2) Divide each second theme into its subsections.
   (3) Note which subsections rely mainly on melodies, which are basically motivic, which consist chiefly of figuration, and so on.
   (4) Does each second theme express a single key and mode or does progressive harmonic movement and/or change of mode take place?
   (5) Observe the type of cadence with which each second theme closes. Is there room for disagreement as to the point at which it ends and the closing theme begins?

11–E.
CONTINUATION OF RELATED KEY
SECTION (CLOSING THEME OR
GROUP)

The closing theme or theme group does not perform a tonal function of its own; rather, it reinforces and confirms that of the second theme. But in continuing the *key* it does not necessarily continue the *mode*, for the related key sections often make use of both major and minor modes, particularly in Beethoven and the composers who followed him.

Since the closing section of the exposition in a sonata form does not introduce a new tonal area, it is not an indispensable feature of the form, and its omission from time to time is not particularly remarkable. In Haydn's *Symphony No. 103* ("Drumroll"), for example, its place is taken by a brief codetta (first movement, mm. 88–94).

Nevertheless, the majority of sonata forms do include a closing theme or theme group, often of considerable length and importance. Ex. 11–9 presents the essentials of the closing theme from the first movement of Brahms' *Symphony No. 1*, with whose first theme and transition we have already become acquainted.

Example 11–9

BRAHMS: *Symphony No. 1*

The four phrases of this closing theme are in reality only two, for the second is a varied repetition of the first, the fourth of the third. The theme is a period with a varied repetition of both the antecedent and the consequent in the key of E♭ minor—identical to the key but not the mode of the second theme. The minor mode of E♭, however, was prominent in the transition which led to the second theme (see Ex. 11–6). We find an almost identical tonal structure in the first movement of Beethoven's *Sonata, Op. 57* ("Appassionata").

The first eight bars of Ex. 11–9 (mm. 161–168 in the score) present a theme basically in two-part counterpoint. The upper voice is new, with a distinctly energetic character of its own, contrasting with that of the previous themes. The lower voice begins as an inversion of the first theme (compare Ex. 11–2) and continues by a sequential repetition of the second phrase member of that theme. Measures 169–176 present the same two-part contrapuntal texture in exchanged positions: the upper voice is now in the lower position and vice versa, a technique known as invertible counterpoint (see Section 14–D). Phrase 3, and its varied repetition (mm. 177–185) have a new upper voice supported by motives from the previous phrases.

Upon concluding the closing theme Brahms introduces a single phrase as a bridge which leads either back to the beginning of the exposition or on to the development. This phrase is based on a motive of the first theme.

From this example, and from closing themes in the sonata forms of other composers, the following general observations are especially to be noted:

1. The closing theme usually has a *character* of its own, different from and contrasting to that of the first and second themes.

2. Nevertheless, *motivically* the closing theme is often related to one or more of the previous themes. In Schubert's sonata forms the closing theme is customarily based on the second theme; other composers frequently prefer it to be based on the first theme.

3. The closing theme is clear and emphatic in its delineation of key, consisting of one or more complete harmonic movements in the key of (usually) III or V and closing with a perfect authentic cadence. Often, especially in works stemming from the Classic period, the closing theme consists harmonically of a series of reiterated cadential formulas, e.g., I–ii–V–I.

4. A codetta often follows the closing theme. Not infrequently this codetta makes reference to the first theme, preparing the ear for its return in the repetition of the exposition and its appearance, when such is the case, at the beginning of the development section.

5. The closing theme or codetta, when present, often leads to a transition serving to introduce first the return of the exposition and, after its repetition, the development. This transition may refer to the first theme, as in the last twelve bars of the exposition in the first movement of Beethoven's *Sonata Pathétique, Op. 13*.

EXERCISES

4. Examine the closing themes of the expositions of the sonata forms of the preceding exercises and comment on their characteristics. Is there a codetta? (Note: Hindemith's *Piano Sonata No. 2*, First Movement, has no closing theme.)

5. Analyze the entire exposition of:
   a. Haydn, *Sonata No. 52*, First Movement
   b. Beethoven, *Sonata, Op. 53*, First Movement

11–F.
THE DEVELOPMENT SECTION

GENERAL CHARACTERISTICS

There is no standard design for the development section of the sonata form as there is for the exposition. Rather, each composition of the great composers is unique in this regard. The development can normally be divided into a series of subsections, each consisting of a single phrase, a phrase chain, phrase group, or period.

The material of the development consists of anything that the judgment of the composer deems appropriate. It might be based on one or more of the chief themes from the exposition, or it might use only motives from the transition. A favorite device of Mozart and Haydn is to base the initial subsection of the development on a seemingly unimportant fragment of the closing theme or codetta which concluded the exposition. Sometimes this little fragment appears throughout the development so that what at first seems trivial takes on great importance as the movement progresses. Usually the methods of motivic construction discussed in Chapter 3 play an important part. In addition, new material may be introduced, either as melody or figuration. Any of these possibilities may appear in combination with any others. One reason for the intense interest that many developments arouse is the fact that the listener cannot possibly guess in advance what is in store for him.

To illustrate a short development section, Ex. 11–10 presents that from Haydn's *Sonata in C Major, No. 35*. (See Ex. 11–3 for the first theme and transition in this sonata.)

Example 11–10

HAYDN: *Sonata in C Major, No. 35*

The opening phrase, taken from the first theme, is clearly introductory. It ends with a semicadence (V/vi), leading the listener to expect the next phrase to begin on vi. Phrases 2 and 3, however, offer a surprise in that they bring in the first theme not in vi but IV. (This theme, stated as it was in the exposition, is not reproduced in our example.) From m. 79 on, the development is nonmelodic, expressing its harmonies through figuration which is a continuation of the triplet arpeggio characterizing most of the

203

exposition. We conclude, then, that this development comprises three subsections.

Bars	Subsection	Material
67–71	1. Introduction (phrase 1)	Consequent of PT
72–79	2. Period (phrases 2 and 3)	PT
79–103	3. Figuration (phrase 4)	New, but using triplet figure from exposition

The tonal structure of this development section, as that of the *departure* of Ex. 10–3, involves a succession within a succession. First the cadential V of the exposition moves down a third to V/vi. By chord succession this V/vi is prolonged (mm. 71–98), after which it moves by descending fifths to the interrupting V_7 (mm. 98–103). Example 11–11 is a harmonic outline of the development showing its basic tonal structure.

Example 11–11

Harmonic outline of Ex. 11–10

Example 11–11 shows how logical the tonal structure of a development section can be. When one hears of the "constantly shifting tonalities" and the "modulations to remote keys" which are commonly supposed to be characteristic of the development sections of this or that composer, it is easy to conclude that these "remote keys" are chosen almost at random. The whim of the composer leads him into strange realms from which somehow he must find his way back. Careful consideration of the tonal structures of the development sections of the great composers will, however, generally show that the various secondary tonics and modulations employed are only elaborate ways of stating a chord succession or progression which, whether simple or complex, is fundamentally reasonable.

THE LENGTHY DEVELOPMENT: DESIGN

Subsections 1 and 2 of the development discussed above (Ex. 11–10, though different from each other, are related in that they both make use of the first theme, the former of the consequent only, the latter of both antecedent and consequent. The grouping together by means of thematic relationships of the various subsections becomes an important method of attaining unity in a long development section. Beethoven in particular, does so systematically in lengthy sonata forms. A survey of the development section to the first movement of his *Symphony No. 9* in D minor will illustrate both this procedure and some other of Beethoven's developmental methods.

Themes from the first movement's exposition which are used in the development section are shown in Ex. 11–12. The exposition begins strikingly. Tiny motivic fragments hint at the principal theme (PT), finally gathering themselves together for the initial unison statement. Particular note should be taken of motives a, b, and c of the principal theme. The second theme (ST) consists of a number of subsections, ST_1 through ST_5, and is followed by a closing theme (CT) made up of CT_1 and a codetta, CT_2. ST_5 is a melodic and rhythmic variant of motive c.

Example 11–12

BEETHOVEN: *Symphony No. 9*

The development begins with a subsection presenting fragments of the principal theme as at the beginning of the movement. This passage can be considered the introduction to the development, just as formerly it served as introduction to the exposition. The development proper begins with three contrasting phrases (subsections 2, 3, and 4; mm. 179–197). The first phrase presents the first theme as a dialogue between winds and strings, the second restates the codetta (CT_2), and the third builds a melodic phrase for woodwinds out of motive b of the first theme (see Ex. 11–13).

Example 11–13

Measures 198–218 also consist of three phrases (subsections 5, 6, and 7) which closely correspond to the preceding three, subsection 5 with subsection 2, 6 with 3, and 7 with 4. By this grouping Beethoven achieves a degree of unity, for the six subsections are felt as being two large groups of three subsections each.

While each phrase has a clear cadence, that cadence always connects by elision with the beginning of the next phrase. The elision of phrase cadences is characteristic of developments, for this is the section in which, more than any other, a sense of urgency and movement is customarily maintained.

Subsection 7 similarly overlaps with the beginning of subsection 8 (m. 218). This section uses a developmental technique of which Beethoven, in his later years, was particularly fond: fugal treatment (see Chapter 14). The theme of this fugal subsection appears in the bass and is constructed by using motives b and c and continuing with an expansion of c in the rhythmic guise in which it appeared as ST_5. It is marked in Ex. 11–14 by the Roman numeral I. The theme is accompanied throughout by two new themes (II and III) in the manner of a triple fugue (see Section 14–G).

Example 11–14

BEETHOVEN: *Symphony No. 9*

Subsection 8, the fugue, as the lengthiest division of the development, can be considered equivalent to a group in itself. Subsection 9 uses motive b in the melody and accompanies it with a variation of ST_5—the same two motives of which the fugue theme consists. Here, however, they are not juxtaposed but are sounded simultaneously. Subsection 10 (mm. 275–286) brings in, for the first time, the initial melody of the second theme, ST_1. Subsection 11 (mm. 287–296) corresponds to subsection 9. Thus the last three subsections group themselves together in the mind of the hearer as a kind of ternary form and comprise a larger unit within the development

Development of the First Movement of Beethoven's Symphony No. 9 from the Point of View of Design	Bars	Division	Material	Description
	160–178	Subsection 1 (introduction)	Motive a	Fragments of PT as at beginning of movement
	179–197	Group I		
	179–188	Subsection 2	Motive a	Dialogue between strings and winds
	188–192	Subsection 3	CT_2	Full orchestral statement
	192–197	Subsection 4	Motive b	Motivic phrase
	198–218	Group II		
	198–206	Subsection 5 (= Subs. 2)	Motive a	Group II similar to
	206–210	Subsection 6 (= Subs. 3)	CT_2	Group I, varied and transposed
	210–218	Subsection 7 (= Subs. 4)	Motive b	
	218–259	"Group" III: Subsection 8	Motive b, ST_5 (= motive c), also new material	Triple fugue; Subject I built of two motives from exposition; Subjects II and III new
	259–297	Group IV		
	259–275	Subsection 9 (like Subs. 4)	Motive b, ST_5	Motive b accompanied by ST_5 in a *cantabile* dialogue
	275–286	Subsection 10	ST_1	As in exposition
	287–296	Subsection 11 (= 9)	Motive b, ST_5	Transposed restatement of Subsection 9
	297–300	Subsection 12 (retransition)	Motive b	Tutti unison cascade built from single motive

section, just as subsections 2, 3, and 4 and subsections 5, 6, and 7 did. Measures 297–300, a furious cascade in the strings and woodwinds, based on motive b and punctuated by sharp outbursts in the brass and timpani, act as retransition and usher in the tonic chord (now altered to its major form) which begins the introduction to the recapitulation.

Although this development section is a long one of 140 bars, its design is easily comprehensible to the alert listener, for Beethoven has not presented an array of small subsections with little or no clear relationship. Instead, he has gathered the various small divisions into four large groups flanked by the introduction and the retransition.

THE LENGTHY
DEVELOPMENT:
TONAL
STRUCTURE Consideration of the tonal structure of this development section reveals an unusual feature at its inception. It will be remembered that normally a sonata form in which the secondary and closing sections of the exposition are in a nondominant key has a development section which progresses from that key to the interrupting V ushering in the recapitulation. In this symphony the exposition ends with a perfect authentic cadence in VI, that is, B♭ major (mm. 149–150), after which the codetta continues to sound this VI chord. Rather than beginning the development from there, however, and progressing gradually to the V, Beethoven drops without modulation from VI to V. From the point of view of the tonal structure, the development is an enormous chord succession prolonging this V and connecting it with the interrupting V immediately preceding the recapitulation. The harmonic outline of the development section in Ex. 11–15 shows its essential tonal structure.

Example 11–15

BEETHOVEN: *Symphony No. 9* (harmonic outline of development in first movement)

After the exposition has come to its close on VI, the development moves abruptly to V and thence to iv, through V₆/iv. Group I (subsections 2, 3, 4) all express the subdominant key, but with the appearance of group II this iv becomes, by means of a chromatic change, the dominant of vii. The fugue begins on vii and progresses by means of descending fifths and chromatic passing tones in the bass to V/v, expressed in subsection 9.

Subsection 10 brings the return of v, pianissimo in trumpets and kettle-drums, this v very gradually growing in strength throughout subsection 11. Just before subsection 12 the chord becomes a V⁷. An unusual feature here is that the low stringed instruments sometimes drop below the recurring dominant of the kettledrum, so that there are moments when the V⁷ is not in fundamental position.

The significance of the key relationships in this development is shown by the summary bass outline in Ex. 11–16. The Roman numerals above the notes indicate the real scale steps expressed, while those below the notes show the function of these scale steps.

Example 11–16

BEETHOVEN: *Symphony No. 9* (key relationships in development of first movement)

A consideration of the function of the various keys which participate in a development section will point up the significance of each key chosen. As in this instance, the great composers follow an essentially straight-forward tonal plan in spite of surface complications.

VARIATIONS OF USUAL TONAL STRUCTURE

Sonata forms based on the usual tonal structure reach, during the last bars of the development section, the V (or V₇), following which the harmonic movement begins again with the recapitulation. Occasionally another chord serves for this interrupting V. In the first movement of Haydn's "Farewell Symphony," for instance, the vii⁰₇ appears in its place.

In the second movement of his *Sonata, Op. 109,* Beethoven's intention at the opening of the recapitulation is apparently to startle the listener. He accomplishes his purpose in two ways. Most of the development is to be played *piano,* the last part *una corda* and *pianissimo,* with interspersed periods of silence. Suddenly the first theme bursts in, opening the recapitulation *fortissimo.* The dynamic surprise here is paralleled by the tonal structure. The V at the end of the usual development section leads predictably into the recapitulation. Here the substitute chord (V/V) does not "lead" into it at all. The effect of the recapitulation's opening is thus doubly abrupt.[1]

---

[1] Two discussions of this singular passage are: Edward T. Cone, "Analysis Today," *Musical Quarterly,* Vol. XLVI, No. 2 (April 1960), p. 172; and Robert Smith, "This Sorry Scheme of Things . . . ," *Music Review,* Vol. XXII, No. 3 (August 1961), pp. 212–213.

EXERCISES

6. Study the development sections of the first movements of the sonata forms under examination.
    a. Find the point at which the recapitulation begins and locate the V pedal point preceding this, if one is present. How far back does this V extend?
    b. Note which chord closes the exposition. Does it relate with the V that closes the development by chord succession or does it progress to that V?
    c. Analyze the development section to discover its design.
    (1) Note whether and how it divides into subsections.
    (2) Identify the material on which each subsection is based.
    (3) Relate the subsections to each other. Do any group themselves together?
    (4) Which subsection acts as retransition?
    d. Follow the progress of the bass line from the end of the exposition to the first appearance of the V pedal point.
    e. Make a summary harmonic outline of the tonal structure.

7. Analyze in a similar manner the development section of:
    a. Haydn, *Sonata No. 52,* First Movement
    b. Beethoven, *Sonata, Op. 53,* First Movement

11–G.
THE RECAPITULATION

THE PURPOSE OF THE RECAPITULATION
The recapitulations of a large number of sonata forms restate in the tonic key all the themes of the exposition in the same order in which they were first heard. This fact has caused many to believe that the purpose of the recapitulation is to provide balance through symmetry—the recapitulation is a counterpart to the exposition, just as part three of the sectional ternary form is a counterpart to part one. There is no question that there is some truth in this supposition, yet it falls far short of revealing the essence of the recapitulation. If the purpose of the recapitulation were to create a symmetrical balance with the exposition, then it would follow that those sonata forms of the great composers which do no such thing must be considered defective to the extent that the recapitulation is altered, a conclusion that would eliminate from the rank of "perfect" works many of the great sonata forms of the classical composers. Nor is there justification for believing that the recapitulation that reproduces the exposition (partially transposed) is "normal" and others "exceptional." From the earliest examples of sonata form, deviations from this mythical "norm" have been too frequent to warrant considering them exceptional cases.

The real purpose of the recapitulation becomes clear when the tonal structure of the sonata form as a whole is considered. It will be remembered that a complete harmonic movement involves a move away from I with a return to I, while a progressive harmonic movement is to a different tonal area without a return (see Section 5–E). The exposition, moving from I of the first theme to III, V, or VI of the second and closing themes is a progressive movement and therefore incomplete. The development does nothing to alleviate this condition; on the contrary, it prolongs it. With the appearance of the recapitulation, however, the situation changes. Beginning the harmonic movement again, it presents the material of the exposition not as a progressive movement from I to some other key, but as a complete harmonic movement within the original tonality.

The most basic function of the recapitulation is to complete a harmonic movement previously left incomplete.

Since this function can be performed perfectly well without an exact restatement of themes, we find that composers often vary them in the recapitulation. Since it can be performed without a restatement of *all* the themes, occasionally certain themes or even whole sections are omitted. Nor is there any absolute necessity for restating the whole of any one theme.

TRANSPOSED RESTATEMENTS IN THE RECAPITULATION If the basic function of the recapitulation is only to complete the harmonic movement and not necessarily to provide thematic symmetry by balancing the exposition, one might well ask why it is that throughout the late eighteenth century and the nineteenth most sonata forms do in fact include a restatement in the tonic of at least most of the material which had been stated in a related key in the exposition. The answer to this question has perhaps less to do with formal patterns than with musical grammar. When an important idea is first heard in a key other than the tonic, whether the piece is a sonata form or not, composers tend to restate the idea in the tonic (or at least to relate some part of it to the tonic). In the typical classical rondo, we have seen how the first episode, stated in a related key, returns transposed to the tonic as the third episode. Similarly, in Mozart's opera arias and ensembles where there is no question of a standard sonata or rondo form, musical ideas in keys other than the tonic often return transposed, whereas themes first heard in the tonic are frequently not referred to again. (See, for instance, *Le Nozze di Figaro*, Finale to Act Two, mm. 1–120, and *Die Zauberflöte, No. 17*, Pamina's aria, comparing mm. 12–15 with mm. 30–32.) This tendency is present even in music of the late Romantics, as is evidenced by Mahler's "Der Abschied" from *Das Lied von der Erde*. A main musical idea is the passage in B♭ major from rehearsal number 23 to 36. This is the only lengthy statement not in the principal key of C minor-major. It returns transposed to the tonic to become the last part of the movement (rehearsal number 58 to end). (See also Strauss' *Don Juan*, discussed on pp. 299–303, theme G.)

The tendency of composers to refer in the coda to a middle episode in, say, a ternary structure is evidence of the same urge to relate everything to the tonic key (e.g., the coda of Chopin's *Prelude No. 13*, referred to on p. 141). Even when the theme in the related key is not specifically stated, a reference in the coda to the key of that theme will bring the theme to mind and thus into a close relationship with the tonic. For instance, Chopin's *Etude in E♭ minor, Op. 10 No. 6* is a ternary form with a middle part which emphasizes the "Neapolitan" key (E major = ♭II in E♭ minor). In the fifth bar before the end of the piece, as part of the final cadence, this ♭II is suddenly stressed as a secondary tonic prolonged for one-and-a-half bars. In context this passage is very noticeable and can be explained only by reference to the middle part of the piece. A somewhat similar case occurs in Berlioz' *Symphonie Fantastique*, as pointed out on p. 141.

One concludes, then, that transposed restatements in the tonic are a way of writing which was very natural to a composer during the tonal era. That they appear so often is only to be expected. But to assume that transposed restatements are therefore a definitive aspect of sonata form in particular—indeed *necessary* to it—is to confuse the purpose and function of the recapitulation with an aspect of the grammar of tonal music.[2]

DIFFERENCES IN DESIGN BETWEEN EXPOSITION AND RECAPITULATION

Summarized under the six headings below are common means by which recapitulations are made to differ from expositions.

Condensation The recapitulation can be altered by shortening one or more of its divisions, especially the first theme. This device gives to the recapitulation all the themes of the exposition, but with one or more of them in condensed form. (See Mozart's "Prague Symphony," First Movement.)

Abbreviation The elimination of one or more sections results in the abbreviated recapitulation. Since the recapitulation restates themes from the exposition in a transposition to the tonic, there is no basic need for a modulating transition, and composers sometimes find they can do without it, as in the first movement of Haydn's *Symphony No. 103* ("Drumroll"). But Haydn is reluctant to do away with the transition entirely, for in this case it includes an interesting phenomenon—a speeded up version of the Adagio introduction, first heard in mm. 74–75. Accordingly, he begins the coda with a return of the Adagio (m. 202) and immediately goes into a restatement of the previously omitted transition. In this way the slow and the quick versions of the introduction's tune are juxtaposed in time, and

---

[2] The interested student who wishes to read further regarding the essence of sonata form would do well to refer to Chapter III of Edward T. Cone's *Musical Form and Musical Performance*, New York: Norton, 1968, and to Chapter II, "Theories of Form," in Charles Rosen's *The Classical Style*, New York: Norton, 1972.

any listener who may have failed to perceive their relationship during the exposition is virtually forced to perceive it during the coda!

In a monothematic movement the chief difference in the exposition between the first and second themes is of course their keys. Since the recapitulation presents the two in the same key, a restatement of both, unless there is some important difference between them, would be redundant. For this reason there are sonata forms in which the second theme is omitted from the recapitulation. Since its material is taken from the first theme, it has already been brought into relationship with the tonic key. An interesting case is the first movement of Mozart's *Oboe Quartet, K. 370.* In the exposition the first theme is presented as an oboe tune with a fairly homophonic accompaniment for the strings. The second theme (m. 37ff.) has a more contrapuntal texture, with the violin and oboe in dialogue and the viola playing a melodic line against them. The recapitulation does away with the second theme but makes up for it by presenting the first theme as a synthesis of the exposition's two themes: the oboe tune is restated intact but with the violin and viola parts in the contrapuntal texture of the exposition's second theme. In spite of a five-bar extension at the end, the recapitulation is thus able to restate in only forty-five bars the essence of a sixty-three-bar exposition.

Variation A varied form of one or more subjects in the recapitulation is rather common. In the last movement of his *Sonata, K. 279,* Mozart varies the first theme of the recapitulation by giving the melody to the left hand and the accompaniment to the right hand, the reverse manner of its appearance in the exposition. Beethoven sometimes lets the reappearance of the first theme be elaborately ornamented, as in the *Adagio sostenuto* of the *Sonata, Op. 106* ("Hammerklavier"). The original theme is given as Ex. 4–3, the ornamentation as Ex. 11–17. There is seemingly no limit to the possibilities for variation of any of the themes in the recapitulation.

Example 11–17

BEETHOVEN: *Sonata, Op. 106*

Special mention should be made of the recapitulation of a minor-mode movement. If in the exposition the second and closing themes were in a major mode, the composer often recapitulates them in the major mode of the tonic key, the parallel major. But, since the movement is itself in the minor mode, he may decide to alter the mode of these themes as well as their key, restating them in the tonic minor. A change of mode from major to minor drastically alters the character of most melodies, shedding on them a new and different light. Mozart was fond of taking advantage of this fact in his minor-mode compositions. By changing the secondary theme from the major mode of the exposition to the minor mode, he was able to endow his recapitulation with a dramatic significance. The effect is as if the theme, through the struggles and conflicts of the development, had become somehow altered, just as the character of, say, Hamlet alters during the course of the play. In the Finale of his *Symphony No. 40 in G Minor*, Mozart goes even further, for in changing its mode the melodic contour itself is completely transformed.

Rearrangement The various parts of the exposition are sometimes recapitulated in a different order. Occasionally the order of first and second themes is reversed (e.g., first movements of Mozart's *Sonata, K. 311*, and Prokoviev's *Piano Sonata No. 7*). An extremely interesting rearrangement is found in the first movement of Mozart's *Sonata in C Major, K. 279*: part of the first theme is omitted in the recapitulation and inserted later in the middle of the second theme! This gives the impression that somehow the phrase was forgotten and the pianist must interrupt the second theme to run back and fetch it.

Expansion With both the first and second themes normally being recapitulated in the main tonality, the composer runs the risk of monotony from overuse of a single key. Often he likes to utilize the intervening transition to provide key contrast. In its wanderings away from and back to the original key this transition is sometimes lengthened.

A less common but more startling expansion of the recapitulation can occur from further motivic development of one of the themes during the course of the recapitulation. Mozart interrupts the closing section to insert a short development of part of the second theme in the Finale to his *Sonata, K. 279*, and Haydn, in his *Symphony No. 101* ("Clock"), interrupts the recapitulation of his second theme to introduce a lengthy development of its initial motive similar to the first portion of his development section.

Variants Used in Combination A single recapitulation may make use of more than one of the preceding methods of alteration. A movement that expands one portion will be likely to condense or omit another in order that some proportion between the large sections may be maintained. In the first movement of the "Clock Symphony," for instance, Haydn makes up for the enormous expansion of the second theme, referred to above, by substituting a new, much shorter, transition. Furthermore he omits the original closing theme entirely and replaces it with a transitionlike passage leading into the coda which concludes the movement.

We have been dealing with differences between an exposition and its recapitulation from the point of view of design. Some recapitulations exhibit tonal structures which call for special comment.

IRREGULAR
TONAL
STRUCTURES IN
THE
RECAPITULATION *Appearance of Recapitulation Before Completion of Interrupting V_7* The first theme of Haydn's "Surprise Symphony" does not begin with tonic harmony but with a secondary tonic of ii (V/ii–ii) which then moves to V–I. In this case Haydn does not follow the usual practice of closing his development section on an interrupting V_7. Instead he ushers in the recapitulation with vi, which in its major form is identical with V/ii.

Example 11–18

HAYDN: *Symphony No. 94* ("Surprise")

The first movement of Haydn's "Oxford Symphony" is similar. Here the first theme begins on V_7 and is ushered in by a V^4_3/V. In both these symphonies Haydn has incorporated the V_7–I progression within the opening bars of the recapitulation because of the nature of the first themes. In Ex. 11–19 the first theme begins with tonic harmony and therefore a variant from the normal tonal structure is not strictly necessary. Nonetheless, the composer has chosen to begin the recapitulation without waiting for the completion of the interrupting V_7 chord. The result is an exceptional tonal structure corresponding to that with which we have already become familiar in ternary form (see Ex. 8–6).

Example 11–19

MENDELSSOHN: *Symphony No. 4 ("Italian")*

The example shows the final retransition measures of the development and the beginning of the recapitulation in the first movement of Mendelssohn's "Italian Symphony." The restatement of the first theme begins in the upper strings just as the cellos and winds reach the interrupting V in the following version:

Thus the recapitulation begins four bars before the harmonic movement of the development has completed its course. The conflict produced between design and tonal structure at this point results in a tight dovetailing of the development and recapitulation sections.

Example 11–20

MENDELSSOHN: *Symphony No. 4*, First Movement (bass outline)

A similar variant of the normal relationship between design and tonal structure is to be found in the first movement of Tchaikovsky's *Symphony No. 5 in E Minor*.

Commencement of Recapitulation in Nontonic Key The characteristic progression in the exposition of most major-mode sonata forms is from I to V, that is, upwards a fifth. Occasionally, particularly in works by Mozart, Clementi, and Schubert, this progression up a fifth finds reflection in the recapitulation. In this case the first theme of the recapitulation does not express the main tonality of the piece but appears in the subdominant key. It then progresses up a fifth to the tonic for the secondary and closing sections. The development section thus becomes a progressive harmonic movement from V to $I\flat_7$ (that is, V_7/IV).

Part One	Part Two	
(Exposition)	(Development)	(Recapitulation)
I → V———→ $I\flat_7$		IV → I
	(= V_7/IV)	

This tonal scheme results in a kind of equilibrium, for the tonic key is nicely balanced between its upper fifth (last part of exposition, V) and lower fifth (first part of recapitulation, IV). Some examples of its use are the first movements of Mozart's *Sonata in C Major, K. 545*, and Schubert's *Symphony No. 5*, as well as the last movement of Schubert's *Sonata, Op. 120*, ("Little A Major").

From time to time the composer, especially the Romantic composer, elects some other nontonic key for the beginning of the recapitulation. In the Finale of Schubert's *Symphony No. 9 in C Major*, the recapitulation commences with E$\flat$ major, III by mode mixture of the main tonality. The entrance of the first theme in this key is particularly surprising because the retransition of the development emphasizes the V and thus seems to be preparing for tonic harmony. The bass G, reiterated over seventy-six very quick bars (mm. 515–590) as a dominant pedal point in the tonic key of C, is, eight bars before the recapitulation, suddenly reinterpreted as the third of an E$\flat$ major tonic chord (mm. 591–598).

In Tchaikovsky's *Symphony No. 4 in F minor* the first movement's recapitulation begins with a statement of both the first and the second themes in D minor. Though unique, such a choice on Tchaikovsky's part is extremely logical when one considers the tonal structure of the movement as a whole. The tonality of F has been expressed by partitioning the octave into four equal segments at a distance of a minor third from each other (F–A$\flat$–B–D–F). These are used as important structural key areas (see Ex. 11–21).

Example 11–21

TCHAIKOVSKY: *Symphony No. 4, First Movement* (summary of tonal structure)

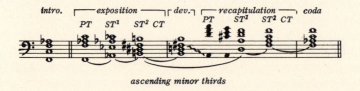

ascending minor thirds

EXERCISE

8. Make a detailed comparison of the recapitulations of the sonata forms of the preceding exercises with their respective expositions.

11–H.
SUMMARY

The sonata form, like the continuous binary forms from which it evolved, is in its very nature rooted in tonality. Tension set up by sharply defined key centers is possible only to tonal music and it is this tension that constitutes the foundation of sonata form. A key center is established (first theme), undermined (transition), and a new key center set up (second and closing themes). The establishment of a second key center causes a tense situation demanding a reconciliation, which comes about after a period of harmonic fluidity (development) when the original key center dominates (recapitulation). More briefly, the tonal structure of the normal sonata form can be explained as a progressive harmonic movement (exposition) that is prolonged (development) and finally begun again and completed (recapitulation).

The specific design that provides flesh and blood for this tonal skeleton is constantly varied. The monothematic sonata form has but one tune which serves as both first and second themes. The two themes of the bi-thematic sonata form are often contrasting in character (one dramatic, the other lyric, and so on). In either of these cases the closing theme, unless it is absent entirely, may introduce still a third idea. Sonata-form expositions which include five or six ideas are not rare. The development is even less susceptible to summary description for here there is no standard subdivision. The material on which subsections of the development are based may include anything from the exposition, even that which had seemed trivial. And new material is not infrequently introduced. The recapitulation is also not predictable, often differing considerably from the design of the exposition.

When analyzing a sonata form, students can avoid a good deal of trouble and misunderstanding by attempting to rid themselves of *a priori* requirements. Rather than constantly referring the work under examination to notions about what it "should" or "should not" do, the student should observe what the composer has done, then attempt to discover the reason or principle lying behind the composer's decision.

The most important features of the main sections of the sonata form have been discussed in this chapter. Optional sections (introductions, codas) and modifications of sonata form will be dealt with in the next. The description of many of the features of sonata form's main sections holds true when they occur in other forms as well. For instance, the development section of the first movement of a sonata rondo (Chapter 12) or a concerto (Chapter 13) is constructed along lines identical to those set forth here. The same is true of transitions. A thorough acquaintance with the principal sections that make up the sonata form will enable students not only to understand works in this form but, by noting their appearance elsewhere, to be immensely aided in their understanding of other forms, both standard and unique.

EXERCISE

9. Analyze:
    a. Mozart, *Sonata, K. 333*, First Movement
    b. Beethoven, *Sonata, Op. 31, No. 2*, First Movement

12

FURTHER ASPECTS OF SONATA FORM

12–A.
THE INTRODUCTION

Symphonies and overtures of Classical and Romantic composers often open with a solemn introduction in slow tempo which leads into the sonata form of the first movement. Example 12–1 is a reduction of the introduction to the first movement of Mozart's *Symphony No. 36 in C Major*.

Example 12–1

MOZART: *Symphony No. 36 in C Major ("Linz")*

The first three bars present a strong unison statement followed by powerful chords. They might be said to herald the opening of a solemn event and have been labeled here the heraldic section. The next four bars consist of a lyric melody with a quiet accompaniment, called the melodic section. The following seven bars present a one-bar motive stated seven times by imitation and sequence, the motivic section. The last five bars, the cadential section, bring the introduction to a close by dwelling on V, treated as a secondary tonic. The entire introduction expresses the key of C; the first two sections are in the major mode, the last two in the minor.

DESIGN OF THE INTRODUCTION   The heraldic, melodic, motivic, and cadential sections which comprise this introduction are the chief section types to be found in the introductions of most of the great composers of the tonal era. Not every introduction, however, includes all four types and some introductions bring in others. Only infrequently does the introduction to a work for a small group of instruments contain a heraldic section. Few things are more absurd than an unsuccessful attempt at grandeur, and a handful of stringed instruments or a piano and violin are simply incapable of mustering the solemn dignity that a full orchestra has at its command. Introductions to chamber-music works can be expected to consist mainly of melodic and motivic types. In orchestral works, however, the heraldic opening is common. Sometimes it is very short. In Haydn's *Symphony No. 103*, a single roll on the kettledrum suffices to produce one of the most impressive openings in symphonic literature. On the other hand, the heraldic opening of Mozart's *Symphony No. 39* comprises six very slow measures for full orchestra. Tchaikovsky, in his *Symphony No. 4*, seems to think almost literally of a herald, for the work opens with a great summoning call in the wind instruments (see also, Schumann, *Symphony No. 1*).

Not infrequently an introduction opens with a short heraldic fragment, continues with a melodic phrase, and then returns to the heraldic opening.

Example 12–2

HAYDN: *Symphony No. 102*

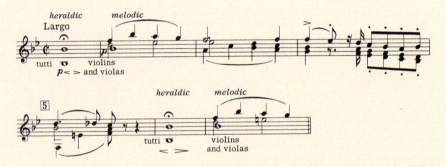

At times the introduction does not come to a cadence but leads directly into the first theme of the first movement. In that case the cadential section is replaced by the transitional section. Usually the transitional section anticipates the opening motive of the first theme.

Example 12–3

SCHUBERT: *Symphony No. 9*

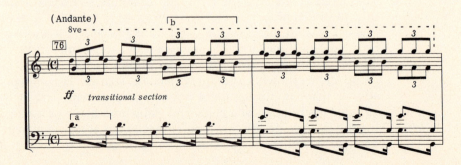

Since the introduction does not form a complete movement in itself, an obvious symmetry of parts is less usual than in a movement that stands alone. Few introductions, for instance, show a binary or ternary form. Rather, they are laid out as a series of sections, a phrase chain or phrase group. Sometimes there are rhythmic or melodic relationships among the various sections; often, as in Ex. 12–1, there are not.

TONAL STRUCTURE OF THE INTRODUCTION

The introduction does not necessarily share the mode of the movement proper. That to Haydn's "Clock Symphony" in D major is in the minor mode. Many introductions, like Ex. 12–1, begin in the major mode, then about halfway through change to the minor. Still others constantly fluctuate between major and minor.

In essence the basic tonal structure of most introductions is a progressive harmonic movement from I to V, V often being treated as a secondary tonic. An outline of the basic harmonic movement of Ex. 12–1, for instance, shows a chord succession on I in which the bass descends an octave, with a change from major to minor en route, followed by a move to V.

Example 12–4

Harmonic outline of Ex. 12–1

When the introduction does not begin on I, the progressive harmonic movement to V is no less likely. The tonality of Tchaikovsky's *Symphony No. 6* is B minor, but the introduction begins in the subdominant key, E minor. By means of a bass line that descends stepwise from the note E to A′♯ the essential harmonic move is from IV to V_6 in B minor, at which point the movement proper begins. Tchaikovsky has here devised his introduction so that the listener assumes the symphony is in the key of E, realizing later that this is only the subdominant aspect of the real key.

Beethoven attempted something quite different in the introduction to his *Quartet, Op. 59, No. 3*, a harmonic outline of which is offered in Ex. 12–5.

Example 12–5

BEETHOVEN: *Quartet, Op. 59, No. 3* (harmonic outline of introduction)

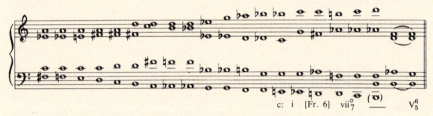

c: i   [Fr. 6]   vii$^{o}_{7}$ $(\overline{\overline{\,\,}})$ V$^{6}_{5}$

In this introduction no key is established by the chord series, and only near the end does the listener begin to get an inkling of the key of C. The harmonic scheme can be understood without initial reference to a key by the purposeful stepwise descent of the bass line from the note f♯ to B' an octave and a half below (presumably the upper B is used here only because the range of the cello would not permit the use of the lower). The bass-soprano framework encloses a series of chords which gradually spreads outward from the opening chord until, as the cello reaches D, the upper instruments supply the remaining tones of a vii$^{o}_{7}$ on that note. This chord moves through a passing chord to its root position, the a♭ then moves to a g, and we hear a V$^{6}_{5}$ in the key of C.

On those rare occasions when the introduction does not end on V, the reason is likely to be that the first theme of the exposition does not begin on I but on some other chord. Examination of the first theme of the opening movement of Haydn's *Symphony No. 92* ("Oxford") shows that it begins with four bars of the V$_{7}$ chord. It is therefore incumbent on the introduction to progress to a chord that will lead into this V$_{7}$. Although the harmonic sequence of the introduction does reach the V (mm. 12–15, not quoted), this V is not prolonged to the beginning of the movement. It progresses instead to the chord of the augmented sixth on its own leading tone, hovering there in mid-air until its resolution to the V$_{7}$ opens the exposition.

Example 12–6

HAYDN: *Symphony No. 92* ("Oxford")

G: [Ger. 6]

THEMATIC
RELATIONSHIPS
BETWEEN THE
SONATA FORM
AND ITS
INTRODUCTION

In the last chapter we observed how, in the "Drumroll Symphony," Haydn related the theme of the Adagio introduction to the main body of the movement (p. 212). In a number of other works there is a definite melodic relationship between the movement and the introduction preceding it. Sometimes this relationship is only a slight one—a similarity of melodic curve or a single motivic resemblance, as in Berlioz' *Symphonie Fantastique*. At other times some melody of the introduction may definitely anticipate a theme of the movement proper. Example 12–7 shows the close resemblance between the opening melody of the introduction and the first theme of the movement in one of Haydn's symphonies (see also Brahms' *Symphony No. 1*, first and last movements).

Example 12–7

HAYDN: *Symphony No. 100 ("Military")*

There may be no clear resemblance between the themes, and still a relationship between the introduction and the movement may exist, for a part of the introduction sometimes returns once or twice during the course of the movement (Mozart, *The Magic Flute*, Overture; Beethoven, *Sonata, Op. 13*). Or a theme from the introduction might take part in the development section (Beethoven, *Sonata, Op. 13*, First Movement; Brahms, *Symphony No. 1*, Finale; Hindemith, *Organ Sonata No. 1*, First Movement).

EXERCISE

1. Consider the introductions to some of the following compositions. Note first the tonal structure, then the various section types employed (heraldic, melodic, motivic, cadential or transitional, or perhaps some other nonstandard types). Be sure to compare the mode (or modes) of the introduction with that of the ensuing sonata form.
   a. Beethoven, *Quartet, Op. 135*, Finale
      (The following are not in Burkhart's *Anthology*.)

b. Mozart, Overture to *Don Giovanni*
c. Mozart, Overture to *The Magic Flute*
d. Haydn, *Symphony No. 101* ("Clock")
e. Haydn, *Symphony No. 103* ("Drumroll")
f. Beethoven, *Piano Sonata, Op. 13* ("Pathétique")
g. Beethoven, *Symphony No. 2*
h. Beethoven, *Symphony No. 4*
i. Schubert, *Symphony No. 9*

12–B.
THE CODA

Many sonata forms possess either no coda or a brief one. As far as the short coda goes, nothing need be added here to the discussion of the coda under ternary forms (Section 8–E). But sometimes composers have provided their sonata forms with lengthy codas so full of significance that they are heard as equaling in importance any of the preceding sections.

THE AFTER-DEVELOPMENT Beginning with the Finale from Mozart's *Symphony No. 41* ("Jupiter") and continuing with the late symphonies and chamber music of Haydn, and especially those of Beethoven, the coda to the sonata form frequently takes on immense significance, serving not merely as an appendage to the movement proper, but as a section with developmental properties of its own. In addition, it sometimes adds a new dimension to the tonal structure. As we are already familiar with the development section of the first movement to Beethoven's *Symphony No. 9* (Section 11–F), it will be convenient to examine the coda of that movement in illustration of the "after-development," as this type of coda is sometimes called.

There is no counterpart in the coda to the introductory section of the development, subsection 1 of the coda corresponding to subsection 2 of the development. Both are dialogues between the strings and winds on the first theme, but formerly only the initial motive, a, was involved while now motive b is added to the portion of the dialogue allotted to the strings (Ex. 12–8a).

Example 12–8

BEETHOVEN: *Symphony No. 9*

The second subsection of the coda is concerned with ST_2, a theme that had not participated in the development (Ex. 12–8b). A subsection making use of a variation of CT_2 (Ex. 11–12d) then appears, corresponding to subsection 3 of the development. This leads into the fourth subsection, based on the fugue theme of the development. Subsection 5 takes up ST_2 again, which leads into subsection 6, corresponding to subsection 4 of the development. The seventh subsection is made up of new material. Over an *ostinato* figure in the strings, possibly derived by diminution from ST_2, the wind instruments sound a new melodic motive which gradually builds up to a tremendous climax leading into the final subsection. This consists of the principal theme, expanded in the middle, sounding in a fortissimo unison by the full orchestra.

In design half of the coda is based on the development section, the other half being divided between restatement of material from the exposition and the newly invented *ostinato*.

Outline Summary of Beethoven's Symphony No. 9, First Movement, Coda, from the Point of View of Design

Bars	Sub-section	Material	Corresponding Subsection of Development	Description
427–453	1	Motives (a), (b)	2	Dialogue between strings and winds
453–463	2	ST_2	—	Statement, as in exposition
463–469	3	CT_2	3	Melodically altered
469–494	4	Motive a; ST_5 (= motive c)	8	Fugue theme; accompanied first by motive b, then by countersubject from development
494–505	5	ST_2	—	Statement; repetition with imitation
505–512	6	Motive b	4	Motivic phrase, as in development
513–538	7	New	—	Melodic motive repeated and developed over *ostinato* figure
538–547	8	Motives a, b, c	—	Unison statement with 4-bar expansion between motives a and b

From the examination of the outline summary we can draw the following conclusions regarding the design of the after-development, conclusions which are verified by reference to other codas of the same type (for instance, Beethoven, *Symphonies No. 2*, first and last movements; *No. 4*, Finale; *No. 5*, Finale; *No. 6*, First Movement).

1. The coda divides into subsections on the basis of material employed.
2. New as well as previously heard material may appear.
3. Previously heard material may (a) be restated without change (other than transposition) from the exposition, (b) be restated without change (other than transposition) from the development, or (c) undergo new development.

227

4. Material from the exposition that had been neglected by the development section is apt to be restated or developed in the coda.

5. Many of the subsections of the coda, particularly the first, correspond closely to subsections within the development. This correspondence sets up a definite relationship between the coda and the development, analogous to that between the exposition and recapitulation.

```
     Exposition                    Recapitulation
     |_____|
          Development                      Coda
          |_____|
```

THE EPILOGUE Short codas not infrequently are based largely or entirely on new material. Occasionally large codas, too, show little or no specific thematic relationship with the movement to which they are appended. Though universally referred to as codas, many such passages would seem better served by the term "epilogue." The long *Adagio* closing Haydn's "Farewell Symphony" is a special case.[1] But the coda of the first movement of Tchaikovsky's *Pathétique* is no less an epilogue. In both these instances the slower tempo and the change of mode from minor to major combine with the nature of the new material to produce a subdued, consoling quality in contrast to that which dominates the movement itself. Beethoven's Overture to *Egmont* and the Finale to his *Quartet, Op. 95,* are alike in that both are in the key of F minor and both end with long epilogues in F major made up entirely of new material. Unlike the Haydn and Tchaikovsky examples mentioned before, these epilogues have a faster tempo than the movement and end on a note of triumph. Brahms' *Academic Festival Overture* ends with a joyous setting of the student song *Gaudeamus Igitur.*

TYPES OF TONAL STRUCTURE IN THE CODA In our previous discussion of the coda (Section 8–E) it was pointed out that there are three distinct types of tonal structures. Sonata-form codas, too, group themselves according to these three types of tonal structure.

1. Codas that prolong the final I by chord succession. This type is very common (for example, the first movements of all Beethoven's symphonies).

2. Codas that prolong the final I by a tonic pedal point. Though common in short compositions, especially ternary forms, this type appears infrequently as the tonal structure of a sonata-form coda. A rare case is the coda, all but a few bars, of the first movement of Brahms' *Violin Sonata No. 3.*

---

[1] Written with gradually reduced instrumentation so that each player, upon finishing his part, snuffs out his candle and leaves the stage. The movement closes with two violinists playing alone in the dim candlelight.

3. Codas that delay the final I by means of a deceptive cadence. This type of coda occurs rather frequently in sonata forms (for instance, Haydn, *Symphony No. 100*, First Movement, and *Symphony No. 104*, Finale).

APPENDED
HARMONIC
MOTION

Often the coda prolongs the final tonic by remaining almost entirely within the area of the home key, except for brief secondary tonics. This is the case with the coda to the first movement of Beethoven's *Symphony No. 9*: each of its eight subsections expresses the key of D minor.

Not infrequently, however, the coda begins with a surprise jump into another key, where it remains for a phrase or more. This sudden change of key is as apt to happen with codas that prolong the final I (type 1) as with those that delay the final I by deceptive cadence (type 3).

Example 12–9

BRAHMS: *Clarinet Sonata, Op. 120, No. 2*

In Ex. 12–9 the coda begins with a deceptive cadence from V_7 to V_7/IV. Rather than resolving to IV, however, it moves in another deceptive resolution to ♭II (expressed enharmonically as E major rather than F♭ major). The key of E major (♭II) is maintained for two phrases (eight bars) before returning to the home key of E♭.

When a foreign key is thus emphasized, the coda may be accurately thought of as supplying appended harmonic motion rather than merely as prolonging the final I. Appended harmonic motion often involves a move to IV, VI, ♭VI, or ♭II, and occasionally to some other key.

FUSION OF CODA
AND
RECAPITULATION

When a sonata form has no coda, each of its two parts will naturally end with the last passages of the closing theme or with the codetta. The resulting similarity between the end of part one (Exposition) and the end of part two (Development-Recapitulation) emphasizes the binary aspect of the sonata form with a musical "rhyme" (see p. 78). The addition of a coda to the piece can undermine the effect of this "rhyme." The Classical composers, sometimes apparently reluctant to give up either the similarity of endings between the two parts or the coda, have managed on these occasions to eat their cake and have it. In Mozart's *Symphony No. 40 in G minor, K. 550,* First Movement, the recapitulation follows the order of themes as first stated in the exposition almost until the point where the codetta would be expected to enter (m. 80). It then takes a different turn: a twelve-bar coda is heard, and only afterwards does the restatement of the codetta make its appearance. The result is to fuse the coda *into* the recapitulation. (See also Mozart's *Symphony No. 36 in C Major, K. 425.*)

EXERCISES

2. In the sonata forms under consideration in the exercises of the preceding chapter, examine the point at which the recapitulation seems to end, then consider the music that lies beyond this point.
    a. Do all have codas?
    b. On what material is each coda based?
    c. Does any coda consist of a number of subsections? Which? How many?
    d. Does any coda act as an "after-development"?
    e. What type of tonal structure does each exhibit?
    f. Does any coda supply appended harmonic motion?

3. Do the same for other sonata-form codas.

4. Analyze the Finale of Beethoven's *Quartet, Op. 135.*

12–C.
MODIFICATIONS OF SONATA FORM

THE SONATINA
FORM

The term "sonatina" originally referred to sonatas which were shorter, lighter, and easier than usual and is still used in this sense today. The sonatina form, however, is not inevitably associated with the sonatina. Some sonatinas include movements in sonata form (Kuhlau, *Sonatinas, Op. 20, Nos. 1* and 3) and some sonata movements are in sonatina form. From the point of view of musical structure the sonatina form is a sonata form without a development section, its place being taken by a link or transition leading to the recapitulation.

The sonatina form has found a place in the sonatas, chamber music, and symphonies of Classical and Romantic composers, not as first but as second movements (Mozart, *Sonata, K. 332, Quartet, K. 465*; Beethoven, *Symphony No. 8*; Schubert, "Unfinished Symphony"; Brahms, *Violin Sonata No. 3*). The sonatina form is also common in the overtures of the Classical period (Mozart, *Marriage of Figaro*; Beethoven, *Prometheus*; Rossini, *Barber of Seville*).

EXERCISES

5. Contrast:
   a. Sonatina and sonatina form
   b. Sonata form and sonatina form

6. Analyze:
   a. Beethoven, *Sonata Op. 10, No. 1*, Second Movement
   b. Franck, *Violin Sonata*, First Movement

FUSION OF DEVELOPMENT AND RECAPITULATION (ENLARGED SONATINA) When the exposition of a sonata form is not repeated, composers often like to begin the development with a statement of the principal theme in the tonic key. The initial effect of such a procedure is to give the impression of a repetition of the exposition, but the listener soon finds that the development section is underway (Beethoven, *String Quartet in F Major, Op. 59, No. 1*, First Movement; Mendelssohn, "Italian Symphony," Finale; Brahms, *Violin Sonata No. 1 in G major, Op. 78*, First Movement). In a number of such cases Brahms apparently considered that since the first theme has been twice heard in the tonic key—at the start of both the exposition and the development—he could do without it at the beginning of the recapitulation. The Finale of Brahms' *Symphony No. 3*, outlined below, is such a piece.

	Part One (Exposition)			retrans.	Part Two (Development and Recapitulation)					trans.	Coda
Mm. 1	30	52	75	102	108	134	172	194	217	246	251
	PT	trans.	ST	CT		PT	dev.	trans.	ST	CT	
	i		V	v		i			I	i	i I

The phenomenon which has occurred here is a fusion of the recapitulation and development sections, for part two contains both, as in the normal sonata form, but delays the development, inserting it in the middle of the recapitulation. Looked at another way, the form is a mixture of the sonatina and the sonata forms. Like the sonatina, part two begins with the restatement of part one. Yet it does not give up the sonata form's development section. For this reason the scheme is sometimes referred to as the "enlarged sonatina." Other well-known compositions in which Brahms made use of a similar procedure are the Finales of the *Violin Sonata No. 1 in G major,* and the *Symphony No. 1 in C Minor,* as well as the *Tragic Overture, Op. 81.*

THE SONATA RONDO The sonata rondo is a hybrid, combining the rondo and the sonata form. The typical Classical rondo bears a certain resemblance to sonata form in that part one (refrain, episode, refrain) is restated, partially transposed, as part three (see outline in Section 9–B), just as the recapitulation of a sonata form is a partially transposed restatement of the exposition. In sonata rondo another resemblance is brought about by substituting a development section for the second episode C (part two), the result being:

		Part Three
Part One	*Part Two*	*(Quasi-*
(Quasi-exposition)	*(Development)*	*recapitulation)*
A–B A		A–B A
I V I	$xxxx$ V$_7$	I I I
(III)		

Not infrequently one of the refrains in part three is omitted. Applied to the small rondo design, sonata rondo is A B A Dev. A, as in Beethoven's monumental *Marcia Funebre* from the "Eroica Symphony."

The sonata rondo, representing a compromise between the sonata form and the ordinary rondo, gains a development section but loses an independent second episode. To this extent it might be considered "less of a rondo" than a simple rondo. When occasion demands, as in Mozart's *Sonata, K. 333,* the contrasting second episode is included but, instead of being followed immediately by the refrain, it leads into a development section. Part three picks up from there.

Classical composers used the sonata rondo almost exclusively for finales and labeled it simply "rondo" without differentiating it from the simple rondo. Most of Brahms' rondos are of the sonata-rondo type, as is the *Scherzo* from Mendelssohn's *Midsummer Night's Dream.* More recent uses include Prokofiev's *Sonata No. 5, Op. 135,* from which, however, the third refrain is omitted.

EXERCISES

7. Contrast:
   a. Sonata form and sonata rondo
   b. Sonata rondo and the typical classical rondo

8. Analyze the third movement of Mozart's *Sonata, K. 333.*

OTHER
MODIFICATIONS

We have by no means exhausted the possibilities for modification of the standard sonata form. For instance, in the first movement of his *Quartet, Op. 77, No. 1,* Haydn fuses the development and recapitulation sections of his sonata form differently from the enlarged sonatina. He begins his development section like a normal sonata form, inserts the recapitulation of the section theme (tonic key) into the development, and later recapitulates the other themes in rearranged order. To take another example, in Beethoven's *Leonore Overture No. 2* and the Finale to Mendelssohn's "Italian Symphony," the recapitulations are omitted completely, the developments leading straight into the codas. The same is true of Schumann's *Symphony No. 4 in D Minor,* First Movement.

The interested student will not find it difficult to discover still other special sonata-form procedures which imaginative composers, particularly Haydn and the late Beethoven, have created and found useful (Beethoven, *Quartet, Op. 132,* First Movement; *Symphony No. 8,* Finale; Haydn, "Surprise Symphony," First Movement).

12–D.
SUMMARY

This chapter has dealt with optional aspects and modifications of sonata form. The introduction is a section, normally in slow tempo, which opens most overtures, many symphonies, and some piano sonatas and chamber music. Occasionally finales are also preceded by introductions. Introductions usually subdivide into a number of distinct sections, some short solemn bids for attention, some stating a clear melody, others based on motivic interplay. Designed to lead into the first theme of the ensuing sonata form, the introduction ordinarily involves a progressive harmonic movement from I to a secondary tonic on V.

The majority of sonata forms end with a coda, some short, others quite long. The long coda, in addition to its role in prolonging the tonic chord and appending a new harmonic motion to the close of the movement, is often given over to thematic development. Less commonly, a coda will be devoted largely or entirely to new material. In either case it is possible for the coda to act not as a mere appendage, but as the culmination of the entire movement (Mozart, "Jupiter Symphony," Finale; Brahms, *Symphony No. 1,* Finale).

A common modification of sonata form is the sonatina form, which omits the development section. The sonatina form may be enlarged by inserting a development between the first and second themes of the recapitulation. The sonata rondo incorporates the sonata form's development section within the framework of the typical Classical rondo, substituting it for the second episode. Special modifications occurring in isolated works are very frequent.

13

THE CONCERTO

HISTORICAL NOTE ON THE BAROQUE CONCERTO The practice of alternating sonorities of different timbre and dynamics is a very old one. In the phenomenon of the echo we have in nature a prototype of this principle. The antiphonal psalm singing of the ancient Jews, the alternating choruses of Greek tragedy, the dialogue between priest and choir in the liturgical worship of the Christian church exemplify the principle of contrast in sounding bodies. In folk song we hear a solo singer or leader answered by the group. In instrumental music the principle of alternating sonorities on which the concerto is based developed in the rich sounds of the *canzone* and *ricercari* written by the Gabrielis in Venice in the late sixteenth century, works which themselves grew out of the polychoral music of the same composers. The rapid development of instrumental technique and the rise of a school of violin virtuosos led to an exploitation of several genres, particularly the concerto. By the end of the seventeenth century Corelli, Torelli, Albinoni, and others had established the concerto as an important medium without crystallizing any particular scheme of movements. This was left for Antonio Vivaldi, whose three-movement plan of fast-slow-fast was used by J. S. Bach and is still considered the norm. Handel, on the other hand, does not follow the three-movement plan, but uses varying movement schemes in the manner of Corelli.

The impact of the Vivaldian concerto on J. S. Bach was so far reaching that we find him composing works of quite different genres along the lines of a Baroque concerto. Several of the longer organ preludes, for instance, such as those in E minor and B minor, are constructed like typical concertos of the period. The same is true of the first movements of the *Organ Sonatas II* and *VI* and the Prelude to the *English Suite in G Minor, No. 3*, for harpsichord.

In postbaroque times the usual concerto was written for one soloist and orchestra. During the Baroque era, however, the concerto for more than one soloist was fully as common as the solo concerto. If there are several soloists, perhaps two violins and a cello, or two trumpets, these as a group are referred to as the *concertino* and the orchestra is called the *concerto grosso*, *tutti* ("all"), or *ripieno* ("full"). The composition itself is also often called a *concerto grosso*. During the first half of the eighteenth century the ripieno consisted not of the orchestra as we know it today, but usually of no more than a group of stringed instruments and an accompanying (and improvising) harpsichord.

13–A.
OUTER MOVEMENTS OF THE
BAROQUE CONCERTO: CONCERTO
GROSSO MOVEMENT

PROCEDURE IN THE BAROQUE CONCERTO

In discussing the *da capo* aria (Section 8–I) we observed that a distinctive feature of the Baroque aria was the use of orchestral ritornellos. These passages, preceding, interrupting, and following the vocalist's part, act as contrast to it. There is an antiphonal give-and-take between two different bodies of sound: the full orchestra on the one hand, and on the other a soloist with a portion of the orchestra lending support.

In the concerto a similar principle is at work except that both opposing bodies of sound are made up entirely of instruments. The forms that are associated with the concerto are a structural result of this opposition. The specific way in which the principle of alternation operates in a given piece of music can be thought of as the procedure of the work. To analyze and discover the form of a concerto movement it is necessary to consider the procedure as well as the design and tonal structure.[1]

As far as the formal procedure of the late Baroque concerto is concerned, it makes little difference whether there is one soloist or several to be pitted against the orchestra. In either case the basic idea of contrasting the two bodies of sound gives rise to a scheme of alternation. Just as in the Baroque aria the orchestral ritornello alternates with the solo voice (Section 8–I), so here the tutti sections, which are in effect ritornellos, alternate with the soloist or with the *concertino*. The result is like a debate or struggle, the tutti at times gaining the upper hand and at others giving way to the soloist or *concertino*. Not until the Romantic era were concertos written which could be considered works for a single instrument with orchestral accompaniment. In the concertos of the Baroque era (and also in the Classical, as we shall see) the main function of the orchestra was not so much to furnish an accompaniment to the soloist as to act as a sparring partner on an equal basis.

[1] Those works of Vivaldi and his contemporaries which are "orchestral concertos" (see Bukofzer, *op. cit.*, p. 226) are not being spoken of here. Nor do many movements of the *concerti grossi* of Handel's *Op. 6* belong to this category.

FORM OF THE CONCERTO GROSSO MOVEMENT The slow movements of Vivaldi's concertos exhibit various forms but need not occupy us here as they present little in the way of structure that is exclusively an aspect of concerto writing. It is to the two outer movements—those in fast tempo—that we must turn our attention. These generally proceed by alternation between the *concertino* and the tutti, as mentioned before, but the precise form thus achieved varies from concerto to concerto. Examination of one of Vivaldi's better-known concerto movements—chosen for an organ transcription by J. S. Bach—will provide an illustration of one *concerto grosso* movement.[2]

Example 13–1

VIVALDI: *Concerto in A Minor, Op. III, No. 8*

[2] Reproduced in *HAM, No. 270.*

The concerto opens with a sixteen-bar asymmetrical period made up of four phrases, marked a, b, c, and c'. Though the first two phrases contain some motivic resemblances, they are not clearly related thematically, as are the last two. The first perfect authentic cadence is found in m. 13. It is on i; thus phrase c, the third, completes a harmonic movement. The fourth phrase acts as codetta, prolonging the final i until m. 16. At this point most of the orchestral players drop out and the soloists, who are also expected to play during the tutti, are left virtually alone, their sound greatly contrasting with that of the full body of strings. The soloists have two phrases, marked d and e. These are essentially new, but d is derived from the second bar of a, and e from b. In m. 22 an imperfect cadence is reached and the tutti begins again, this time performing only the codetta phrase, c'. Another passage is then given to the soloists. This begins like the former solo passages except that the first and second violinists have exchanged parts. The accompaniment, which had been provided by the violas, is soon taken over by the bass instruments and harpsichord, while the first violin has solo figuration. This solo leads from i to a perfect authentic cadence on III (mm. 36–37), whereupon the figuration is taken up by the tutti in a prolongation of this III (mm. 37–39). Continuing with material first introduced in the opening ritornello, it is interrupted several times by short interjections from the soloists. During its course it progresses from III to a perfect authentic cadence on v (m. 47), immediately followed by another on iv (m. 48), at which point the next solo section begins. This section continues to express iv. The tutti then sounds a transposition to iv of phrase a (mm. 51–55). The ensuing solo section combines the figuration of the second solo section with motivic treatment based on phrase b, ending with a semicadence, V of iv. The tutti enters with phrase c, which brings a permanent return to i (mm. 62–65). A three-bar passage for solos recalls the first two solo sections. Measures 68–71, ending with a semicadence, bring in phrase a. After the next solo section the tutti performs phrases b and c', having this time skipped over phrase c. Another solo section intervenes before the final tutti plays phrase c'. In all, the tutti has been entrusted with eight sections in this movement and the soloists with the seven intervening ones. In addition, the soloists "invaded" the third tutti section several times.

The procedure can be represented graphically by assigning appropriate letters and numbers to the various sections. Thus, R1 stands for the first ritornello or tutti section, S1 for the first solo section, and so on. The design of the movement can be indicated by the use of the letters assigned to the various phrases of the opening ritornello and the other letters representing the themes of the solo sections. Beneath the representation of the procedure and the design, a summary of the basic tonal structure can be indicated. In this way we shall have conveniently before us the necessary data for drawing a conclusion regarding the form of this movement.

Measures	1–16	16–22	22–25	25–37	37–48	48–51	51–55	55–62	62–65	65–68	68–71	71–78	78–86	86–90	90–93
Procedure	R1	S1	R2	S2	R3 (solo interjections)	S3	R4	S4	R5	S5	R6	S6	R7	S7	R8
Design	abcc′	de	c′	dfg	gbah	b g	a	b g	c	d	a	b g	c′	b	c′
Tonal Structure	i	i	i	i	III v	iv	iv		V^7	i	i	i	i	i	i

Although the movement contains a number of perfect authentic cadences, none of these have a strongly divisive effect, due to the fact that in every case, except of course the last, these cadences are elided, occurring simultaneously with the beginning of the next section. In spite of the contrast in sound between the concertino and the ripieno the work is characterized by a striking continuity of movement. It would seem, then, that these perfect authentic cadences do not possess a divisive quality strong enough to act as a basis for analysis into parts.

Reference to the tonal structure line of our graphic representation shows that the first twenty-five bars are essentially concerned with expressing i. Measures 25–65 show a progressive harmonic movement from i to III to v to iv and from there to V_7, which resolves in m. 65 on i. This i is then retained for the remainder of the piece.

As the perfect authentic cadences are nondivisive and no other aspect of design—such as far-reaching contrasts in quality—creates a divisive force, our conclusions regarding form must be based on tonal structure alone. The movement consists of three parts, the two outer parts expressing I, the middle part a move from i through III, v, and iv and thence back through V_7 to i. Certain aspects of design combine to confirm this three-part analysis. Part one introduces all the important themes (e, f, and h are not striking; they occupy inconspicuous places and, once stated, are never referred to again; g plays an important role, but it is not a theme, only violinistic figuration). Four of these are stated by the *concerto grosso*, one by the *concertino*. Part two takes up these themes, adding figuration g, detaches them from one another, and treats their motives separately. At the conclusion of part two phrase c is restated exactly and is therefore the only important theme omitted from restatement in part three. Restatement here is particularly interesting in that the order of themes is entirely rearranged, though c′, because of its singular codettalike quality, continues to close the sections. On the whole the design might be summarily described as A-BA′ and the form of this particular movement considered as closely allied to the sectional ternary.

The observations listed below are the result of examination of a quantity of Vivaldi's concerto movements.

Regarding tonal structure
1. First and last ritornellos are always in the tonic key. The penultimate ritornello is very often in the tonic key.
2. The second ritornello begins by expressing III or V; it may remain there or make a progressive movement to IV or VI.

Regarding design of ritornellos
3. The phrases of the ritornello are detachable. Any phrase theme can be used separately or omitted, or the phrases can be arranged in a different order.
4. Only occasionally does any ritornello present material not included in the first ritornello. (The very term "ritornello" implies a "return" of previously heard material.)
5. The final ritornello is often an exact restatement of the first, the intervening ones being shorter. The penultimate ritornello is generally the shortest of all.

Regarding design of solo sections
6. Soloist(s) may present a harmonic progression as a figuration of some kind idiomatic to the instrument employed. When this occurs, the accompaniment often includes some melodic motive derived from the opening ritornello.
7. Solo instrument(s) may play one or more of the ritornello's themes. Often the solo begins with a theme from the ritornello, varies it, then gradually moves into a figuration of some kind.
8. The solo instrument may be given a new melody of its own.

Regarding procedure
9. The movement invariably ends with a ritornello and usually begins with one; initial solo sections are not rare enough, however, to be considered really exceptional.

10. The soloists of a Baroque concerto, unlike their counterparts in the Classical and Romantic concerto, play during the tutti sections, their part consisting merely of a doubling of the orchestral voices. Occasionally, however, the soloist is given brief passages of his own in a tutti section. Conversely, the orchestra sometimes invades the solo passages with short outbursts.

EXERCISE

1. Make a summary outline similar to the preceding, showing the procedure, design, tonal structure, and form of Bach's *Brandenburg Concerto No. 2,* First Movement.

> *Note:* In this movement the orchestra consists of strings and harpsichord while the soloists are trumpet, flute, oboe, and violin. As in all normal Baroque concertos, the soloists play during the tuttis. Rather than always merely doubling the music of the string orchestra, the soloists often play music which is idiomatic to their respective instruments. Thus it is not always immediately obvious which are the tutti sections and which the solo sections. Doubts can generally be dispelled by listening to a recording of the work.

HISTORICAL NOTE ON THE CLASSICAL CONCERTO Emulating the form and style of Vivaldi's concertos during the first half of the eighteenth century were a number of Italian composers who, like Vivaldi, were either Venetians or were living in the vicinity of Venice. In other parts of Italy, however, the tendency of the younger generation was away from the sweeping drive and fiery energy of the Baroque concerto toward a more vocally conceived melodic style that led finally to the concertos of the Classical composers of Vienna. The desire was for more melodious themes, greater rhythmic variety, and fewer alternations of the tutti and solo sections. Often the finales were no longer constructed according to the same principles as the opening movements, but were dancelike pieces in binary form. The concertos of Locatelli, Tartini, Padre Martini, Leo, Pergolesi, Durante, and Hasse show the early stages of the new type of concerto. A further stage in its development can be clearly followed in the concertos of J. S. Bach's youngest son, Johann Christian Bach, and others.

As a very young boy Mozart came under the influence of J. C. Bach, going so far as to convert, in 1765, three of the older composer's sonatas into piano concertos. Mozart's concertos, of which there are about fifty, exhibit in their first movements the same basic structural plan found in those of J. C. Bach. Although Mozart's greater genius produced concertos which far outshine the pleasantries of his model, he did not deviate from his adherence to this standard procedure in the first movements. The first movements of the concertos of Haydn and Beethoven are laid out according to the same pattern. This pattern will be examined in the discussion to follow.

The concertos of Mozart, Haydn, and Beethoven regularly follow the standard movement scheme of the Vivaldian concerto: two fast movements surrounding a slow one. Many of J. C. Bach's concertos, on the other hand, have only two, rather than three, movements.

13–B.
FIRST MOVEMENTS OF THE CLASSICAL CONCERTO: CONCERTO-SONATA FORM

PROCEDURE IN THE PRECLASSICAL CONCERTO

By the middle of the eighteenth century the structural pattern of the first movement of a concerto had become fairly well standardized. It usually consisted of four ritornellos, of which the penultimate was still the shortest, with three intervening solo selections. The usual tonal structure was:

	R1	S1	R2	S2	R3	S3	R4
Major Mode:	I	x	V	x	vi or I	x	I
Minor Mode:	i	x	III	x	v or i	x	i

The solo and tutti sections did not, as a rule, exhibit obvious melodic resemblances. The tutti parts tended to have themes of their own not shared by the soloist, and vice versa.

The first movements of the concertos of J. C. Bach composed in Berlin while he was still in his teens follow the general outline given above. However, after his move to Italy and thence to London his concertos show important changes from his earlier essays in this genre. The basic outline of four ritornellos alternating with three solo sections remains the same. But R3, the short ritornello, is now usually, rather than sometimes, in the tonic key. Moveover, in design the solo sections have taken on characteristics of sonata form. S1, for instance, is patterned after the exposition of a sonata form. Its themes may or may not have been previously presented in R1. S2 prolongs the V and corresponds to the development section of the sonata form. The brief third ritornello, R3, is either omitted or merges with S3 to form a single section that recapitulates S1, now entirely in the tonic key. In all, then, there are six discernible sections in the first movements of the majority of J. C. Bach's London concertos (1763–1777)[3]:

---

[3] The first movements of Leo's *Violoncello Concertos* in D major and A major (1737) show an almost identical procedure more than a generation earlier. The concertos of J. C. Bach's contemporary, Luigi Boccherini, are also the same in this regard.

Section 1. R1	Orchestral ritornello	I
Section 2. S1	Solo and orchestral exposition	I → V(III)
Section 3. R2	Orchestral ritornello	V(III)
Section 4. S2	Solo and orchestral development	V(III) → V₇
Section 5. R3–S3	Solo and orchestral recapitulation	I
Section 6. R4	Orchestral ritornello	I

A cadenza improvised by the soloist was sometimes inserted between S3 and R4. In later Classical concertos, however, the cadenza is an interruption of R4.

The regular appearance of these six sections as the chief structural principle of the first movements of the Classical concerto is enough to warrant considering these movements a standard form. Because of the resemblance of sections 2, 4, and 5 to the exposition, development, and recapitulation, respectively, of the sonata form, the first movement of the Classical concerto can be labeled the concerto-sonata form. Within the broad outlines of the six sections of the concerto-sonata form there is room for much variety. It is doubtful whether any two first movements of Classical concertos are patterned just alike. Moreover, the grouping of the sections into parts is not the same in every case. Our approach, then, must be to select certain movements for examination, with the warning that identical designs are not likely to be found elsewhere. We shall concern ourselves with two of the greatest piano concertos, Mozart's in C minor, *K. 491* (in Burkhart's *Anthology*), and Beethoven's in E♭ major, *Op. 73*. The former will be discussed in some detail, the latter briefly.

MOZART'S CONCERTO IN C MINOR, FIRST MOVEMENT

The opening ritornello for orchestra comprises a complete harmonic movement, interrupted by the V at mm. 58–62 and closing with the authentic cadence on I at mm. 90–91, prolonged until m. 99. It can be labeled R1 and makes up part one of the concerto movement.

This great ritornello divides itself into five sections and presents altogether six distinct melodic ideas. The first of these contains three different motives, marked a, b, and c, from which spring many of the themes or accompanimental figures appearing later in the movement.

Example 13–2

MOZART: *Concerto, K. 491*, ritornello themes

Section 1 (mm. 1–34), a phrase group of three phrases, deals with theme A, and carries the harmonic movement to a half cadence. Section 2 (mm. 35–62) is a chain of three phrases; Ex. 13–2 quotes the first of these (B_1). The place of this phrase chain in the tonal structure is to prolong the V with which section 1 ended. This V acts to interrupt the harmonic movement that begins again with the presentation of A as section 3 (mm. 63–73), concluding with a deceptive cadence (V–VI in m. 73). Section 4 (mm. 73–91), an extended phrase (C_1), completes the harmonic movement with an authentic cadence on i (mm. 90–91) and this i is prolonged by section 5 (mm. 91–99), which serves as codetta to the ritornello (D).

The bass outline in Ex. 13–3 shows how the whole ritornello is, in effect, a balanced period, magnified to immense proportions, which is based on the principle of interruption.

Example 13–3

MOZART: *Concerto, K. 491*, bass outline of opening ritornello

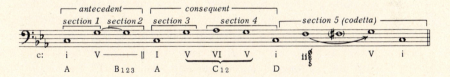

The opening ritornello is followed by the first solo section, S1, designed as a sonata-form exposition. Each division of this exposition except the transition presents not a single theme but a group of themes, entailing its division into subsections. The solo piano introduces the exposition with a new theme of its own, E (Ex. 13–4a), after which the orchestra and solo combine to present theme A. This turns out to be the transition leading to the mediant key of E♭, the relative major. (Phase 2 of this modulation occurs at m. 130, phase 3 at m. 134.) The second theme group (mm. 147–220) divides itself into three subsections, the new theme F being presented in the first (Ex. 13–4b). The second subsection G (mm. 165–200) refers to motives c and b, introduces the new bass motive d (Ex. 13–4c), and then continues with a fragment of D. The third subsection (mm. 201–220) presents a new theme, H (Ex. 13–4d).

Example 13–4

MOZART: *Concerto, K. 491,* exposition themes

The closing theme consists first of an extended phrase based on A (mm. 220–241) followed by an eight-bar codetta, with its varied repetition and eight-bar extension. Immediately R2 (mm. 265–282) bursts in, its first chord coinciding with the last of S1. It begins with a melody made up of motives b and c and concludes with the final bars of D. In the tonal structure R2 has done no more than extend the final chord of S1 and repeat the authentic cadence on III (that is, E♭ major) with which S1 had ended. S1 and R2 group themselves together to become part two of this concerto movement.

The second solo section, S2, is designed like the development of a sonata form. On the basis of its material and phrase organization it falls into five subsections. Subsection 1 (mm. 283–301) deals with theme E. Starting on III it progresses to iv, the chord that opens subsection 2 (mm. 302–329). Here the orchestra is given over to the sounding of A with particular stress on motives b and c, while the piano furnishes brilliant scales and figuration. Subsection 2 moves from V back to III, then to V_7/V, but the cadence resolves deceptively to a V_5^6 (m. 330), which opens subsection 3. Subsection 3 deals with a rhythmic variation of motive d, first heard as the bass of G in the secondary section of the exposition. This version of motive d is so disposed as to prolong the V_5^6 for four bars, then repeats sequentially three times, each time prolonging a $^6_5$ chord in descending fifths (mm. 330–345) until subsection 4 begins in m. 346 on III (E♭). This is the chord that closed the exposition and opened the development. So far, then, the tonal structure of the development has consisted of movement within an area, a great chord succession prolonging III. A harmonic outline of the development section shows that the long chord succession on III is in essence a move to the chord whose root is a second above III, then to the chord whose root is a second below III, then through the series of $^6_5$ chords in descending fifths back to the beginning III. The succession is a gigantic slow turn around the note E♭.

Example 13–5

MOZART: *Concerto, K. 491*, development of first movement (harmonic outline)

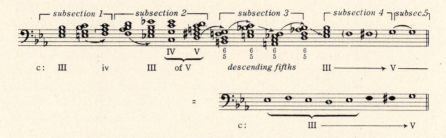

The development continues with subsection 4, thematically based on motive a, which appears in diminution in the bass. In mm. 352–354 the III that had been prolonged by succession from the beginning of the development finally moves to V, which is itself prolonged by means of pedal point throughout subsection 5, the retransition (mm. 355–361). Here the woodwind parts are particularly interesting. They play the descending broken triad derived from H, but by preceding this motive with a sixteenth note and indicating that it is to be played staccato, Mozart contrives to give it the aspect of motive b'.

It has been observed that the penultimate ritornello, even in Baroque times, was customarily much shorter than the others and that in the preclassical concerto it shrank still further. The same holds true during the Classical period, so it should afford us no surprise that R3 in this concerto consists of no more than a six-bar presentation of A. There is not even a cadence, for R3 merges immediately into S3 (m. 367), and the two together become the fifth section, the recapitulation.

The recapitulation of Mozart's *Concerto in C Minor* is quite different from the exposition in design as well as in tonal structure. Theme A (mm.

Outline Summary of Mozart's Piano Concerto, K. 491, First Movement

Bars	1–99	100–265	265–282	283–361	362–473	473–509	509–523
Procedure	R1	S1 (exposition)	R2	S2 (development)	R3–S3 (recapitulation)	R4	Coda
Design	AB ‖ AC–D	*PT* tr. *ST CT* (EA) (FGH) (A)	bcD	E A G A H (bc) (d) (a) (b")	*PT ST CT* (A) (HF) (bB) A Cad. C D		H b"
Tonal Structure	i (i → V ‖ i → V I)	i → V i i ⟶ of III III	III	III ⟶ V₇	i	i	i
Form	Part One	Part Two		Part Three			

245

363–387) begins as it did in S1 (see mm. 118–134) and concludes as in R1. The transition to the second theme group, being no longer necessary for modulatory purposes, is reduced to a mere four bars. The second theme is reduced to two subsections and entirely rearranged, now beginning with H and closing with F—the reverse order of their original appearances—G being omitted completely. Moreover, theme F is altered considerably and incorporates in its final bars a motive from C_2. The closing theme (mm. 428–473) is entirely different from that of the exposition, for it opens with a new section, based on a rising octave derived from motive b'', and continues with the three phrases of B, taken from R1. The third phrase is especially to be noted, for this time it is presented in canonic imitation (mm. 452–456). The whole recapitulation has been concerned only with the tonic key and has completed the harmonic movement i-V-i. This final tonic chord coincides with the opening chord of the last ritornello, R4 (m. 473). It begins as a phrase stating theme A, but halts on a i_4^6 for an improvised cadenza. The piano soloist is expected to close his cadenza with the V or V_7 foreshadowed by the orchestral i_4^6 with which it began. The ritornello then continues, taking its material from R2 and themes C and D. The tonal structure of R4 has re-emphasized the tonic key. A coda, which corresponds thematically to subsection 5 of the development, with piano figuration from the end of the recapitulation, prolongs the i by means of pedal point. S2, R3–S3, and R4 (with cadenza) group themselves together as part three of the concerto.

THE PROBLEM OF THE DOUBLE EXPOSITION

The initial ritornello of Mozart's *Concerto in C Minor* presents a half-dozen melodic ideas, and the exposition several more. While the exposition included some of the themes from R1, it by no means stated all of them. Yet these other themes, "exposed" only in the orchestral ritornello, are certainly an integral part of the work. Writers on music often speak of a "double exposition" in the concerto-sonata form—the opening ritornello being considered exposition one, the first solo section exposition two. The pros and cons of this view of R1 have been much debated with no universal agreement. But whether or not one applies the term "exposition" to both R1 and S1, it can hardly be denied that the recapitulation, R3–S3, is usually based on both of them and can be thought of as a synthesis of the two. The fact that R1 is used along with S1 as material on which to base the recapitulation would seem to lend weight to the argument in favor of considering it an exposition. Thus there is no harm in calling it that, provided of course that one keeps in mind that R1 is nothing like the exposition of a *sonata form,* for it remains throughout in the tonic key.

THE PARTS OF A CONCERTO-SONATA FORM

In this concerto Mozart employs R2 as a means of prolonging the final chord of S1. These two sections, then, group themselves into a single part, part two, in the mind of the listener (see the foregoing outline summary).

In some concertos, however, R2 does not merely prolong the final chord of S1, but instead leads directly into the beginning chord, whatever it may be, of the development section, S2. J. C. Bach's *Concerto, Op. 13, No. 2*, and Mozart's *Sinfonia Concertante for Violin and Viola, K. 364*, both contain this type of R2. Except for the first two piano concertos all of Beethoven's works in the genre follow this procedure in their first movements. The result is a grouping of sections into parts different from that in the Mozart *Concerto in C Minor*. For if R2 concludes its connective motion with a semicadence, it will inevitably be grouped with the part that follows rather than with the part that precedes. There are concertos, then, in which part two is made up of S1 alone, part three consisting of the final four sections.

THE FLOURISH In his *Piano Concerto in B♭ Major, K. 450*, Mozart treats the first entrance of the piano in a new way. Rather than waiting until the orchestra has completed R1 and then beginning with the principal theme of S1 (exposition), the piano enters just *as* the orchestra is completing its R1 cadence, presenting not a theme but a passage in running sixteenth notes which embellishes the orchestra's tonic harmony. This passage, rather brilliant in nature, can be called a *flourish* and serves several functions: (1) it embellishes and prolongs the orchestra's final tonic chord of R1; (2) it provides an introduction to the statement of the first theme of S1; and, perhaps most important, (3) it furnishes an effective first entrance of the solo instrument.

In a famous essay Donald Francis Tovey writes of the artistic need for a solo to "hold its own by doing that which most distinguishes it from the orchestra," and that it "should therefore be florid just in proportion to the amount of orchestral impressiveness."[4] In a note he goes on to write of the necessity for the solo part in Mozart's concertos to be more difficult technically and more brilliant than those of his predecessors simply because the orchestra had become more powerful and its use more varied. Similarly, Beethoven's solo parts had to be more dazzling than Mozart's, and Brahms' more than Beethoven's. The flourish sets the stage appropriately by arranging for a brilliant *first* entrance of the solo instrument. In two later piano concertos, *K. 467* and *K. 503*, both in C Major, Mozart also brings in the piano by means of the flourish. In *K. 503* the effect is different in that the piano begins almost hesitantly with short fragments, and only gradually do these form themselves into brilliant passagework.

The flourish is to be found several times in the concertos of Beethoven and Brahms and similar passages appear at the beginning of several Romantic concertos (Weber, Chopin, Schumann, Liszt, and others).

[4] "The Classical Concerto" in *Essays in Musical Analysis*, Vol. III. Oxford: Oxford University Press, 1936, p. 20.

BEETHOVEN'S CONCERTO IN E FLAT MAJOR, FIRST MOVEMENT

The first movements of Beethoven's concertos exhibit the same six sections as do Mozart's, disposed as orchestral ritornellos with intervening exposition, development, and recapitulation for soloist with orchestra. They differ from most of Mozart's in having fewer themes, for Beethoven sought to be economical in the use of his melodies. In all but the first two of Beethoven's concertos the exposition consists entirely of material heard in the opening ritornello, usually in approximately the same order.

In the *Concerto in E♭ Major, K. 271*, the twenty-one-year-old Mozart brought in the solo piano at the very beginning, letting it help state the first theme of the opening ritornello. Although Mozart never did this in his later concertos, Beethoven took up the idea in his *Concerto No. 4 in G Major*. In his *Concerto No. 5 in E♭ Major*, after a single chord from the orchestra, he allows the piano to enter not with the theme but with a flourish, moved from its place separating R1 and S1 in order to act as a brilliant introduction to the opening ritornello.

This ritornello is a gigantic affair in eight subsections, ABCA'DEF, concluding with the codetta, G, which is related to A. The third subsection, C, is a remarkable melody, always appearing first in the minor mode, then in the major.

Example 13–6

BEETHOVEN: *Concerto, Op. 73*, ritornello themes

The piano re-enters for the exposition before the orchestra has quite finished the ritornello, a device that had appeared in Mozart's *K. 364* and *K. 413* and that Beethoven had previously used in the *Piano Concerto No. 4*. The exposition uses most of the themes presented in the opening ritornello, but transposes to V those serving the secondary and closing sections. Beethoven achieves a striking effect in his presentation of C as secondary theme. It appears first not in V (Bb major) but in the enharmonically notated minor mode of bVI (B minor), moves into the major mode (Cb major), in which it appears in a variation, and finally bursts out in the orchestra in the traditional dominant key. This use of a progressive harmonic movement in the secondary section is occasionally to be found in sonata-form expositions as well, as was pointed out in Chapter 11 (see p. 198).

At the end of the development the repetition of the introductory piano flourishes leads into the recapitulation. The themes here are presented in the same order as in the exposition, but Beethoven is again unorthodox in regard to the key of the secondary section. In the exposition it had appeared first in a key a half tone higher than that for which it was ultimately destined. Now it appears first a whole tone lower (Db major), but with its orchestral statement it settles into the tonic key.

Outline Summary of Beethoven's Concerto, Op. 73, First Movement

Bars	1–11	11–111	111–224				
Procedure	Intro.	R1	S1 (exposition)				
Design	Flourish	ABCA' DEFG	PT tr. ST (A) (B) (C)			tr. CT (B') (A'D)	
Tonal Structure	I–IV–V⁷	I	I	bvi–bVI–V	V⁷/V	V	
Form	Part One		Part Two				

Bars	224–263	263–272	273–362	362–373	373–485					485–562	562–582
Procedure	R2	Intro.	S2 (development)	Intro.	R3–S3 (recapitulation)					R4	Coda
Design	AA'DFG (Cf. mm. 104–7)		A G A F B A'	Flourish	PT tr. ST (A) (B) (C)			tr. CT (B') (A'D)	A A' CA'EFG (quasi-cadenza)		G
Tonal Structure	V → III	III (= V/vi)	vi → V		I–IV–V⁷	I	bvii–bVII–I	V⁷	I	I–I⁶₄ : V⁷–I	I
Form	Part Three										

The fourth ritornello enters normally and comes to the usual halt on I_4^6, preparatory to the cadenza, which begins accordingly. But after a few bars the listener is astonished to find the orchestra accompanying the pianist and realizes that this is not an improvised cadenza after all but a composed cadenza and only the beginning of one at that. It leads into a final restatement of all but D of the ritornello themes. This is the only concerto in which Beethoven eschewed the improvised cadenza in the first movement. It was perhaps for the use of other soloists that he wrote out cadenzas to all his other piano concertos, including three for *Op. 15* and two for *Op. 58.*

EXERCISE

2. Make an outline summary similar to those in the text of the first movement of a concerto by Mozart or Beethoven, or the first movement of Brahms' *Violin Concerto.*

13–C.
THIRD MOVEMENTS OF THE
CLASSICAL CONCERTO:
CONCERTO-RONDO FORM

A few Classical concertos end with a set of variations on a theme. The finales of the others are rondos (see Chapter 9), a custom that was largely continued throughout the nineteenth century. The rondos that conclude the concertos of Romantic composers do not differ substantially in form from the ordinary rondo or sonata rondo already discussed. The rondos of many Classical concertos, too, are essentially the same. But there is a special type of rondo, first developed by Mozart in certain early concertos and used with some consistency in his later ones, which, being especially designed for use in the concerto, we shall call the concerto-rondo form.

The finales of Beethoven's first four piano concertos are ordinary rondos, as is that of the *Triple Concerto, Op. 56,* and the *Violin Concerto, Op. 61.* But in his last concerto, the *Piano Concerto in E♭ Major, Op. 73,* he followed Mozart's concerto-rondo form.

The form bears many resemblances to the concerto-sonata and may be considered an application of that form to the rondo. It proceeds as follows.

Refrain 1. In the concerto-rondo the refrain plays approximately the same role as did the ritornello in the concerto-sonata form, with two differences: (1) the refrain of the concerto-rondo usually begins with the solo instrument rather than with the orchestra, and (2) the refrain always recurs in the tonic key. Like the ritornello it consists of several detachable parts.

Episode 1. The first episode is constructed as a compressed version of the exposition in a concerto-sonata form except that normally no theme from the refrain appears in this exposition. There are a few exceptions to this general observation, an example being Mozart's *K. 466*, in which the refrain melody makes up the second half of the exposition's first theme. The first, second, and closing themes are presented as in any sonata form, after which a retransition leads back to the refrain.

Refrain 2. The return of the refrain is sometimes shortened. Normally the solo instrument states it first, as in refrain 1, then the orchestra takes over. Progressive harmonic movement to the initial chord of episode 2 may occur during the orchestral statement of the refrain (compare similar treatment of R2 in concerto-sonata form, Section 13–C).

Episode 2. In some concertos this episode consists of new material, as in the second episode of any typical Classical rondo. In that case it is likely to express IV or vi. In many concertos, however, this episode is replaced by a development, as in the sonata-rondo form. Mozart's *Clarinet Concerto, K. 622*, includes both: an episode of new material expressing vi, followed by a development (compare similar treatment in sonata-rondo, p. 232).

Refrain 3. The third refrain of the concerto-rondo is frequently omitted (analogous to the extreme brevity of R3 in concerto-sonata form).

Episode 3. This episode comprises the recapitulation section of the movement and hence is normally a restatement, entirely in the tonic, of episode 1. Often it is highly abridged. If, for instance, episode 2 was a development including treatment of the first theme of episode 1, that theme is likely to be absent here. If there is to be a cadenza, the closing theme will lead to a halt on the I_4^6 and the improvisation will begin at that point.

Refrain 4. The final appearance of the refrain is generally shortened and sometimes merges with the coda.

(Frequent omissions are indicated by enclosure in brackets)

Outline of the Concerto-Rondo Form	*Refrain 1*	*Episode 1*	*Refrain 2*	*Episode 2*	*[Refrain 3]*	*Episode 3*	*Refrain 4 and Coda*
	Solo, orch.	Exposition *PT* tr. *ST CT*	Solo, orch.	New, develop-ment, or both	Solo or orch.	Recapitulation *[PT]* tr. *ST CT* [Cadenza]	Orch., solo
	I	I V(III)	I*	IV (VI)**	I	I	I

* Or progressive movement to beginning of episode 2.

** Or, when episode 2 is a development, progressive movement to V_7.

251

The chief distinction between the ordinary rondo with which many concertos end and the concerto-rondo form lies in the sonata-form construction of the first episode. In the usual rondo, it will be remembered, the first refrain is followed by a modulating transition leading to the key of episode 1 (III or V). In the concerto-rondo the refrain is concluded on I by

Outline Summary of Mozart's Concerto, K. 466, Finale

Bars	1–63	64–161	161–167	167–195	196–240	240–345	346–353	354–428
Procedure	Refrain 1	Episode 1 (exposition)		Refrain 2	Episode 2 (develop-ment)	Episode 3 (recapitulation)	Refrain 4* (Refrain 3 omitted)	Coda
Design	A–AA'BC	*PT* tr. *ST CT* retrans. (DA) (EF) (G)		A–A'	DA	*PT* tr. *ST CT* + Codetta (D) (EF) (G) (FC and cadenza)	A (abbre-viated)	GB'G'
Tonal Structure	i	i iii III III V$_5^6$		i–i V/v	v iv V$_5^6$ i	i i	i	I
Form	Part One (A)	Part Two (BA)			Part Three (Dev.–C, B'A)			

* For a different but still plausible point of view, see p. 164.

Outline Summary of Mozart's Concerto, K. 488, Finale

Bars	1–61	62–193	193–202	202–229	230–293	293–312
Procedure	Refrain 1	Episode 1 (exposition)		Refrain 2	Episode 2 (new)	
Design	A–ABCDE	*PT* tr. *ST CT* + Codetta retrans. (F) (G) (H) (I)		A–AA'	J K retrans.	
Tonal Structure	I	I v V V	V–V^7	I–I → vi	vi IV ⟶ V^7	
Form	Part One (A)	Part Two (BA)			Part Three (C)	

Bars	312–423	423–441	441–480	480–524
Procedure	Episode 3 (recapitulation)		Refrain 4 (Refrain 3 omitted)	Coda
Design	*PT* tr. *ST CT* + Codetta (F) (F') (G') (H) (I)		A–ABC	I D E
Tonal Structure	I i I–i I	I	I	I
Form	Part Four (BA)			

the orchestra, and the solo instrument enters not with a modulating transition but with a new theme also expressing I. Thus the first episode does not begin on III or V but on I. After the first theme of the exposition episode has been stated, a transition leads to the related key for the statement of the second and closing themes. This difference has caused a great deal of confusion among annotators of phonograph record jackets, a confusion which has, no doubt, been passed on to their readers.

Outline summaries of two of Mozart's concerto rondos are given.

EXERCISE

3. Make an outline summary, similar to the foregoing, of the third movement of one of Mozart's later piano concertos (*K. 450* and upwards, except *K. 453*, *K. 482*, and *K. 491*) or of the *Clarinet Concerto, K. 622*.

13–D.
SUMMARY

Throughout the Baroque and Classical periods the fundamental characteristic of the concerto, contrast between sounding bodies, was maintained, demanding the constant use of the device of the orchestral ritornello. The first and third movements of the typical late Baroque three-movement concerto proceeded by alternation between the orchestra (*concerto grosso*) and the soloist or soloists (*concertino*). No standard "concerto grosso form" emerged from this systematized procedure, since the number of these alternations was not fixed and there was no typical tonal structure. The *concerto grosso* movement regularly has the following general features:

1. *Ritornellos*. The movement usually begins with an orchestral ritornello comprising several sections in the tonic key. It always ends with one in that key. During the course of the movement other ritornellos appear in related keys (III, IV, V, or VI), although the next-to-last ritornello is often in the tonic key. The middle ritornellos are much abridged; the final one sometimes is.
2. *Solo sections*. Between ritornellos the *concertino* performs with an accompaniment of a portion of the orchestra. These solo sections may include new themes or simply figuration of a nature idiomatic to the instrument. Occasionally the soloist presents a theme first heard in the ritornello. The solo sections generally modulate from the key of the preceding ritornello to that of the following.

Though musical style underwent a great change during the course of the eighteenth century, the structure of the ritornello itself remained much the

Relation-ships Among the Concerto Forms	Concerto Section	1. Concerto Grosso	2. Concerto-Sonata Form	3. Concerto-Rondo Form	Rondo Section
	Tutti R1	A B C . . . I	A B C . . . I	A A B C . . . I	Solo, tutti Refrain 1
	Solo S1	D (or A', B' . . .) I → V(III)	Sonata-form exposition of new or partially new themes *Pt tr. ST CT* I → V(III)	Sonata-form exposition of new themes *PT tr. ST CT* I → V(III)	Solo Episode 1
	Tutti R2	A (B C . . .) V(III)	A (B C . . .) V(III)*	A (B C . . .) I	Solo, tutti Refrain 2
	Solo S2	E (or A", B" . . .) V(III) → VI(IV)	Sonata-form development V(III) → V₇	Sonata-form development V(III) → V₇ *or* new material VI(IV)	Solo Episode 2
	Tutti R3	(A B) C . . . VI, IV, or I	Sonata-form recapitulation A (short) I	Sonata-form recapitulation A (short) I	Solo, tutti Refrain 3 (perhaps omitted)
	Solo S3	F (or A''', B''' . . .) VI(IV) → I or I	Recapitulation (continued) *PT tr. ST CT* I	Recapitulation (continued) *PT tr. ST CT* I	Solo Episode 3
	Tutti R4**	(A) B C . . . I	(A) B C . . . (interrupted by solo cadenza) Plus coda	(A) B C . . . (possibly preceded by solo cadenza) Plus coda	Tutti Refrain 4

* Or progressive movement to initial chord of S2.

** The *concerto grosso* frequently has more than four ritornellos.

same. The usual number of ritornellos, however, shrank to four, and of these the third was often extremely short. In certain concertos of the preclassical composers (Leo, Boccherini, J. C. Bach) the first solo section takes on the characteristics of the exposition of sonata form, the second solo those of the development, and the third those of the recapitulation, resulting in what is now called the concerto-sonata form. It appears (much enlarged) as the first-movement structure of the concertos of Mozart, Haydn, and Beethoven. Though the ordinary rondo often served for the concerto finale, Mozart developed a special concerto-rondo form by combining features of the concerto-sonata with the recurring refrains in the tonic key characteristic of the rondo. The outline above shows the relationships among the various types of concerto forms.

HISTORICAL NOTE ON THE CONCERTO AFTER BEETHOVEN The shadow of Beethoven loomed so large over the musical world that for a number of years after his last concerto was written many composers dared not attempt anything structurally very different. Weber's and Chopin's piano concertos, for instance, are constructed along lines similar to Beethoven's. When Weber disregarded the principles of the Classical concerto, he called the result not a concerto, but a *Konzertstück*, that is, a piece in the style of a concerto. But the Romantic spirit could not forever take on a Classical body, and soon a new type of first movement began to appear. Mendelssohn ushered in the new Romantic type with two concertos for piano and the *Violin Concerto in E Minor*. An essential characteristic of the concerto had hitherto been the contrast in sounding bodies, the opposition of soloist and orchestra. Now it became a different thing entirely—a brilliant piece of music for a virtuoso performer with an orchestral accompaniment. Mozart and Beethoven wrote concertos for piano and orchestra. It is significant that Schumann called his *Op. 129* a concerto for violoncello "with the accompaniment of an orchestra."

Since the idea was no longer the contrast between sounding bodies, the form was altered to eliminate the orchestral ritornellos. The result in some cases is an ordinary sonata form, each theme usually being presented by the soloist and immediately taken up by the orchestra, or vice versa. In some cases entirely unique forms were devised. The concertos of Liszt and Schumann are among the great products of the new concerto type.

In his four concertos Brahms restored the orchestral ritornello to a place of prominence, in the *Violin Concerto, Op. 77* and the *Double Concerto, Op. 102* even including the six sections of the Classical concerto-sonata form. The opening of the *Piano Concerto No. 2 in B♭ Major, Op. 83*, takes its cue from both Beethoven's *No. 4* and *No. 5*, for the piano is allowed to help with the first theme of the ritornello, as in Beethoven's *No. 4*. It then proceeds with a flourish similar to Beethoven's *No. 5*, remaining silent throughout the rest of the first tutti section.

One often hears the statement that Brahms' *Piano Concerto No. 2* is not a concerto at all but a symphony with piano obbligato. It is true that this piece, like most symphonies, has four movements, while concertos ordinarily have only three, but in its treatment of the contrast between soloist and orchestra it is a concerto in the true and historic sense of the word. Along with Brahms' other concertos it is one of the few nineteenth-century concertos about which this can be said.

After Brahms had re-established the Classical concerto-sonata form, Romantic composers had two choices open to them. They could continue along the path first opened by Mendelssohn and followed by Liszt and Schumann—to eliminate the tutti sections and concentrate on the soloist's part, providing it with an interesting and elaborate orchestral accompaniment—or they could retain the tutti sections and thus achieve the contrast between sounding bodies which had been in the past the concerto's most characteristic feature. The great majority disregarded Brahms and chose the former way—Grieg, Tchaikovsky, and Saint-Saëns, being outstanding among these. One of the few who chose the latter way was Dvořak in his *Concerto for Violoncello in B Minor*.

The twentieth-century concerto generally continues to be essentially a work for a solo performer with accompaniment. In spite of highly elaborate orchestral writing contrast between a large and a small sounding body is no longer in evidence as a structural principle, for in the modern concerto, as in that of the nineteenth century, the soloist is very prominent most of the time. The three-movement scheme, fast-slow-fast, continues to appear with regularity. Nevertheless, other movement schemes occur from time to time, as in Berg's *Violin Concerto* (four movements played as two) and Schoenberg's *Piano Concerto, Op. 42* (four movements played as one).

14

FUGUE AND RELATED GENRES

HISTORICAL NOTE ON THE FUGUE The fugue is properly considered to have emerged as a distinct genre in the seventeenth century, although its origins can be traced back several centuries in the imitative contrapuntal texture of polyphonic vocal music.

So far as is known, the term *fuga* was first used by Jacobus of Liège in his theoretical treatise *Speculum musicae* (c. 1330), where it is equivalent to *caccia*, a work in which two voices move by canonic imitation over a free third voice. In the latter part of the fourteenth century it was sometimes synonymous with *rondellus* or *rota*, a round. Fugal treatment was defined around 1475 by Tinctoris in his *Diffinitorium musicae* as "the identity of rhythmic and melodic writing in various parts of a composition," that is, equivalent to what we think of today as canonic writing. In the fifteenth and sixteenth centuries composers frequently made great use of fugal procedures in both their sacred and secular vocal works—the masses and motets on the one hand, the *canzoni* or French chansons on the other— procedures which were sometimes reflected in the title: Dufay, Josquin des Prez, and Palestrina each composed a *Missa ad fugam*.

During the sixteenth century the motet and the chanson or *canzona* became models for similar instrumental genres, the *ricercare* and the *canzon da sonar*, respectively, such as the organ *ricercari* of Cavazzoni. The style of the *ricercare*, derived as it was from the sacred motet, was generally of a solemn character, while that of the secularly inspired *canzona* was rhythmic and lively. The *canzona* differed further from the *ricercare* in being less rigidly contrapuntal and in introducing contrasting sections of a different nature. The two styles persisted in the fugal writing of the seventeenth and early eighteenth centuries and are exemplified in the first two fugues of Bach's *WTC*, that in C Major being of the *ricercare* type, that in C Minor the *canzona*.

The early seventeenth century saw the organ *ricercare* and *canzona* established in Italy, chiefly by Frescobaldi. An important northern counterpart was the fantasia, a term referring in the late sixteenth and early seventeenth centuries to an instrumental piece in imitative counterpoint that often combined features of the *ricercare* and the *canzona*. The English fancy (or fantasia) for a consort of viols, such as those of Orlando Gibbons, the early works of John Jenkins, and, much later, Henry Purcell, foreshadowed fugal writing in many respects. The keyboard fantasias of Sweelinck in the Netherlands, however, came even closer to the fugue in that they were composed on a single theme throughout.

The most important organ fugues of the latter half of the seventeenth century occur as sections within the toccatas or "praeludia" (now often called preludes and fugues) of Buxtehude, though fugues as independent pieces were also being composed (Krieger, Pachelbel, J. K. F. Fischer). The evolution of the fugue reached its peak in the works of J. S. Bach—not only in the famous organ fugues and those of his *WTC,* but in the mighty fugal choruses from the sacred vocal music, although the best fugal choruses of Handel are equally impressive.

In Bach's time it was customary to precede the independent keyboard fugue with a composition of a less contrapuntal, or even of a completely homophonic, texture. The result is the two-movement prelude and fugue, toccata and fugue, or fantasy and fugue.

After Bach the majority of important fugal composition occurs in choral music. The masses, oratorios, and other large choral works of Haydn, Mozart, Beethoven, Mendelssohn, Berlioz, Brahms, Verdi, and others are rich with *fugato* (that is, fuguelike) passages as well as entire fugal movements. Although most nineteenth-century composers wrote instrumental fugues, only Beethoven can be compared with Bach in this field. As he advanced in years, Beethoven came to rely more and more on the fugue as a means of artistic expression (*Quartets, Op. 131, Op. 133; Piano Sonatas, Op. 101, Op. 106, Op. 110;* the *Diabelli Variations, Op. 120;* and so on).

The fugue cannot be said to play an important role in twentieth-century music as compared with the late seventeenth and early eighteenth centuries. Nevertheless, certain important works with a fugal texture continue to appear from time to time (Hindemith, *Ludus Tonalis;* Schoenberg, *Variations on a Recitative,* Finale; Stravinsky, *Symphony of Psalms,* Second Movement; Bartók, *Music for Strings, Percussion, and Celesta,* First Movement).

14–A.
FUGUE AND FORM

The fugue is not a form. Two Bach fugues may have much in common, but the relationship between them is not of the same kind as the relationship between, say, two of Beethoven's sonata forms. Fugues are classed together in a single species not because of similarities of form, but because they exhibit in their texture similar contrapuntal procedures. From the point of view of form each fugue is independent. It may show a binary or ternary form; it may exhibit resemblances to the rondo. The Finale from Brahms' *Violoncello Sonata in E Minor, Op. 38*, is a fugue in sonata form. Frequently a particular fugue has a unique form of its own.

In this chapter, then, we shall be dealing not with standardized patterns of musical structure like the rounded binary form or the Classical rondo, but with pieces in any form which are based on certain contrapuntal practices.

14–B.
CHARACTERISTICS OF FUGUE

A fugue is a polyphonic composition with a texture made up of a constant number of melodic lines, usually three or four, occasionally five, rarely two or six. It is customary to refer to these melodic lines in vocal terminology, that is, the uppermost line is called the soprano voice, the lowest the bass. In a three-voice fugue the middle line is the alto, the fourth voice, when it exists, being the tenor. The fugue is based on a theme that begins in one voice, is imitated by another, again by a third, and so on, until each voice has stated it. The theme is called the subject, its imitation the answer. The subject and answer then reappear at intervals throughout the piece. Imitation in fugal writing is generally of two types: real (or exact) imitation and what is known as "tonal imitation."

14–C.
THE FUGUE SUBJECT AND ANSWER

THE PRINCIPLE
OF TONAL
IMITATION

Example 14–1

HANDEL: *Messiah*, Part II

259

The familiar passage in Ex. 14–1 illustrates a procedure in imitative writing which is exceedingly important for the study of fugue. For convenience in explication the system will be employed here whereby 1 stands for the tonic note, I for the tonic chord, 2 for the supertonic note, ii for the supertonic chord, and so forth.

The subject as sung by the altos begins with three upward leaps of a perfect fourth each, separated by downward leaps of a sixth (5–1, 3–6, 1–4); then it descends to 1 by stepwise motion. When answered by the sopranos, however, it has a slightly different melodic contour. The sopranos' answer is not a literal imitation of the subject, for the first upward leap is a fifth rather than a fourth (1–5). Except for this difference the remainder is an exact transposition of the subject a fifth higher. If Handel had allowed the sopranos to enter on the note *e"* rather than on *d"*, the imitation would have been altogether exact. The purpose behind his alteration of this first note has to do with the maintenance of the tonality, D major. If the altos were to enter on *a'* and the sopranos on *e"*, and, similarly, the basses on *a* and the tenors on *e'*, the resulting impression on the listener would be of the tonality of A, not of D. Here, then, is the first observation regarding imitation:

As it enters, each voice sounds either 1 or 5 of the main tonality.

The second observation also has to do with the expression of tonality by emphasis on the tonic and dominant aspects of the main key.

The answering voice transposes the subject up a perfect fifth or down a perfect fourth (i.e., to the dominant level).

The principle of tonal imitation, then, is that the subject and the answer together shall, while remaining basically in a single key, state both the tonic and dominant aspects of that key. (Historically speaking, the most likely reason for an imitating voice being at the fifth above or fourth below has to do with vocal range—sopranos and tenors sing comfortably approximately a fifth higher than do altos and basses.)

In Ex. 14–1 the subject begins by outlining I with its first three notes and continues until it settles on I at its conclusion (m. 48, third beat). In accordance with the second observation the sopranos answer with a transposition a fifth higher, implying dominant harmony. But for an exact transposition up a fifth the first note of the answer should have been 2, *e"*. It is changed to *d"* in accordance with the first observation—the note 5 is answered by the note 1. Due to this alteration of the first note the initial melodic interval of the answer is an inexact imitation. Because the distance from 1 upward to 5 is greater than that from 5 upward to 1, the answer has a slightly different shape from that of the subject. But because of this change the first note of the answer helps to express the main tonality of D major.

Consideration of the following fugue subjects and their answers gives rise to a third observation.

Example 14–2

a. BACH: *Art of the Fugue, Contrapunctus No. 1*
b. BACH: *Musical Offering, Ricercar à 3*

Both these subjects begin on 1. Therefore their transposition up a fifth or down a fourth, in accordance with observation two, automatically also complies with observation one. But in these cases there is a prominent 5 very near the initial 1. Observation three is:

A prominent 5 near the beginning of the subject is answered by 1, not by 2.

The reason for this again has to do with maintaining the chief tonality.[1] Were the opening fifth *d'–a'* of Example 14–2a to be answered by the fifth *a'–e"* the implication would be that of two different keys, rather than the tonic and dominant aspects of a single key. Similarly, in Ex. 14–2b, even though the fifth *c"–g"* is divided by the *e♭,"* the answer, to express the tonality of C minor, must be the fourth *g'–c"*.

TONAL IMITATION IN PRACTICE It is important to bear in mind that adjustments of a theme required by tonal imitation normally occur only at the beginning of the theme. Every 5 throughout the whole subject cannot be answered by 1 without resulting in some very unmusical answers. An examination of one of Bach's well-known fugue subjects will illustrate this. We shall observe the possibilities open to him and then what he actually did.

The tones 1 and 5 appear prominently several times in the subject (Ex. 14–3a). Two 5s occurring toward the end of the second bar are short passing notes, not prominent enough to take into account for the purpose of tonal imitation.

---

[1] Still, it has a history prior to the era of tonality and is rooted both in the overtone series with its direct influence on natural wind instruments and in the duality of authentic and plagal modes during the Middle Ages and the Renaissance.

Example 14–3

BACH: *WTC*, Vol. 1, *Fugue No. 2*

If Bach had transposed the subject to the upper fifth in an exact imitation, the answer would have been Ex. 14–3b. This answer takes into account the first and second observations but not the third. While 1 is answered with 5, 5 in this version is not answered with 1 but with 2. If, then, the prominent 5s are answered throughout with 1s, the result is Ex. 14–3c. A single playing will convince anyone that this version is unsatisfactory due to the change of the first note of the second bar from *d″* to *c″*. One of the intriguing elements in this seemingly innocent subject is what we might call an implied lower voice, consisting of a four-note descending scale fragment, one of whose notes falls on each strong beat. Thus in the subject, Ex. 14–3a, the *a♭′* in the first bar moves down to *g′*, the first note of the second bar, and thence to *f′* on the third beat, and *e♭′* on the next first beat. This pattern is an essential characteristic of the melody and should reappear in the answer as *e♭″*, *d″*, *c″* and *b♭′*. Bach therefore employs the tonal imitation only in the first part of the answer, where it destroys no essential characteristic of the subject, and continues with real imitation (Ex. 14–3d).

Sometimes a fugue subject is susceptible to more than one version of tonal imitation. The subject in Ex. 14–4 was answered by Buxtehude with a tonal imitation for the first note but a real imitation for the fourth. Bach, on the other hand, answers it tonally throughout.

Example 14–4

a. BUXTEHUDE: *Organ Fugue in E*
b. BACH: *Organ Fugue in E♭* (BWV 552)

THE REAL ANSWER If the subject does not stress the 5, the answer is a real imitation at the upper fifth or, essentially the same thing, at the lower fourth.

Example 14–5

BACH: *WTC, Vol. 1, Fugue No. 1*

SUBJECTS WITH THE SEVENTH SCALE DEGREE Transposed up a fifth, a 3 in the subject will be answered by 7 (see Ex. 14–2b). Theorists of the seventeenth and eighteenth centuries maintained that a 7 in the subject need not be answered by 4—a fifth above—but by 3. The practice of composers bears this out.

Example 14–6

BACH: *WTC, Vol. I, Fugue No. 19*

In Ex. 14–6 the first note of the subject, 1, is answered in a normal manner by 5. The second note, 7, is answered by 3. The second note of the subject leaps up a perfect fourth to the third note. This perfect fourth, being a characteristic feature of this melody, must be preserved in the answer. Therefore the third note of the answer is 6, not 7. But the remainder of the subject can be answered satisfactorily at the normal interval of the lower fourth. This example should be compared with the two excerpts given as Ex. 14–4. The first five notes of the subject of Ex. 14–4 is, transposed, the answer of Ex. 14–6, and vice versa.

Example 14–7

BUXTEHUDE: *Organ Fugue in E Minor*

In the minor mode, 7 is often raised to become the leading tone ♯7. In Ex. 14–7 the subject includes both the natural 7 and the raised ♯7. The corresponding notes of the answer are 3 and ♯3. These notes govern the remainder of the subject so that the last note 4 is not a fifth but a fourth higher than the original (expressed as a fifth lower). Similarly, in Ex. 14–8 the ♯7 which appears as the second note of the subject is answered by ♯3, a fourth rather than a fifth higher, and the remainder of the answer follows suit.

Example 14–8

BEETHOVEN: *Quartet, Op. 131*

In spite of the cases cited above and a number of other similar ones, a prominent 7 or ♯7 in the subject is not necessarily answered by 3 or ♯3. In his "Hammerklavier Sonata," for instance, Beethoven's fugue subject opens with a situation similar to that of Ex. 14–8. Yet his answer is not as in that example, but appears at the perfect fifth above throughout, with the one exception of the initial 5 answered by 1.

<mark>SUBJECT WITH A SECONDARY TONIC</mark> **Example 14–9**

BACH: *Magnificat, No. 11*

In this subject V is stressed to a marked degree by the vigorous upward drive from 1 to 5 in the first two bars, by the threefold repetition of this 5, and by the expression of V as a secondary tonic in the fourth bar.[2] We can anticipate that the answer will reflect this emphasis of the dominant by a corresponding emphasis of the tonic. If Bach had answered the subject entirely at the upper fifth, as in Ex. 14–10a, the emphasized scale degree would not have been the tonic but the supertonic. This situation could have been rectified by a substitution of 1 for 2, as in Ex. 14–10b, but this spoils the effect of the eighth notes rising energetically to their goal. Bach's solution (Ex. 14–10c) transposes only the first note to the upper fifth. Thus

---

[2] Many theorists call this secondary tonic on V a "modulation to V" and refer to this as a "modulating subject."

the initial 1 is answered regularly by an initial 5. The remainder of the melody is transposed to the upper fourth. Though such a solution delays the beginning of the ascent, the vitality of the second bar is not impaired. The rise from 1 to 5 in the subject is answered by a rise from 5 to 1, this 1 is now repeated three times, and the implied authentic cadence on V is answered by a similar cadence on I.

Example 14–10

BACH: *Magnificat, No. 11*

METHOD FOR ANSWERING A FUGUE SUBJECT

From the foregoing examination it is possible to arrive at a five-step method for constructing the answer to a fugue subject.

Step 1. Examine the subject and note whether it exhibits (a) an initial 5, (b) use of V as a secondary tonic (that is, ♯4–5), or (c) a conspicuous 7 or ♯7 near the beginning.

Step 2. If none of these conditions exists, one has merely to answer with real imitation: Transpose the subject a perfect fifth higher (or perfect fourth lower). Even though condition (c) above should exist, real imitation is nevertheless possible (see Bach, *WTC*, Vol. 1, *Fugue No. 4*).

Step 3. If condition (c) exists but real imitation is not desired, or if conditions (a) and/or (b) are present, it is necessary to note further in the subject any characteristic feature displayed, a feature that must be maintained.

Step 4. (a) Subjects with a prominent 5 near the beginning: Transpose the subject a perfect fifth higher, substituting in the answer a 1 for the initial 5. (b) Subjects with a secondary tonic on V: Do the same, but answer the ♯4–5 in the subject with 7–1 (or ♯7–1). (c) Subjects with prominent 7 or ♯7: If real imitation has not been employed, answer the 7 or ♯7 of the subject with 3 or ♯3.

Step 5. Now play or sing the result, observing whether any characteristic feature noted under step 3 has been destroyed in the answer. If the subject was a satisfactory melody and the answer is not, one can be certain that an important melodic characteristic has been destroyed. The final step, then, is to adjust the melody to restore this characteristic. Usually a subject exhibiting only condition (a) can be restored simply by reverting at some inconspicuous point (for instance, a weak beat or fraction of a beat) to real imitation at the fifth above. The characteristic feature of subjects exhibiting condition (b) can usually be restored by preceding the implied authentic cadence of the answer (7–1) with transposition at the fourth above.

An application of the various steps of the method for answering a fugue subject is given in Ex. 14–11. The subject chosen is unusual in that conditions (a), (b), and (c) are all present.

Example 14–11

BACH: *Mass in B Minor*

THE LENGTHY SUBJECT

Tonal imitation often makes it possible for the composer to begin his answer with tonic harmony even when that answer will later stress the dominant (see Ex. 14–1, Ex. 14–4b, Ex. 14–6). Thus too abrupt an establishment of a secondary tonic on V can be avoided. Very long fugue subjects, such as that of the "Little G Minor Fugue" for organ, are frequently answered by real rather than tonal imitation. In these cases since the answer does not enter until some time after the beginning of the piece, there is no necessity to postpone stress on dominant harmony.

EXERCISES

1. Copy all the fugue subjects in the Burkhart *Anthology* or *WTC*, Vol. 1, without glancing ahead at the answers. Following the five-step method just presented, construct answers to these subjects. Compare with Bach's answers and explain any differences.

2. Consider the two-voice fugue in E minor from *WTC*, Vol. I, (No. 10) (not in Burkhart). What features of the answer are unusual? Speculate as to the reasons for Bach's decision to write the answer in this way for this particular fugue.

14–D.
CONTRAPUNTAL DEVICES
COMMONLY OCCURRING IN FUGUE

In fugue the composer often employs any or several of the technical devices with which we are already familiar: augmentation, diminution, inversion (rarely retrograde, though Beethoven makes use of it in the fugue of his "Hammerklavier Sonata"). In addition two other devices regularly appear.

STRETTO We speak of stretto when the subject is presented in one voice and imitated in one or more additional voices, the imitation beginning before the original statement has run its course. It is thus made to overlap itself. Here is a stretto that occurs in the fugue of Ex. 14–4b.

Example 14–12

BACH: *Organ Fugue in E♮ Major* (BWV 552)

Sometimes the whole subject is used for stretto (*stretto maestrale*), sometimes only the first part. Stretto may occur at any time in the course of the fugue. It is particularly valuable, however, as a means of building up excitement and tension at some climactic point. The subject does not make its first appearance in stretto, although an exceptional case occurs in the *Fugue No. 4* of Bach's *WTC*, Vol. 2.

INVERTIBLE COUNTERPOINT Most fugues employ to a great extent a device known as *invertible counterpoint*. When two melodic lines exchange places so that the line which first appears in the lower position is put in the upper, the composer has *inverted* their positions. Invertible counterpoint involving two voices only is spoken of as double counterpoint.

Example 14–13

BEETHOVEN: *Grosse Fuge, Op. 133*

Triple counterpoint occurs when three different melodic lines exchange places. There are a few cases of quadruple and quintuple counterpoint, a famous example of the latter being in the Finale to Mozart's *Symphony No. 41.*

EXERCISE

3. Examine the following passages for technical contrapuntal devices:
   a. Bach, *Fugue No. 1* from *WTC*, mm. 14–20
   b. Bach, *Fugue No. 2* from *WTC*, comparing mm. 3–4 with 15–16; and comparing 17–18a with 5–6a and with 18b–19
   c. Bach, *Fugue No. 8* from *WTC*, mm. 77–82

14–E.
FUGAL PROCEDURE

Example 14–14

MARCHAND: *Organ Fugue in G Minor*

In Ex. 14–14, the four voices, making use of tonal imitation, enter singly in descending order: soprano, alto, tenor, bass (mm. 1–12). The original version of the subject alternates with that of the answer. As each completes its statement it continues with a counterpoint flowing against the new presentation of the theme. After the bass statement, the four voices continue for four bars (mm. 12–17), with no reference to the subject. The subject reappears in mm. 18–20 in the bass, and again in the tenor (mm. 21–24). Here the last three notes are augmented to cover two bars rather than a single one. The theme is absent from mm. 25–28, enters as answer in the soprano voice in mm. 29–31, and is absent from the final bars of the fugue. Twice it is shortened: in the first bass entrance the theme is diverted a half bar before its conclusion (m. 12), and in the final entrance it is diverted three quarters of a bar before (m. 31). It is to be noted that the passages in which the theme does not appear (mm. 12–17; mm. 25–28; mm. 31–37) are, by virtue of the chains of suspensions they contain, motivically related to each other but not to the theme. Having the nature of digressions from the subject, they are called episodes. Passages that present, or "expose," the theme are called expositions. Thus, in this fugue the first exposition (mm. 1–12) comprises an entrance of the theme in each of the four voices (subject-answer-subject-answer). Relief from the theme is afforded by episode 1 (mm. 12–17) after which exposition II presents, in bass and tenor, two appearances of the theme, both subjects. Episode 2 (mm. 25–28), recalling episode 1, affords a few bars' digression, following which is exposition III, a single entrance of the answer in the soprano. Episode 3 brings the fugue to a close.

Before attempting to draw any general conclusions from this single short composition, let us consider one of the fugues of J. S. Bach. The first twelve bars appear as Ex. 14–15, the entire fugue being included in Burkhart's *Anthology of Musical Forms*.

Example 14–15

BACH: *WTC*, Vol. 1, *Fugue No. 16*

The theme of the fugue is clearly made up of two motives, marked a and b, which are separated by a rest. It appears as subject low in the alto voice and is imitated tonally by an answer in the soprano. During the soprano's statement the alto continues with a counterpoint against it. This counterpoint is ingeniously devised from inversion of the two motives of the theme (Bach chooses the answer for the inversion), which are placed in reverse order. A perusal of the rest of the fugue will show that when the subject appears it is nearly always accompanied by this same counterpoint. The counterpoint, then, is spoken of as the *countersubject* of the fugue. Sometimes it appears beneath the subject, sometimes above it; that is, it is composed in double counterpoint.

One might expect the third entry of the subject to follow immediately after the entry of the answer in the soprano, but instead we find a one-bar episode treating motive b in sequence. Only in m. 5 is the subject heard in the bass, followed in mm. 6–7 by the tenor answer. Although an episode intervenes between the first pair of subject entries (subject and answer) and the second pair, the four first entries taken together are considered to comprise a single exposition. Later on in the fugue only those entries not separated by episodes group themselves into a single exposition. Exposition I leads into the second episode which, like episode 1, is based on motive b. This episode is much longer than the first, covering four bars (mm. 8–12) rather than a single one. Although motive b is derived from the subject, as used here it offers a certain amount of contrast by reason of the absence of motive a and the new countermelody in the uppermost voice. The episode leads to a cadence on the first beat of m. 12, at which point the alto begins a new exposition. This second exposition contains five entries of the theme, the last two occurring in stretto. Episode 3 (m. 19) is again based on motive b and like episode 1 is only a single bar in length. Exposition III (mm. 20–24) contains three entries of the subject. Episode 4 corresponds to episode 2 in length and in the use of the new countermelody against motive b. This melody is now used in both upper voices. Exposition IV is very short (mm. 28–29) but by means of stretto squeezes in two complete statements of the subject in the soprano and tenor, plus motive a in the bass. Episode 5 (mm. 29–31) uses only motive b. Exposition V (mm. 31–34) closes the fugue with two statements of the subject. In the last two bars the alto voice divides to provide a climactic close in five voices.

271

A comparison of this fugue with Ex. 14–14 will show some similarities and some differences:

Comparative Observations		*Fugue in G Minor* *by Marchand*	*Fugue in G Minor* *by Bach*
Exposition I		1. Order of entry: S-A-T-B.	1. Order of entry: A-S-B-T.
		2. Each entry follows immediately after previous entry.	2. Episode separates entries into two pairs.
		3. Subject and answer versions of the theme alternate.	3. Same.
Later expositions		4. No standard arrangement of subject and answer versions.	4. Same.
		5. No fixed number of entries.	5. Same.
		6. Sometimes entire theme is not stated, final notes being diverted.	6. Same. In addition, in m. 23 the first note of the subject is halved in its rhythmic value.
Episodes		7. Only new material is employed.	7. Without sacrificing their value as relief from the subject, episodes are motivically related to it.
		8. Episodes related to each other.	8. Same.
Over all		9. Except for mm. 19–20, once the four voices have entered, they all continue steadfastly to the end. Final chord in five voices.	9. Only in a few passages do all four voices sound at once. Most of the time one of them is silent. Final entry (last two bars) in five voices.
		10. The piece consists of three expositions and three episodes, ending with an episode.	10. The piece consists of five expositions and five episodes, ending with an exposition.
		11. Virtually no use made of any special contrapuntal devices.	11. Relies heavily on inversion, double counterpoint, and stretto.
		12. Each statement of theme accompanied by new and different counterpoint.	12. Theme regularly accompanied by the countersubject.

These are, of course, only two examples chosen from the hundreds of tonal fugues in existence. An examination of a large number of them would certainly reveal the use of still other procedures. Generally speaking, however, the chief methods involved in the construction of a fugue are included in one or the other of the two fugues we have examined. Nevertheless, the following comments on the table of Comparative Observations should be made.

1. Regarding No. 1, an examination of a great number of fugues reveals no preferred order of entry for the voices. One point needs to be made, however: If a "high" voice (soprano or tenor) begins, then it is a "low" voice (alto or bass) which will answer, and vice versa.

2. Regarding No. 3, exceptions occur from time to time (for example, *Nos. 1* and *14* in *WTC*).

3. Regarding No. 10, fugues have been written without episodes (for example, *No. 1* in *WTC*).

4. Regarding No. 11, some fugues use the additional devices of augmentation and/or diminution (*No. 8* in *WTC*). Not infrequently certain entries of the theme are inverted (*Nos. 8* and *23* in *WTC*).

EXERCISE

4. Make a summary outline of the procedure of Fugue No. 13 in F♯ Major, from *WTC*.

14–F.
THE FORM OF A FUGUE

Our examination of the fugue has begun by investigation of the procedure customarily associated with the genre. This serves as an introduction to the study of the form of the fugue. Both tonal structure and design have to be taken into account before a conclusion regarding form can be reached. It is time to reconsider these fugues, first as tonal structures, then as designs.

TONAL STRUCTURE

Very striking in the fugue of Ex. 14–14 is the absence until the last bar of any definite cadence. The final note of each phrase coincides by elided cadence with the first note of the next (first beats of mm. 4, 7, 10, 12, and so on) so that the piece seems to move with an uninterrupted flow. Expected cadences, as in m. 28, are diverted before being completed.

Each statement of the subject and answer expresses G minor by means of i and V. A possible exception is the tenor entrance in m. 21, which, by means of the B♮ in the bass, seems to be leading to iv in its opening bars. But it does not fail to make a quick return to i (mm. 24–25). Nor do the episodes provide relief from this insistence on the home key.

The tonal structure, with its alternations of i and V, devoid of obvious cadential goals, comprises an extended prolongation of i followed by the final full authentic cadence iv V i (mm. 34–37). This fugue, like most others prior to those of Bach and Handel, does not transpose the theme to other pitches than those used for the initial subject and answer.[3]

The tonal structure of the composition, then, is restricted to an essential alternation between i and V.

[3] See, for instance, the organ fugues of Buxtehude or those in the organ masses of François Couperin; also the fugue by J. C. F. Fischer in Schering's *Geschichte der Musik in Beispielen* (No. 265) and that by J. Christoph Bach in Karl Geiringer, *Music of the Bach Family*. Cambridge, Mass.: Harvard University Press, 1955, pp. 34–35.

In Bach's fugue quite another situation prevails. Episode 2, following the prolonged i of the first exposition, moves into the region of the mediant key (III) and closes there with a perfect authentic cadence. Exposition II expresses III and V/III. The ensuing episode moves to the subdominant and the first two entries of exposition III dwell on iv. The third entry of this exposition returns to i and comes to a perfect authentic cadence in m. 24 on i. The remainder of the fugue (episode 4, exposition IV, episode 5, and exposition V) maintains this i and closes with another full authentic cadence. The over-all harmonic movement can be summarized as:

$$i \rightarrow \quad \underbrace{\frac{\text{ii V I}}{\text{of III}}} \quad \rightarrow iv \rightarrow ii° \text{ V i} \rightarrow ii° \text{ V i}$$

EXERCISE

5. Examine Fugue No. 13 in F sharp major from *WTC* from the harmonic point of view:
    a. Consider the expositions and episodes individually, noting which chord or chords is essentially expressed by each.
    b. Compare the relative strengths of the cadences, taking note of any strongly divisive cadence. (*Note*: this particular fugue has so many authentic cadences in such a short period of time, that their divisive qualities are questionable. Thus, the factor of the *breadth* of a cadence, as described on page 9, must be considered when judging the relative strengths of the cadences.)
    c. Note the point at which the final perfect authentic cadence takes place. Is there a coda?
    d. Make a summary of the tonal structure.

DESIGN   The episodes of Marchand's fugue cannot be said to afford any striking contrast to the expositions. In no fugue, for that matter, is any great contrast, such as often occurs between the first and second parts of a ternary form, to be looked for. The episode of a fugue rarely initiates a new mood or emotional quality, or still less a change of basic rhythmic structure or tempo. The contrast it provides is usually a lightening of the texture by restricting itself to fewer voices, and omission of references to the fugue theme or at least to its opening motive. Far-reaching contrasts are contrary to the continuously flowing, unified nature typical of fugal style.

It will be remembered that a composition divides itself into parts either by completion of more than one harmonic movement or by certain divisive factors in design, such as perfect authentic cadences, or strong contrasts in character (see Chapter 6). Since most fugues do not exhibit such contrasts, the usual basis for division into parts would seem to be completion of more than one harmonic movement or the divisive effect of the perfect authentic cadence. Marchand's fugue, possessing neither of these criteria is, then, a one-part form with the design ABA'B'A"B". In this scheme, A stands for the expositions and B for the episodes.

Bach's fugue, on the other hand, is divisible on two accounts. First, two harmonic movements are completed during the course of the fugue, the first at the perfect authentic cadence on i in m. 24, the second at the end of the fugue. In addition, there is an emphatic perfect authentic cadence on III in mm. 11–12. The fugue, then, is in three parts, in an "arched" design.

Part One				Part Two			Part Three			
Ex. I	Ep. 1	Ex. I (cont.)	Ep. 2	Ex. II	Ep. 3	Ex. III	Ep. 4	Ex. IV	Ep. 5	Ex. V
A	B	A	C	A'	B'	A"	C'	A'"	B"	A""
			ii V I of III	III → iv ii° V i			i → ii° V i			

(i ————→)

The presence of the diverse authentic cadences does not necessarily inhibit the continuity which seems to be a genuine and regular feature of fugal style. Measure 12 of Ex. 14–15 reveals that the final chord of part one is not released before part two begins. The continuity is even more marked at the point where parts two and three meet.

Example 14–16

BACH: *WTC, Vol. 1, Fugue No. 16*

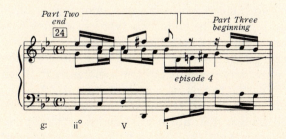

EXERCISES

6. Examine the fugue of the preceding exercises from the point of view of design:
   a. Compare and relate the expositions to each other.
   b. Compare and relate the episodes to each other.
   c. Compare and relate the expositions with the episodes.
   d. By the use of letters, make a symbolic representation of the design.

7. Using information arrived at by the foregoing exercises, make a chart (similar to that in Section 14–G) representing the form, procedure, design, and tonal structure of the fugue presently under examination.

8. Make a complete analysis (procedure, tonal structure, design, form) of the Fugue No. 2 in C Minor from *WTC*.

14–G.
SPECIAL TYPES OF FUGUE

FUGUE IN CONTRARY MOTION
Many fugues make use of the possibility of inversion at various desirable points in their course. A fugue that makes systematic use of inversion is referred to as a *fugue in contrary motion* or *counterfugue*. In this case the answer appears from the start as an inversion of the subject and this inversion recurs during the course of the fugue.

Example 14–17

BRAHMS: *Fugue in A flat Minor for Organ*

DOUBLE FUGUE
Fugues based on two subjects which at some point appear simultaneously are called double fugues. There are two types of double fugue. In the ordinary type the subjects are associated with each other throughout the fugue, appearing together from the start and continuing together much as the subject of an ordinary fugue is often associated with its countersubject. Bach was not partial to this type of double fugue, though one of his most famous compositions, the *Passacaglia*, includes one in its final portion. It was used a great deal during the eighteenth century by Italian composers and also by Haydn and Mozart. The *Kyrie* of Mozart's *Requiem*

Mass in D Minor is a famous example. The two subjects are always well contrasted in character and rarely begin exactly together. The theme that begins first is labeled subject I, the one entering later is called subject II.

Example 14–18

MOZART: *Fantasy for Mechanical Organ, K. 608*

The other type of double fugue presents the first subject alone before combining it with the second in a simultaneous statement. Thus the first section is a short fugue on subject I, with one or more expositions and episodes. A fugue on subject II follows which may combine the two themes. Or this second section may be devoted exclusively to subject II in which case a third section presents the two themes simultaneously.

This larger type of double fugue occurs in the works of certain of J. S. Bach's predecessors and contemporaries, such as Luigi Battiferri and Gottlieb Muffat. Nevertheless, it can be called the "Bachian type" in that examples by great composers other than J. S. Bach are rare. Exceptional cases are Schumann's *Op. 60, No. 6*, and Reger's *Op. 85, No. 4*. A few of Bach's numerous double fugues of this type are *No. 14* and *No. 18* in Vol. 2 of *WTC*, the *Toccata and Fugue in F Major* for organ, and the first part of the *Confiteor* from the *Mass in B Minor*. The organ "fughetta" *Allein Gott in der Höh'* is an interesting case in miniature.

TRIPLE FUGUE We have seen that Beethoven uses triple fugue in the development section of his *Symphony No. 9*, First Movement (Ex. 11–14) and it occurs in part two (mm. 146 ff) of the *Scherzo* of his *Quartet, Op. 18, No. 4*. Both of these illustrate the use of fugal procedures within a movement in sonata form. Triple fugues that comprise entire movements in themselves are so seldom found that we can scarcely speak of any preferred procedure. We are limited instead to description of a few specific cases.

Since the ordinary double fugue begins with a simultaneous statement of the two subjects, one might expect a triple fugue to begin with a combined statement of its three subjects. The portions cited from Beethoven's sonata forms begin in this way, and the triple fugue in the *Concerto for Four Violins* by Leonardo Leo follows a similar procedure. Yet a triple fugue of this type is not to be found among Bach's pieces expressly called fugues. Still, he did write one; it occupies a place in Vol. 1 of his *Well-Tempered Clavier*—not among the fugues but among the preludes! *Prelude No. 19 in A major* turns out on examination to be a triple fugue with the three subjects stated together from the outset (the first note in the bass is to be disregarded).

Example 14–19

BACH: *WTC, Prelude No. 19*

The procedure and form of this fugue can be outlined as follows:

Bars	1–12				12–14	14–24		
Procedure	Exp. I	Episode 1	Exp. I (cont.)	Episode 2	Exp. II	Episode 3	Exp. III	Episode 4
Design*	A	B	A	C	A	B C	A	C′
Tonal Structure	I ⟶			ii⁷ V i vi	i V i vi	⟶ I ⟶		⟶ V I
Form	Part One				Part Two	Part Three		

* In the representation of the design, A indicates the whole complex of the three subjects.

Bach's *Art of the Fugue* contains two triple fugues, *Contrapunctus No. 8* in three voices and *Contrapunctus No. 11* in four. Both of these comprise several parts, and in each case part one presents the aspect of a complete simple fugue on a single subject, the other subjects being kept in reserve for later appearances. Aside from this initial similarity the forms and procedures of the two fugues, *Nos. 8* and *11*, are very different. Part two of *No. 8* begins as a double fugue on subject I—the theme of part one—combined with a new theme, subject II (m. 39). After five expositions and four episodes this double fugue comes to a half cadence, and subject III (a rhythmic variant of the main theme that runs through the whole volume) enters with an exposition of its own (mm. 94–109). A rather long episode which makes use of fragments of subjects I and II brings part two to a close (m. 124). Thus in neither of the first two parts have the three themes been brought together, though subjects I and II have combined a number of times. Bach postpones the simultaneous presentation of the three subjects until he can do so as a kind of climax to the whole fugue. Even part three does not state them together at first. It begins with subjects I and II combined in a rhythmic position different from that in which they previously appeared together. After two expositions of these subjects and two episodes the three subjects are combined (m. 147) and from this point on they keep constant company, even though the fugue contains four more expositions and three episodes. The effect of the three subjects is therefore cumulative: in part one of the fugue, subject I appears alone, but in part two it is joined by subject II, and the two themes are thereafter inseparable. Toward the end of part two, subject III (the main theme of the entire work) appears alone, and after observing, as it were, the other two themes from a distance, decides to join them.

In *Contrapunctus No. 11* subjects I, II, and III are the inversions of subjects III, I, and II, respectively, of *No. 8*. Part one is a simple fugue of two expositions and one episode (mm. 1–27). Part two (mm. 27–71) is another simple fugue on subject II which is here constantly accompanied by a fragment of a chromatic scale as countersubject. Part three (mm. 71–89) is comparatively short, comprising a single exposition (four entries) of the inversion of subject I (this inversion of an inversion returns the theme to the position it had in *Contrapunctus No. 8*). Part four (mm. 89–129) is made up of several entries of the three subjects. While II and III appear together, the combination of the three is reserved for part five, but as in *No. 8*, the combination does not appear until this part is well under way (m. 145). An episode based on subject III follows (mm. 150–158) after which Bach makes clear his reason for devoting part three to an exposition of the inversion of subject I. He was preparing the listener for the presentation of this theme simultaneously with its own inversion (mm. 158–162; mm. 164–168). After another episode, the final exposition of the fugue brings two more statements of the three combined subjects (mm. 174–184).

It would seem that the simultaneous presentation of the three subjects at some point in its course is requisite to the triple fugue. Certain theorists, at least, deny the label to Bach's *Organ Fugue in E♭ Major* ("St. Anne"), even though it possesses three subjects, each with expositions of its own. In part two subject I appears with subject II, in part three with subject III, but all themes are never stated together. For this reason it has been suggested that this fugue be considered a "double fugue with three subjects."[4]

FUGUES WITH UNCERTAIN CLASSIFICATIONS Some fugues are difficult to classify with certainty. If a subject is accompanied throughout the fugue with a distinctive countersubject, might not that countersubject be considered in essence a second subject? Thus, in *Fugue No. 2* of *WTC*, Vol. 1, once the second voice has entered, the countersubject appears constantly in the company of the subject. According to some this should be considered a kind of double fugue, and so should a number of other seemingly simple fugues. Similarly, some which might be classed as double fugues are considered by certain theorists, because of a recurring countersubject, to be triple fugues (for example, the final section of the organ *Passacaglia*).

It would seem best, however, not to regard a consistently recurring countersubject as a second or third subject. In a double fugue the listener is forcibly made aware of the presence of subject II—in the ordinary type because it appears from the beginning along with subject I, and in the Bachian type because it is first presented alone in a new fugal exposition. A countersubject, on the other hand, is first heard along with a later entry of the subject and is, for this reason, partially obscured. It is never given an exposition of its own. If the composer expects the listener to recognize a melody as the subject of a piece, he must present it in such a way that the alert listener cannot fail to grasp its significance.

QUADRUPLE AND QUINTUPLE FUGUES Fugues using more than three subjects are almost nonexistent. The Finale of Haydn's *Quartet, Op. 20, No. 2*, called "Fuga a IV Soggetti," offers a unique case among the works of the great composers. It also provides examples of genuine quadruple counterpoint. The final piece of the *Art of the Fugue* was to have been a quadruple fugue. Bach, however, did not live to complete it and the piece breaks off before the entry of the fourth subject.[5] A single example of quintuple fugue exists in the works of the great composers—this is the celebrated fugal coda in the Finale of Mozart's *Symphony No. 41 in C Major*.

OTHER FUGUE TYPES Bach's last work, *The Art of the Fugue*, being a demonstration of the various forms and techniques of fugue writing, includes a number of

---

[4] Kent Kennan, *Counterpoint*. Englewood Cliffs, N.J.: Prentice-Hall, 1972, p. 241.

[5] For a thorough account of attempts to complete this fugue, see: Walter Kolneder, *Die Kunst der Fugue: Mythen des 20. Jahrhunderts*, Wilhelmshaven, 1977, pp. 301–327.

fugue types that are very rarely met with in other musical literature. A brief statement of the contents of this work will act as a summary of the fugue types described and add a few others not previously mentioned. It should be pointed out that Bach uses a single theme as the basis for all fourteen fugues of the work, this theme appearing in many interestingly varied forms.[6] He added new themes when necessary for those fugues based on more than one subject, and some of these new themes appear in more than one fugue. All fugues except *Nos. 8* and *12* are in four voices. Although Bach did not specifically state what instrumentation he had in mind, all evidence points to the harpsichord as the appropriate medium.

Group I. Simple Fugues.
1. Simple fugue with episodes making use of new material.
2. The same with dotted rhythms.
3. Simple fugue on the inversion of the subject.
4. Simple fugue on the inversion of the subject with episodes derived from the subject.

Group II. Fugues in Contrary Motion.
5. The answer is the inversion of the subject.
6. The answer is the inversion in diminution of the subject.
7. The subject is the diminution of the main subject of the whole work; the first answer is the inversion of the main subject; the second answer is the inversion in diminution; the third answer is the inversion in augmentation.

Group III. Multiple Fugues.
8. Triple fugue on main subject and two new subjects.
9. Double fugue on main subject in augmentation and a new subject.
10. Double fugue on main subject in inversion and a new subject.
11. Triple fugue on subjects of No. 8 in inversion.

Group IV. Invertible Fugues. (An invertible fugue is one which can be played either as written—"rectus"—or with all parts simultaneously exchanged and inverted—"inversus.")
12. Invertible fugue in three voices: in "inversus" the alto becomes the soprano, the bass becomes the alto, the soprano becomes the bass, and the whole is inverted.
13. Invertible fugue in four voices: in "inversus" the bass becomes the soprano, the tenor becomes the alto, the alto becomes the tenor, the soprano becomes the bass, and the whole is inverted. The effect of this fugue is as

---

[6] In addition to the fugues Bach composed four canons based on variants of the main theme.

if "inversus" were a reflection of "rectus" in a mirror. It is usually referred to as a mirror fugue.

Example 14–20

BACH: *Art of the Fugue, Contrapunctus No. 18*

Group V. Quadruple Fugues.

14. Quadruple fugue on three new subjects, the third beginning B-A-C-H (that is, B♭, A, C, B♮ in German), and the main theme. Left unfinished by Bach at his death.

15. There is good reason to believe that Bach's original intention was to add still another fugue to the work. This was to be an invertible ("mirror") quadruple fugue. To prove the possibility of such a fugue, Tovey composed one using two new subjects, the main theme, and B-A-C-H.

EXERCISE

9. Examine some or all of the fugues in Bach's *Art of the Fugue*, particularly those of Groups II and III.

14–H.
THE VOCAL FUGUE

A fugue for voices does not proceed in a manner basically different from an instrumental fugue. The great choral fugues which appear in the sacred works of the eighteenth and nineteenth centuries are, however, provided with a more or less independent orchestral accompaniment—"more or less" because often a seemingly independent orchestral melody turns out on examination to be only an ornamented version of one of the vocal parts.

In the choral fugue the orchestra often provides quite a full independent accompaniment in the beginning section of the fugue, where the choral texture contains first only one, then two, then three voices. After all the voices have entered and the choral texture accordingly becomes more complicated, the orchestral accompaniment tends to be less so, providing, say, an ornamented bass line and contenting itself with little more than a mere doubling of the voice parts.

Occasionally the initial statements of the fugue subject are accompanied not only by the orchestra but by outbursts from the other voices of the chorus (for example, *Patrem Omnipotentem* from *Mass in B Minor* of J. S. Bach).

EXERCISE

10. Analyze the Kyrie from Mozart's *Requiem*, K. 626.

14–I.
THE INVENTION

The thirty short keyboard pieces of J. S. Bach which we refer to today as the *Two-* and *Three-Part Inventions*[7] are similar in some ways to the fugue.

1. Both are polyphonic compositions with a consistent number of "voices" or parts.
2. Both are based on a single theme, normally stated at the outset by each voice in succession,[8] and reappearing at intervals throughout the piece.
3. Both are founded on imitative counterpoint and frequently use tonal as well as real imitation.
4. Both make frequent use of contrapuntal devices such as inversion and double or triple counterpoint.
5. Both are contrapuntal procedures rather than forms.

The chief differences between the invention and the fugue are as follows.

1. The fugue subject is answered at the fifth above (or fourth below); the invention subject is answered either in this way or at the octave.

[7] Bach called those in two parts *Praeambula* or *Invenzioni*; those in three parts *Fantasias* or *Sinfonie*.

[8] Exceptions are No. 2 and 5 of the *Three-Part Inventions*.

2. In fugue, except for those intended for ensembles, the initial statements of the subject are unaccompanied; in the three-part inventions, and usually in the two-part inventions, these statements are accompanied by a counterpoint in the lowest voice.
3. Very short themes, hardly more than motives, are more common in the inventions than in fugues. These motivelike subjects are generally heard in almost every bar of the invention.
4. The fugue is an instrumental or vocal genre; the invention is for a keyboard instrument.

Bach used the idea of the invention for other compositions. The four duets from Part III of the *Clavierübung* and the *Prelude No. 13* from *WTC*, Vol. 1 are two-part inventions. The three movements of *Organ Sonata No. 1* are very much like three-part inventions.

EXERCISE

11. Analyze Bach's *Inventions No. 1* and *No. 15*.

14–J.
THE FRENCH OVERTURE

During the seventeenth century the Venetian opera was distinguished by a certain type of overture consisting of two parts, a slow part followed by a fast one. This overture became the model on which Lully based the overtures to his operas written for the entertainment of the French royalty in the latter part of the seventeenth century, and it is therefore referred to as a French overture. In Lully's overtures the slow part is characterized by dotted rhythms giving the effect of pompous solemnity. The fast part begins with imitation in the various voices, a partially fugal texture rather than a real fugue. Often this movement broadens out toward the end in an *allargando*.

Many eighteenth-century composers continued to write French overtures, both as introductions to their operas and oratorios and as the first movement of instrumental suites. Virtually all of Handel's operas and oratorios, for example, open with a French overture, that to *Messiah* being, no doubt, the most frequently performed. Bach, too, though he wrote no operas and no real oratorios, composed French overtures, among which the opening of his *Suite in B Minor for Flute and Strings*[9] is a celebrated example.

---

[9] In eighteenth-century terminology suites that begin with a French overture are called simply "overtures," though in reality they are overtures followed by a series of dances.

Outline Summary of Bach's Suite No. 2, Overture, Fugal Movement

Bars	21–55	55–78	78–94
Procedure (concerto aspect)	RI	S1	R2
Procedure (fugal aspect)	Ex. I Ep. (4 entries) Ex. II Ep. (1 entry)	First solo episode	Ex. III Ep. (2 entries)
Design	A	B	A
Tonal Structure	i → V i	i → III	III
Form	Part One	Part Two	

Bars	94–102	102–119	119–143	143–151	151–174	175–198
Procedure (concerto aspect)	S2	R3	S3 (with tutti interjections at mm. 127 and 137)	R4	S4	R5
Procedure (fugal aspect)	Second solo episode	Ex. IV (4 entries)	Third solo episode (with tutti interjections at mm. 127 and 137)	Ex. V (1 entry, altered)	Fourth solo episode	Ex. VI Ep. (1 entry) Ex. VII Ep. 1 entry)
Design	C	A	B' (A)	A'	C	A
Tonal Structure	III → V/iv	iv → i	i → V/iv	iv → V	i → V$^6_5$ i	(deceptive cadence in m. 186) i → V^7 V$^4_2$/iv iv^6 → V i
Form	Part Three					

By the eighteenth century fugal procedures had reached a higher stage of development than in the seventeenth century, and we find the fast part of the French overture taking on more and more the appearance of a true fugue. The

Overture to *Messiah*, for instance, contains a genuine Handelian fugue. He continues the seventeenth-century practice of broadening the final few bars to prepare the movement for its close. Some composers during the eighteenth century made this *allargando* at the end of the fugal portion much larger, producing the effect of a second slow movement. This practice has given rise to the opinion that the French overture has three movements: slow, fast, slow. In actuality this final slow part does not appear often enough to justify such a view, although Bach used the idea in his *Suite for Flute and Strings*.

The fugal portion of this suite deserves some discussion, for it presents an interesting case of the form of a composition being influenced by its medium. The fact that Bach used a single flute with a body of strings suggests at once that he probably designed it as a showpiece of some kind for the flute. The music bears this out. While the opening slow movement of the overture, a continuous binary form using Lully's dotted rhythms, lets the flute double the first violins, the fugal portion is constructed to show the flute off to best advantage. Naturally the weak tone of a flute could not hope to hold its own as one of the voices in a fugue against a body of strings. Therefore Bach designed this portion to be a cross between a fugue and a *concerto grosso*. The fugal expositions are entrusted to the orchestral ritornellos as are some of the episodes. Other episodes are given to the solo sections. The third solo section is twice interrupted by tutti interjections which refer to the fugue subject but do not present it in its entirety as full-fledged entries. These interjections may have been provided by Bach for physical as well as musical reasons, for they give the struggling flutist a sorely needed chance to breathe.

14–K.
THE CHORALE PRELUDE

The chorale prelude is simply a sacred melody arranged to be played, usually on the organ, rather than to be sung. For Catholic services this tune is either a plainsong hymn or a segment of some other plainsong melody. For Protestant services it is a chorale, usually one of the German chorales of the Lutheran Church. Its place in the Protestant service was originally to precede the actual singing of the hymn, hence its familiar name chorale prelude, although it was sometimes also performed after the hymn or between stanzas. Today such compositions are performed independently of congregational singing.

The chorale prelude bears the following resemblances to the fugue:

1. It is normally a polyphonic composition with a consistent number of "voices," usually four, not infrequently two, three, or five, occasionally six.

2. Imitative counterpoint (real imitation, tonal imitation, canon) plays an important role.

3. It is not a form; any chorale prelude may exhibit one of the standard forms or have a unique form of its own.

The chief types of chorale prelude are listed below.

1. *Simple chorale prelude.* In this type of setting the chorale is presented in one of the voices, not necessarily the soprano, and surrounded or supported by the others. These accompanying voices are almost always motivic, that is, based on one or two motives which recur by means of repetition, sequence, and imitation. The chief motive or motives on which the accompaniment is based may be either derived from the chorale or newly invented.

2. *Chorale prelude with ritornellos.* The idea of a regular recurring passage, familiar to us from the Baroque aria and concerto, also found a place in the organ chorale prelude. The piece begins with a ritornello, either contrapuntal in texture or not, and the successive phrase or phrase members of the chorale are separated by its return. Very often the melody of the ritornello, or motives derived from it, appears as accompaniment against the chorale tune.

3. *Chorale prelude with prelude and interludes.* The various phrases of the chorale may be preceded and separated not by a recurrence of the same material, as in the ritornello, but by different material. In this case the intervening sections are almost sure to be derived in one way or another from the chorale melody. Brahms provides some interesting organ chorale preludes of this type (*Op. 122, Nos. 4, 7, 10, 11*).

4. *Chorale prelude with fugal expositions* (*the chorale motet*). The technique of this type is similar to the vocal motet technique of the sixteenth century, one of the forerunners of the fugue. The first phrase of the chorale serves as the subject for a short fugal exposition. Sometimes all voices participate in this exposition. Usually, however, one voice is reserved to present the phrase intact as the last entrance. A second exposition, treating the second phrase similarly, follows, and so on through all phrases of the chorale. Often the theme of each fugal exposition is a variant rather than the original form of the chorale melody (for example, Brahms, *Op. 122, No. 1*).

5. *Chorale fugue.* Sometimes rather than using the whole melody, the opening notes of the chorale are chosen as the subject for a fugue or *fughetta* (a "little fugue").

6. *Groups of organ chorale preludes.* Not infrequently two or three settings of a single chorale are grouped together, usually marked Verse 1, Verse 2, and so on. Often in these cases each setting reflects the text of a particular stanza. When a larger number of settings of a single chorale are grouped

together, they are generally entitled *chorale variations* or *chorale partita*. In this case, too, the suggestion for each successive variation normally comes from the text.

One of Bach's final works was a set of *Canonic Variations on a Christmas Song*. It consists of five chorale preludes on *Von Himmel Hoch*, each demonstrating a different type of canonic writing.

7. *The Vocal Chorale*. The technique of the organ chorale prelude also occurs in vocal music, especially in the great choruses of Bach's cantatas and passions. Sometimes while the chorale is sung by the chorus, either in unison or four parts, the orchestra is given an elaborate, independent accompaniment. A unique example of this type of vocal chorale prelude is found in the Finale to Act II of Mozart's *Magic Flute*. Using an old German hymn tune, *Ach Gott, vom Himmel sieh' darein*, to which he added a final phrase, Mozart gives the tune to two men in armor who sing it (with new words) in octaves. Against this the orchestra plays an accompaniment based on two motives, also providing ritornellos between phrases. This type of vocal chorale is analogous to the organ chorale prelude with ritornellos.

EXERCISES

12. Examine, classify, and analyze the following organ chorale preludes by Bach:
   a. Bach, *Jesu, meine Freude* (compare with chorale in Appendix)
   b. *Wenn wir in höchsten Nöten sein*
   c. *Vor deinen Tron tret' ich hiermit*

13. How are the three lower voices of *Wenn wir in höchsten Nöten sein* related to those of *Vor deinen Tron tret' ich hiermit*? (Compare, for instance, mm. 8–10 of the latter with 1–3 of the former.)

14–L.
SUMMARY

Due to the variety of forms exhibited by the fugues of the great composers of the tonal era, the fugue cannot be considered a form at all. It is, rather, a musical genre for instruments, voices, or both, with the following characteristics:

1. It comprises a constant number of melodic lines, referred to as "voices" or "parts," which state and develop a theme by contrapuntal imitation.

2. The theme, or subject, is imitated either by real or by tonal imitation. The imitation, called the answer, has in the latter case a different melodic contour

from the original subject, especially in the opening notes. Both versions of the theme are apt to be used throughout the fugue.

3. Often, particularly as the fugue is nearing its close, the imitating voices begin before the preceding statement of the theme has been completed. The result, an overlapping of the theme upon itself, is termed stretto. Other contrapuntal devices frequently occurring are inversion, double, and triple counterpoint.

4. Occasionally fugues are written in which the theme is constantly sounding in at least one of the voices. But most fugues make use of episodes—passages from which the theme is absent.

Special types of fugue include (1) the fugue by contrary motion, (2) the double fugue, and (3) the triple fugue. Of these the double fugue is by far the most frequently found. Ordinarily Bach gives each of the two subjects of his double fugues an exposition of its own before combining them in a simultaneous statement. Other composers, such as Handel and Mozart, present the two subjects together from the start.

There are several musical genres that are more or less closely related to the fugue. The invention presents and develops a single subject by imitative counterpoint, often using tonal imitation. The French overture includes a fugal movement within its over-all movement scheme. The chorale prelude depends largely on imitative counterpoint, maintains a consistent number of melodic lines, and often includes fuguelike expositions by tonal imitation.

15

UNIQUE
FORMS

HISTORICAL NOTE ON UNIQUE FORMS Unique forms are commonly found in every era of music history. Baroque genres in which they frequently occur are fantasias and toccatas for organ or harpsichord. During the Rococo and Classical periods they were particularly common in keyboard fantasias, such as those by C. P. E. Bach and Mozart. Much music of the nineteenth century displays nonstandard forms, including the many program symphonies, opera preludes, and symphonic poems that appear so regularly on our concert programs. For instance, each movement of Berlioz' *Symphonie Fantastique* except the second is unique in form. And opera, oratorio, and other vocal music abound in such unique forms. Of particular interest are the unique composite forms of the lengthy finales to the individual acts of a Classical opera.

While many composers of the first half of this century have tended to rely heavily on standard forms of the past (Ravel, Hindemith, Berg, Bartók, Prokofiev), the trend in recent years, among composers of the greatest variance in styles, is toward the creation of compositions that display formal singularity.

15–A.
STANDARD AND UNIQUE FORMS

In expressing his musical thoughts the composer is free to make use of pre-existing forms or to invent new ones. In addition, as we have seen, he can use established forms but adapt them to his needs. So far we have dealt, with the exception of the chapter on fugue, only with standard forms—those which are the common property of a number of composers and which with certain modifications recur again and again in their works.

In this chapter we shall concern ourselves with forms which occur in isolated cases, forms not regularly used which were created especially for particular compositions. Clearly a mere description of a unique form is applicable only to the single work in which the form appears and would in itself be of little use to us in this study. However, to consider the *causes* for the unique aspect shown by various special forms would be profitable.

We speak of a standard form when both design and tonal structure conform in their general outlines to a pattern that occurs often enough in music literature to receive recognition as established. But should one of these elements, say the design of a work, be constructed in a way essentially different from the norm, the piece will have a nonstandard form even if this design is applied to an established tonal structure. If, for instance, a three-part form has the design ABC (as in Schubert's *Winterreise, No. 11*) it is not to be considered one of the standard ternaries whatever its tonal structure, for the standard ternaries are in design laid out as ABA. Conversely, some works bear frequently used designs but these are applied to a unique tonal structure. Here, too, the result will be a special form. There are in addition other procedures that result in nonstandard forms. In this chapter several compositions that illustrate these various methods will come under scrutiny.

15–B.
COMBINATION OF STANDARD FORMS INTO A UNIQUE COMPOSITE FORM

Brahms' *Rhapsody, Op. 53,* is a setting of part of Goethe's *Harzreise im Winter* ("Winter Journey in the Harz") for contralto solo, men's chorus, and orchestra. Against the background of snowy desolate mountain scenery the poem contrasts the natural happiness of a band of hunters with the bitter loneliness of the misanthrope. From this ode Brahms selected for musical treatment those stanzas which make up the chief picture of the misanthrope. Each of the three stanzas presents him from a different point of view. In the first he is seen from without, the second stanza reveals his inner self, and in the third he is the recipient of a prayer for grace.

> But who is it there apart?
> His way is lost in the thicket,
> Behind him the branches clash together,
> The grass rises again,
> The waste land devours him.

Ah, who can heal his pain
For whom balm has become poison,
Who has drunk hatred of mankind
From the fullness of love?
Once the scorned, now the scorner,
Unknowingly he consumes his own worth
Through insufficient self-concern.

If on Thy psalter, Father of Love,
There be one tone audible to his ear,
Revive his heart!
Open his darkened eyes
To the myriad springs
Beside the thirsty one in the desert.

Brahms has chosen to reflect these three aspects in the form of the music, and the result is three relatively independent parts, unified only by general mood and by identity of key: C, minor mode, changing at stanza 3 to major.

Part one divides into two sections. The first is given to the orchestra alone and seems to be a musical representation of the scene described in the first stanza. It is a phrase group that moves from i to V. The second section is given to the alto soloist, who sings the words in an arioso style, while the orchestra sounds an expanded version of section 1. The basic tonal structure of both sections is the same, as is the basic design. Section 2, being a varied repetition of section 1, adds nothing essential to the form. The rhapsody, then, begins with a one-part form and its varied repetition.

The second stanza is treated by Brahms as a continuous ternary form (ABA'), the first section comprising the initial four lines, and the middle section the last three lines. The return to the opening section is accomplished by repeating the first four lines in the manner of a *da capo* aria. The repetition of these lines, far from making nonsense of the poem—as occasionally happens when careless composers attempt the trick—actually points up with increased clarity the connection between the second and third stanzas. The reiterated question "who can heal his pain . . . ?" leads with great plausibility into the third stanza's prayer.

Since part two is not to be the final part of the work, the harmonic movement does not complete itself as in an independent continuous ternary form. Rather, like part one, it moves from i to a secondary tonic on V. A short transition provides a bridge to the third and final part.

In the third stanza the men's chorus is heard for the first time. As in the second stanza, the opening lines are here repeated to make possible a ternary form, and by further repetitions of the line "revive his heart" Brahms manages to have words for a coda.

The first section of part three is a complete harmonic movement ending with a perfect authentic cadence on I. Section 2 begins on ♭III, then leads by descending major thirds through VII to V, then to V^7 and back to I for the return of the opening as section 3. Part three, then, is a sectional ternary (A–BA). The coda uses material from both A and B.

Outline
Summary
of Brahms'
Rhapsody,
Op. 53

Bars	Division	Design	Tonal Structure
1–47	Part One: initial part (one-part form, repeated)	A	i V (C Minor)
1–18	Section 1: orchestral statement	a	i V
18–47	Section 2: solo statement, varied repetition	a	i V
48–115	Part Two: middle part (continuous ternary form)	B	i $\dfrac{V^7\ i}{\text{of V}}$ (C Minor)
48–69	Section 1	a	i VI
69–73	transition		VI vii^{o7}/VI
73–90	Section 2	b	$V \to V_7$
90–108	Section 3 (= Sec. 1)	a'	$i \to \underbrace{V_7\ I}_{\text{of V}}$
108–115	transition		$V–V_7–V^6_5$
116–175	Part Three: closing part (sectional ternary form)	C	$I \to V_7\ I$ (C Major)
116–127	Section 1	a	$I \to V_7\ I$
128–141	Section 2	b	$\underbrace{V_7\ I}_{\text{of ♭III}}\ \underbrace{V_7\ I}_{\text{of VII}}\ \underbrace{V_7\ I}_{\text{of V}}$
141–145	retransition		$V \to V_7$
146–156	Section 3 (= sec. 1)	a	$I \to V_7\ I$
157–175	Coda	ba	$V_7/♭III \to IV\ I$

Taken as a whole the tonal structure of the three parts can be succinctly expressed as i → V, i → V, I → V–I, and the design as ABC. The rhapsody shows a composite continuous form in three parts, but since part three is not in any sense a restatement of part one, there is no analogy here with the standard continuous ternary form, or with any of the composite ternaries. Rather, the form is unique, having grown out of the particular situation for which it was created—the musical expression of the selected stanzas of Goethe's poem.

Another formal masterpiece achieved through a combination of various standard forms is the Finale to Act I of Rossini's *The Barber of Seville*. The form here grows out of the dramatic situation, and yet Rossini has so fashioned it that it is perfectly intelligible as pure music. The four large parts into which it divides itself correspond in quality but not in form to the usual four movements of a symphony. Unlike most ·symphonies, however, the Finale has transitions which connect these movements.

Part one: first movement, *marziale* (Count, *"Ehi di casa!"*)	I
transition (Rosina, *"Ecco qua"*)	i → V$_3^4$/♭III
Part two: scherzo, *allegro* (Figaro, *"Che cosa accadde"*)	♭III → V I
transition (chorus, *"Fermi tutti"*)	I → V
Part three: slow movement, *largo* (Rosina, *"Freddo ed immo-bile"*)	♭VI
transition (orchestral, two bars)	♭VI → V$_7$
Part four: finale, *allegro*	I

    1. Introduction (recalling first movement)
    2. Movement proper (Sextet, *"Mi par d'esser"*)

Taken as a whole, the tonal structure has involved a move from I up a third to ♭III, a return to I, a move down a third to ♭VI and a return to I. The design, ignoring the transitions, is A–BC–D. Though the entire finale can be labeled a sectional composite four-part form, it has nothing to do with the standard four-part form which has an entirely different tonal structure and design (see Section 6–F).

<h3 style="text-align:center">15–C.
DESIGN OF ONE STANDARD FORM
COMBINED WITH TONAL
STRUCTURE OF DIFFERENT
STANDARD FORM</h3>

The Prelude to Handel's *Suite in E Major* for harpsichord is given as Ex. 15–1.

Example 15–1

HANDEL: *Suite in E Major, Prelude*

The first two bars, virtually in one voice, are an introductory phrase. Beginning with the last quarter-note value of m. 2, the musical texture flows uninterruptedly, linking the phrases or avoiding an expected cadence in such a way that the entire piece shows a remarkable coherence. The endings of phrases 1 and 2 are obscured by the sixteenth-note movement in the alto voice, and the third phrase is extended to great length by avoiding the expected cadence in m. 16. The tonal structure is basically a move from I to a secondary tonic on V and a return to I with a brief secondary tonic on IV. Judging from the single harmonic movement and the absence of conclusive cadences within the composition, one would conclude that it is a normal one-part form. But a comparison of the thematic content of the four chief phrases of the piece shows that they are related in a way which recalls a different standard form. Except for the opening two beats the second phrase is a transposed repetition of the first, while the others in spite of motivic resemblances differ from the previous two. The design, then, is AA'B, a clear reference to the design of the barform. The prelude cannot be considered a real barform which, being a type of sectional binary, has a different tonal structure (see Section 6–D). We have, rather, a unique form: one part, because of the tonal structure and absence of divisive cadences, but designed like the barform.

15–D.
STANDARD DESIGN APPLIED TO
UNIQUE TONAL STRUCTURE

Debussy's preludes contain a number of interesting and unusual forms. *Prelude No. 10* ("The Engulfed Cathedral") from the first volume is selected here because it demonstrates the technique of providing a unique tonal structure with a commonly used design. In this case the design is ABAB.

Example 15–2

DEBUSSY: *Prelude No. 10* ("The Engulfed Cathedral"), themes

The work opens with introductory chords using motive a. Then theme A, a melody that includes three appearances of motive a in augmentation, is stated. The introductory chords reappear to close the section, after which a transition leads to the second section, a statement of theme B. The transition uses motive a and anticipates theme B by emphasizing the descending scale fragment, motive c. Theme A then returns with a short development of motive a in its augmented version. Finally theme B is restated and a short coda, beginning with the introductory chords (motive a) and continuing with motive b (from theme A) in the left hand, concludes the work. There is nothing extraordinary in the design itself. It is only when the tonal structure is viewed in conjunction with this design that the singularity of the form can be appreciated. Here is the harmonic outline.

Example 15–3

DEBUSSY: *Prelude No. 10* (harmonic outline)

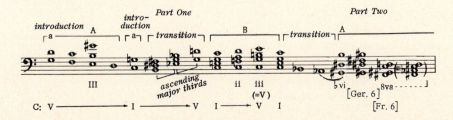

The opening harmonies begin on V and move stepwise down to I. Halfway through this progression, on III, theme A is stated. The tonality of theme A is ambiguous. Taken alone it seems to imply the Dorian mode, transposed to C♯. As presented here, however, the theme is stated with an inner pedal point on E. The listener hears the theme as expressing the major mode of the mediant key, and the A♯'s are understood as implying V/V in that key. This E major is, of course, but a temporary secondary tonic on III and the movement continues down to I. The transition begins by dropping a half step to VII, from which it leaps upward, in two jumps of a major third each, to V, soon expressed as a ninth chord with omitted third, in preparation for theme B, which enters on I. At the conclusion of B a short transition follows in which the bass moves down two whole steps to ♭VI, changing enharmonically from the note A♭ to G♯. This G♯ becomes a pedal point underlying the second presentation of theme A. The tonal ambiguity of this theme is again utilized, for without transposition of the theme itself, Debussy makes it sound as if it were expressing the key of G♯ minor, that is, the low submediant (by enharmonic change) of the tonality of the whole work. This ♭VI pedal point remains throughout the development of motive a, whereupon it moves to I through the French augmented sixth (mm. 68–70). Theme B appears for the second time on I, closing the harmonic movement. The coda prolongs I.

Though unusual, the resulting form is entirely logical: sectional binary with the design AB–A′B. Theme A is first heard on III, that is, a major third above I; after B has expressed I, Theme A is heard again, untransposed but this time expressing ♭VI, a major third below I; the final return of B is again on I. The two statements of B are like a tonic pivot which balances the two statements of A presented at equidistant points above and below.

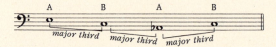

It may be pertinent here to point out the reason for the omission of any remarks regarding the shape of the prelude: how the various sonorities, motives, and themes gradually build so that the listener seems to see the mysterious cathedral rising from the depths of the sea and sinking again beneath the waves. The shape of the prelude, the title, and the images evoked in the listener's mind by the knowledge of the legend behind the title, are not without significance to the musician as performer or listener. But these extra-musical factors are not in the province of the musician in his capacity as analyst. An understanding of the form of a textless piece of music comes about only by preoccupation with the music itself as the composer left it, not by speculation about what he was attempting to express through the music, valuable and interesting as that speculation may be.

The work to be discussed next is Richard Strauss' tone poem, *Don Juan, Op. 23*, the composition of which seems to have depended to a large extent on certain dramatic incidents and concepts of a psychological and philosophical nature in Lenau's poem. But, as in the case of the Debussy prelude, in our role as analysts we must direct our attention solely to the music.

15–E.
UNIQUE DESIGN APPLIED TO
STANDARD TONAL STRUCTURE

Example 15–4

STRAUSS: *Don Juan* (themes and motives)

299

Richard Strauss' tone poem, *Don Juan*, contains a large number of themes and motives that are presented in Ex. 15–4. See the outline summary opposite.

Outline Summary of Strauss' Don Juan

Bars	Division	Function	Design	Tonal Structure
1–168	Part One	Exposition	Themes A, B, C, D	$I \rightarrow \underline{V\text{–}I}$ of $V \rightarrow V_7$
1–40	Sec. 1	*PT*	A　　B　　A′ abcdef　c″ cf　dec″ ab	$\flat VI\text{–}V\text{–}I \rightarrow V_7\text{–}I$
40–89	Sec. 2	Transition	g (anticipatory), C, i, h (anticipatory), various motives from sec. 1	$I \rightarrow V/V$
89–149	Sec. 3	*ST*	D hj	$\underline{I\ V_7\ iv}$ of V
149–168	Sec. 4	Transition	h, A	$iv/V \rightarrow V_7$
168–196	Part Two	Development	B	$\flat VI \rightarrow vii/\flat\ iii$
197–314	Part Three	Episode	E, F	$\underline{i \rightarrow V_7\ i}$ of $\flat iii$
197–231	Sec. 1	Intro.	E with interjections of e and c	$\underbrace{i\ V_7 \parallel i \rightarrow vii^{\circ 4}_{\ \ 3}\ I}$ of $\flat$ iii
232–296	Sec. 2	Quasi-slow movement	F accompanied by k	$\underbrace{I \rightarrow V_7 \parallel I \rightarrow V_7 \parallel I \rightarrow V_7\ I}$ of $\flat III$
296–314	Sec. 3	Codetta and link	k	$\flat III\ (= V/\flat VI)$
314–567	Part Four	Development and Recap.	G plus all previous themes except E	$\flat VI \rightarrow V_7 \parallel I \rightarrow V_7\ I$
314–350	Sec. 1	Development	G (derived from F?), F in diminution, A	$\flat VI \rightarrow V/V$
351–386	Sec. 2	Development (Scherzo)	i, G (free diminution), A	$\flat VII \rightarrow V_7/vi$
386–424	Sec. 3	Development	H (from d and c) with new motive n, in combination with G	$vi \rightarrow IV \rightarrow V_7$
424–473	Sec. 4	Retransition	Restatement of C, D, F; abc in combination with n	$V \rightarrow V_7$ (pedal point on V)
474–567	Sec. 5	Recapitulation	A abbreviated to abc, B in combination with n, G developing and intertwining with l and m, A, B, final phrase like that of part one, section 1	$\flat VI\text{–}V\text{–}I \rightarrow V_7\ I$
567–606	Coda	Coda	c′, new figuration, I	$I \rightarrow V_7\ iv \rightarrow i$
566–585	Sec. 1		c′, new figuration	$I \rightarrow V_7$
586–606	Sec. 2		New figuration, I related by inversion to k (also to D, F, and G?)	$iv \rightarrow i$

For greater ease in comprehending the essential tonal structure of this complex work, a succinct harmonic outline is presented in Ex. 15–5.

Example 15–5

STRAUSS: *Don Juan* (harmonic outline)

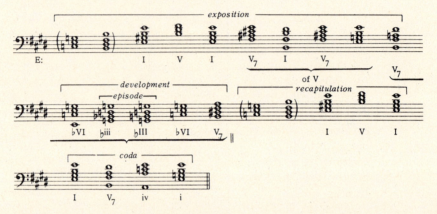

The outline shows the establishment of I (E major) followed by a modulation to V (B major) succeeded by a V_7. This V_7 is prolonged by chord succession which, like Ex. 10–3 (see also Ex. 10–4), shows a succession within a succession: a prolongation of ♭VI (C major) by means of its V (G minor-major). Following the V_7 is a return to the beginning and a complete harmonic movement on I. The basic tonal structure, then, is that of the standard sonata form: I → V–V_7 ‖ I → V_7 I. But in design the work is quite different. The first part, corresponding to the exposition of a sonata form, is, it is true, similar in most respects to the exposition of many sonata forms, nor is the insertion of new material into the development section in itself enough to disqualify it from being considered a sonata-form development. But the great length of the G minor-major episode, its complete harmonic movement, its perfect authentic cadences, and its codetta, combine to stamp it clearly upon the listener's mind as a part in itself, not a subsection within a sonata-form development. Another difference in design is the fact that the recapitulation completes the interrupted harmonic movement with a theme (G) which made its first appearance not in the exposition but in the development, while no theme of the exposition other than A and B is to be heard during the recapitulation.

The tone poem is a continuous four-part form with coda having the over-all design AA'BA" arrived at by the grouping:

A	A'	B	A"
(Part One)	(Part Two)	(Part Three)	(Part Four)
A, B, C, D	B	E, F	G, H, C, D, F, A, B, G–(I)

The work can also be conceived, though not with strict accuracy, as a gigantic sonata form in which a lengthy episode has been inserted into the development section and which, in the recapitulation, substitutes for the original second theme a new theme first heard in the development, transposed here to the tonic. This conception of the work brings up a perplexing question. When a form bears certain strong resemblances to a standard form but also differs from the norm in important ways, is it to be considered a unique form with certain characteristics of the standard form, or should it be thought of as a modified version of that standard form? Only the pedant would insist on a cut-and-dried rule regarding this question, for if the design and tonal structure of the music are understood, it is of no great import what formal label is given the piece. Nevertheless, if a decision is desired, it would seem best to consider whether the form in question is of the same general type as the standard form which it resembles. For instance, we have said that Strauss' *Don Juan* cannot "with strict accuracy" be considered a modified version of sonata form. The reasoning behind this statement is that the standard sonata form is a type of continuous binary. Since the G minor-major episode in *Don Juan* has all the characteristics of a part in itself, the work is not in two parts but four. This fact makes it impossible to consider it a real sonata form, even a highly modified one, in spite of its other similarities. Another example is the first movement of Mahler's *Symphony No. 4*, which has all the earmarks of sonata form except the essential one of being a continuous binary. Since the exposition makes a complete harmonic movement, closing on I (mm. 97–101), the form is an immense sectional binary, and therefore unique. It can be considered a modified version of sonata form only by redefining the term without reference to tonal structure.

15–F.
DESIGN AND TONAL STRUCTURE
BOTH UNIQUE

Example 15–6

CHOPIN: *Ballade in G Minor, Op. 23* (themes)

Chopin's well-known *Ballade in G Minor* makes use of neither a standard tonal structure nor a standard design. Below is an outline summary of the form and Ex. 15–7 is a harmonic outline of the basic tonal structure.

Example 15–7

CHOPIN: *Ballade in G Minor, Op. 23* (harmonic outline)

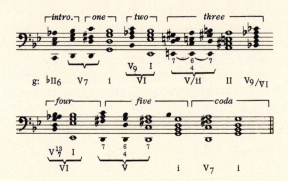

This *Ballade* is a unique type of sectional five-part form. Its over-all design [A–B–Dev. B–A'–(C)] is arrived at by the following grouping:

A	B	Development	B	A'	
(Part	(Part	(Part	(Part	(Part	(C)
One)	Two)	Three)	Four)	Five)	(Coda)
A, B	C, D	A', C, E	C, D	A'	F

· At first glance this would seem to be somewhat like the "arch" design of Bach's *Fugue No.16* in G minor from *WTC* (see Section 14–F); Chopin's *Waltz, Op. 34, No. 1*; and Brahms' *Rhapsody, Op. 119, No. 4* (see Section 8–H). This view of the design might be plausible if part five resembled part one to a greater extent. But although both are based on theme A there is little similarity between them. On the other hand, part five is an almost

Outline Summary of Chopin's Ballade, Op. 23

Bars	Division	Design	Tonal Structure
1–7	Introduction	Independent phrase	$\flat II_6(V)–iv_6(V)$
8–56	Part One	A, B, and codetta	V_7 i, V_7 i
8–36	Sec. 1	A (motive a)	V_7 i iv_6 V_7 i
36–44	Sec. 2	B	i V_7 i
44–56	Sec. 3	Codetta	i–iv–i
56–67	Transition	anticipates C	→ V/V of VI
68–90	Part Two	C, D	V_9 I → V_7 I of VI
68–82	Sec. 1	C	V_9 I → V_7 I of VI
82–90	Sec. 2 (codetta)	D (motive a)	$I–iv_4^6–I$ of VI
90–94	Transition	motive a	VI → V/ii
94–165	Part Three (Quasi-development)	A', C, E	V_7 i V_7 I → V_3^4/V of ii → of VI
94–105	Sec. 1	A'	V_7/ii
106–125	Sec. 2	C	V_7 I of ii ii_7^0 VI
126–137	Sec. 3	Flourish	V_7/VI
138–165	Sec. 4	E (related to B)	I → $V_3^4/V–iv_6$ of VI
166–188	Part Four	Varied repetition of part two	(Same as that of part two)
166–180	Sec. 1	C	(Same as that of part two)
180–188	Sec. 2 (codetta)	D (motive a)	(Same as that of part two)
188–194	Transition	motive a (like transition mm. 90–94)	VI → V
194–208	Part Five	A' (like part three, sec. 1)	V_7 → i
208–262	Coda	New material, motive a	i → V_7 i
208–248	Sec. 1	F	i → V_7 i
248–262	Sec. 2	Motive a, scales	i

exact transposition of section 1 of part three. Such a close tie between the two restatements of theme A, both standing in opposition to the original statement, effectively destroys any resemblance to an arch which the design might otherwise have displayed.

Part three, though labeled in the outline summary "quasi-development" has, except for section 1, nothing to do with the motivic development characteristic of many development sections of the classical composers. But, as we have seen, some developments of the classical composers are, like this one, occupied with presenting either new material or previously heard material transposed intact to a new key.

The unique aspect of the tonal structure of Chopin's *Ballade in G Minor* lies not in its initial delay of the tonic chord, but in the lengthy chord succession which prolongs VI through parts two, three, and four. The harmony of part five, too, is remarkable, for in its essence it expresses no more than a drawn-out V_7 followed by i.

15–G.
SUMMARY

The means of achieving a unique form are summarized as follows:

1. Standard design; standard tonal structure of different form
2. Standard design; unique tonal structure
3. Unique design; standard tonal structure
4. Unique design; unique tonal structure
5. Unique composite of standard forms

Students who make the effort to discover for themselves the characteristics of some of the unique forms will be richly rewarded, for they will gain an insight into the workings of the composer's mind which cannot be acquired by other means.

EXERCISE

1. Analyze some or all of the following music. If unique forms are discovered, indicate the specific factors that have brought about this unique quality.
   a. Chorale, *Es ist genug* (in Appendix)
   b. Chorale, *O Haupt voll Blut und Wunden* (in Appendix)
   c. Wilby, *As fair as morn*
   d. Handel, *Violin Sonata in F major*, Adagio
   e. Mozart, *Fantasia, K. 475*
   f. Schubert, *Erlkönig*
   g. Schumann, *Album, No. 31*
   h. Chopin, *Nocturne in D flat major, Op. 27, No. 2*
   i. Wagner, *Prelude* and *Liebestod* from *Tristan and Isolde*
   j. Brahms, *Intermezzo in C major, Op. 119, No. 3*
   k. Wolf, *In dem Schatten meiner Locken*
   l. Debussy, *Prélude à "L'après-midi d'un faune"*
   m. Ives, *General William Booth Enters Into Heaven*

16

RETROSPECTION

The ancient principle of variety in unity emphasizes that a worthy work of art will inevitably contain a number of diverse elements which cohere to form a single impression in the mind of the beholder. "How all's to one thing wrought!" There can be little doubt about which single factor does most toward achieving unity in tonal music: it is the utilization of the twelve tones in such a way that a set of relationships emerges among them, relationships that point out to the listener a single tone as center.

From another point of view the action might be looked at the other way round: to see the composition as something which has developed from a single tone. A seed is, to all appearances, almost insignificant. Yet, over a period of time, it develops by the processes of nature into the complex organism we call a flower or tree. A single tone, too, may seem almost nothing compared to a symphony. But the great compositions of the recent past have, in the last analysis, "grown" from a single tone, the keynote.

A tone, because of the implication of its overtones, can give rise to a series of chords which are dependent on that tone and which group themselves about it as planets, to use a different analogy, do around a sun. By the phenomenon of secondary tonics and the process of modulation, a composer can focus interest on any of these "planets" in turn, making it act as a temporary "sun" surrounded by its own "planets." A series of chords, then, or what we call the harmonic movement, can either remain within the orbit of the original tonal center or appear to abandon the original and proceed to orbit around a secondary one. Except for special reasons, the composer does not let this secondary tonal center equal the first in importance, for to do so would contribute toward disunity, equivalent to having two suns in our musical solar system. Hence the second is allowed to have temporary significance only.

Harmonic movement which leaves one area to focus its attention on another is progressive. Harmonic movement which, after having left an area, returns to it again is complete.

307

Throughout this study of musical form one particular scheme of harmonic movement has appeared more often than any other. In this scheme a tonal center is first established (I), then a progressive harmonic movement sets in which establishes a second tonal center with a dominant relationship to the first (V). This V is extended in time by a series of harmonies which may focus temporary attention on other scale degrees but which returns to V. At the return, however, V no longer acts as a secondary tonal center, but as a chord dependent on and pointing to I, the original tonal center. Finally, then, a complete harmonic movement on I takes place.

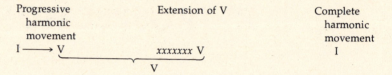

A common variant of the harmonic scheme outlined above comes about when III rather than V is the immediate goal of the first phase of the harmonic movement, a situation not limited to, but occurring most often in, the minor mode. Located midway between I and V, III acts like a steppingstone between them.

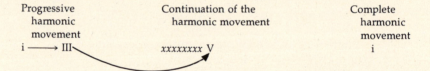

The fundamental harmonic movement underlying the surface of any tonal composition is called its tonal structure. Comprehension of the tonal structure of a composition is of paramount importance in attempting to understand its musical form. Nevertheless, it is not the only factor to be considered, for music displays a number of other contributing elements. Chief among these are cadences and the various relationships (variation, contrast, restatement) discernible in melody, rhythm, and texture. The interaction of all these, grouped together as *design*, is crucial to the form. A cadence, if perceived as relatively stronger than its surrounding cadences, can divide a composition into separate parts regardless of the tonal structure. (In practice, such a cadence is normally the perfect authentic.) Strong rhythmic or melodic contrast is capable of setting off a passage of music as a part in itself. It is just because design plays such an important role in the final form which a composition assumes that the basic tonal structure and its variant, outlined above, can be utilized again and again in works of differing forms. We have seen how it is able to serve the one-part form (Ex. 6–12), the three types of continuous binary (simple Ex. 10–1; rounded, Ex. 6–3 and Ex. 10–3; balanced, page 174), the continuous ternary (Ex. 6–10), the sonata form (Section 11–A), and unique forms (Ex. 15–1, Ex. 15–5). Beethoven introduced a further variant of this tonal structure by substituting VI for V or III as the first goal of the progressive harmonic movement. In this version, the tonal structure has been utilized in sonata form (Ex. 11–16) and even theme and variations (bass outline of tonal structure, Section 7–F). Bach anticipated Beethoven's use of VI in the triple fugue outlined in Section 14–G, page 278.

These tonal structures are, of course, identical or similar only in their broadest outlines. The precise route taken when moving from I to V, or the particular sequence of harmonies which prolong the V, will, to be sure, vary greatly among the different compositions. But the fundamental outline of this harmonic scheme is found frequently enough to stamp it as the chief tonal structure of the continuous forms.

Like continuous forms, sectional forms begin by establishing a tonal center. But instead of a progressive movement to a secondary tonal center they make a complete harmonic movement on I. Only then does the question of a second tonal center present itself. There is little uniformity among the sectional forms concerning the particular relationship of the secondary tonal center to the original. In the typical Classical rondo it will in all likelihood express III or V, but in a sectional ternary IV or VI is preferred as often. Indeed, not infrequently the original key, with a change to the opposite mode, is retained.

In concluding this study, it would perhaps be well to re-emphasize an observation made at several points along the way. We cannot assume that any great composer, in creating a piece of music, has proceeded along prescribed lines with the intention of producing a work that conforms to an established standard or model. It follows that if we approach the first movement of a symphony or the last movement of a concerto with a firmly fixed notion that the former will necessarily be a sonata form and the latter a rondo we will risk missing the meaning of the work. We will also be imposing arbitrary restrictions on the composer, who has never been under any compulsion to accept them. It would be far better to reserve opinion until the piece has been carefully listened to and examined, preferably following the six-step method of analysis outlined in Section 6–H. Moreover, it is usually not particularly revealing or interesting simply to place the label "rondo" or "sonata form" on a piece of music. Should the analysis cease with the discovery that a certain composition falls into a particular category of standard forms, the student's musical insight will have increased but little. Rather, aspects of the structure which contribute to the individuality of the work should be sought out and identified. An interesting variant of the usual tonal structure, an ingenious rearrangement of subsections in a recapitulation, a particularly lengthy episode in a fugue—features like these, once noted, can do much toward spurring the mind to the pursuit of even further degrees of understanding. It is one thing to note a variant from a customary practice, but it is much more to understand the reasons behind that variant. When students find themselves pondering the significance of the note g♭′ in m. 25 of Schubert's *Impromptu, Op. 90, No. 2* (see autograph manuscript on the cover of this book), and postulating for it a reason which takes into account the whole composition, they will know they are progressing toward musical maturity.

Index of Composers and Compositions

Index of Subjects

Boldface numbers indicate definitions or extended discussions.